PUNCHING
ABOVE THEIR WEIGHT

From Newtownmanor, County Leitrim, Sean McGoldrick has worked as a journalist for thirty-seven years. He co-authored *Shooting from the Hip*, the autobiography of Kerry GAA star Pat Spillane and *I Remember It Well*, the autobiography of legendary broadcaster Jimmy Magee. Winner of the GAA's McNamee award in 1999 and 2009 and shortlisted for Sports Journalist of the Year in 2008, he reported on the exploits of the Irish boxers at the 2000, 2008 and 2012 Olympic Games for the *Sunday World*.

PUNCHING

ABOVE THEIR WEIGHT

THE IRISH OLYMPIC BOXING STORY

SEAN McGOLDRICK

THE O'BRIEN PRESS
DUBLIN

First published 2015 by
The O'Brien Press Ltd,
12 Terenure Road East, Rathgar,
Dublin 6, D06 HD27 Ireland.
Tel: +353 1 4923333; Fax: +353 1 4922777
E-mail: books@obrien.ie
Website: www.obrien.ie

ISBN: 978-1-84717-686-8

British Library Cataloguing-in-Publication Data
A catalogue record for this title is available from the British Library

1 3 5 7 8 6 4 2
15 17 18 16

Picture credits

The author and publisher thank the following for permission to use photographs:
Picture sections: all images, courtesy of Sportsfile, except section 1: p1, top: John McNally; bottom:
Conor McCaughley/*Sunday World*; p2, top: Brendan Murphy; bottom: Irish Photo Archive; p4, top
right and p5, top: Colman Doyle, courtesy of the National Library. Front cover: Shutterstock. Back
cover: top, John McNally. Back cover, bottom, Paddy Barnes (Sportsfile).

Text credits

The author and publisher thank the following for permission to quote from: Carruth, Michael
(with Peter Byrne), *Ring of Gold*, with permission from Blackwater Press; from Egan,
Kenny (with Ewan McKenna), *Kenny Egan: My Story*, with permission from Paper Weight
Publications; from Flynn, Barry, *Legends of Irish Boxing: Stories Seldom Told*, with permission
from Appletree Press; from Flynn, Barry, *Best of Enemies: John Caldwell vs Freddie Gilroy*, with
permission from Liberties Press, from Jennings, Andrew, *The New Lord of the Rings: Olympic
Corruption and How to Buy Gold Medals*, with permission from Andrew Jennings; from
Naughton, Lindie & Watterson, Johnny, *Irish Olympians*, with permission from Blackwater
Press; from TV documentary *Tales from a Neutral Corner* with permission from Andrew
Gallimore from *Irish Independent* (Vincent Hogan) and from *Sunday Times* (Denis Walsh).
*If any involuntary infringement of copyright has occurred, sincere apologies are offered and the owners
of such copyright are requested to contact the publisher.*

Printed and bound by ScandBook AB, Sweden

CONTENTS

Dedication

To Mary, Paul, Orla (RIP), and Colm

PROLOGUE

The recent construction in Abbotstown, west Dublin, of a €3.5 million purpose-built training centre and accommodation block for Ireland's Elite boxers is a belated but fitting testimonial to the country's most successful Olympic sport.

Finally, twelve years after its establishment by the Irish Amateur Boxing Association (IABA), the High Performance Unit (HPU) has a facility worthy of its cohort of world-class boxers. HPU coaches have trained Irish boxers to win a total of 241 medals in championships at all levels, up to the end of June 2015, resulting in the unit earning the moniker 'The Medal Factory'.

The taxpayer picked up the tab for the cost of this new, much-needed and long-awaited facility. The IABA hasn't always been so fortunate. Shortly before the start of the Second World War in 1939, Ireland hosted the fifth European Boxing Championships in the IABA's magnificent new headquarters on Dublin's South Circular Road which was built without any financial aid from the government, though they did donate the site.

The organisation, which was just over a quarter of a century in existence at the time, showed remarkable foresight and considerable self-confidence in erecting its own HQ, which they simply named the National Stadium. In 1935, the IABA had taken a lead role in organising a meeting of other sports organisations to look into the possibility of building a national sports stadium. All the organisations supported the idea in principle but none were willing to commit to raising the necessary finance. Undeterred, the IABA pressed on with this ambitious project, even though it would cost more than one million euro in today's money to complete.

The heroine of the project was Mrs Mary Murphy, wife of Major General William Richard English-Murphy, the then president of the IABA and arguably the most influential figure in Irish boxing for the first half of the twentieth century. It has been estimated that she personally raised £3,000 – the equivalent of €240,000 in today's money – through the organisation of carnivals and garden parties for the project.

The National Stadium opened its doors for the first time in March 1939 when it hosted the National Senior Championships. A month later, a sell-out crowd of over two thousand crowded into the arena to see two Dubliners, seventeen-year-old Jimmy Ingle and his teammate Paddy Dowdall, win gold medals in the flyweight and featherweight categories respectively, while welterweight Charlie Evenden claimed a bronze at the European Championships.

They were the first medals won by Irish boxers representing Ireland in international championships. The next official European Championships were not held until after the war. Again they were hosted by the IABA in the National Stadium in 1947 when heavyweight Gearóid O Colmáin won gold and featherweight Peter Maguire landed silver. Five years later, bantamweight John McNally secured Ireland's first Olympic boxing medal at the Helsinki Games. The bold decision to build the National Stadium was the catalyst for the first golden era in Irish boxing.

Arguably, the current golden era in Irish amateur boxing was precipitated by the fall of the Berlin wall in 1989 and the break-up of the Soviet Union two years later. Its dissolution resulted in the creation of fifteen new countries, and seven more states came into existence when Yugoslavia broke up in 1992.

European politics, sport and in particular, boxing, would never be the same again. The rules of engagement had changed dramatically. Irish boxing was ill-prepared for the tsunami which all but wiped out the country's reputation as a respected boxing nation.

This is the story of how that reputation was not only painstakingly restored but embellished way beyond peoples' imaginations.

CHAPTER 1

BUILDING THE
TRADITION

'He [Jake Corvino] was a good-looking guy, but he was the hardest man I ever fought. Once I beat him, I wasn't afraid of anyone.'
John McNally

Eight of Ireland's fifteen Olympic boxing medallists hail from Belfast, bolstering the argument that the city is the spiritual home of the sport in this country. John McNally was the pioneer, fashioning a historic breakthrough at the Helsinki Olympic Games in 1952, when he became the first ever Irish boxer to win an Olympic medal. He minted silver; by all accounts, it ought to have been gold.

His breakthrough marked a watershed moment in the evolution of Irish sport. Until then, athletics was Ireland's showcase event on the world stage. Pat O'Callaghan was crowned Olympic hammer champion in 1928 and 1932, when Bob Tisdall also won the 400-metre hurdles. The new Irish Free State was represented in four sports at the 1924 Summer Olympics in Paris: athletics, water polo, lawn tennis, and a seven-man boxing team, six of whom were members of the Irish army. The exception was bantamweight Robert Hilliard, a Trinity College student. He hailed from Moyeightragh, near Killarney, was a founder member of the college's hurling club and fought on the Republican side in the Civil War. Later he worked as a journalist before being ordained a Church of Ireland minister. He subsequently resigned from his ministry, immigrated to London, and joined the Communist Party of Great Britain. He was killed in 1937 while fighting with the International Brigades in the Spanish Civil War.

At the Paris Games, Thurles-born Paddy 'Rocky' Dwyer became the first Irish boxer to record a win at Olympic level when he beat Great Britain's Joseph J 'Johnny' Basham in the preliminary round of the welterweight category. He followed on with wins over Ko Cornelissen (the Netherlands) and Théodore Stauffer (Switzerland) before being stopped in the third round of the semi-final by Argentinian Héctor Méndez. There was controversy surrounding the fight. The Irish camp contended that Méndez should have been disqualified for deliberately headbutting Dwyer, which resulted in a nasty cut on his brow and effectively ended his involvement in the Games.

Prior to the 1952 Games, semi-finalists who lost had to box off for bronze. Thirty-year-old Dwyer, who had learned to box while serving in the British army, had to concede a walkover in the box-off to Douglas Lewis from Canada due to his head wound. Under current rules he would have been guaranteed a bronze medal.

Four years later, at the Amsterdam Games, Dwyer was the official trainer of the eight-man Irish team, three of whom came from the ranks of the Gardaí and two from the Irish army. This time around it was Dubliner Frank Traynor who was the luckless one. He was disqualified by British referee GH Chandley during the bantamweight semi-final against Italian Vittorio Tamagnini – the eventual gold medallist. Irish journalist AP McWeeney, who was ringside, reported that there was 'no cause' for the decision. Following a protest by the Olympic Council of Ireland, Traynor was reinstated. However, he was not permitted to re-box the Italian. He lost to Harry Isaacs from South Africa in the box-off for the bronze medal.

Only four Irish boxers competed at the 1932 Olympics in Los Angeles. Three failed to win their opening bouts, but light-heavyweight James Murphy, a member of the Gardaí, beat John Miler from the USA in the quarter-finals. Unfortunately, he was forced to withdraw from both his semi-final against Gino Rossi (Italy) and a box-off for the bronze medal with Denmark's Peter Jørgensen due to injury.

Ireland did not compete at the 1936 Olympics in Berlin, and the outbreak of the Second World War caused the cancellation of the 1940 Games. By the time the Olympics resumed in London in 1948, Ireland had established itself as a significant power in boxing at European level.

Dublin hosted the European Amateur Boxing Championships in 1939 in the newly-opened National Stadium – the first purpose-built boxing arena in the world. The Irish team finished second behind Italy in the medals table after seventeen-year-old Jimmy Ingle (flyweight) and Paddy Dowdall (featherweight) won gold medals, while welterweight Charles Evenden secured a bronze. The National Stadium again hosted the European Championships in 1947 and Ireland finished third overall with two medals: gold for Gearóid Ó Colmáin in the heavyweight division and silver for featherweight Peter Maguire.

Maguire didn't make the eight-man team for London, where the boxing took place on a temporary bridge laid out over the Empire Pool at Wembley. Ó Colmáin, a Dublin-based blacksmith, was beaten in the first round by

Italian Uber Baccilieri, but Mullingar lightweight Michael 'Maxie' McCullagh underlined his potential by reaching the quarter-finals. Middleweight Mick McKeon, a twenty-five-year-old plumber from Dublin, was the unlucky Irish fighter. Having defeated Canadian and Iranian opponents, he beat the defending European champion, Frenchman Aimé Escudie, in the quarter-final. But, later on the same day, he lost to England's John 'Johnny' A Wright in the semi-final. There was outrage in the Irish media about the decision. Writing in *The Irish Press*, Dick Wilkes was apoplectic:

'Mick McKeon whacked the British champion, Johnny Wright, in the Olympic at Wembley, London yesterday, and by rights should be the first Irishman ever to contest the final of an Olympic championship today. But he won't. Through one of the greatest pieces of boxing injustices I have ever seen, he was not given the verdict against the Britisher and now joins the ranks of boxers from all over the world who have been "robbed" of the decision they earned and richly deserved.'

Ireland lodged an official protest, though other countries took more drastic action when they were the victims of dodgy decisions. Argentinian officials stormed the judges' tables, while France withdrew their boxers, and their international president resigned. Just to compound McKeon's misery, he had to withdraw from the box-off for the bronze medal after the medical officer advised him not to box due to a broken nose. In fact, McKeon had broken his nose in training before the Olympics started but had battled through four fights despite the obvious discomfort. Wright was beaten in the Olympic final by the famous Hungarian southpaw László Papp, the first boxer to win three successive Olympic gold medals.

But there was one positive outcome – for all boxers. The injury-enforced withdrawal of McKeon, American lightweight Wallace Smith – a future world professional champion – and Swiss heavyweight Hans Mueller led to both beaten semi-finalists getting bronze medals from the following Games onward. According to boxing historian and writer Gerry Callan, the fact that three boxers at the one Games lost the chance of fighting for a medal through no fault of their own made the authorities realise the unfairness of the rule.

The eighth European Championships held in Oslo in 1949 were significant insofar as they were the last in which Russian boxers did not compete. Irish featherweight David O'Connell was awarded a bronze medal by the jury – he had lost to the eventual winner Jacques Bataille in the semi-final. Maxie McCullagh was the Irish hero, however, as he was crowned European light champion. Forty-two years would pass before another Irish boxer would win a European title.

John McNally's silver medal in 1952 launched boxing on a journey which has seen it becoming Ireland's pin-up sport at Olympic level. Since then, Irish boxers have won sixteen Olympic medals, whereas all the other sports combined have accumulated just nine. Athletic aficionados will argue that they have won four gold medals compared to just two in boxing, but the overall trend is undeniable. Furthermore, only three of the six athletic medals have been won post 1932, whereas all of the boxing medals have come since 1952.

Nowadays octogenarian McNally makes the daily commute by bus from his home in south Belfast into the city centre, where he regularly reminisces with his boxing acquaintances in the Grapevine Café. Born in Cinnamon Street, situated in the city's Pound Loney area, he can recall an era when the nearby Falls Road was dotted with flax mills. His formative years were dominated by the Second World War. He was nine when, on Easter Tuesday night, 15 April 1941, two hundred bombers from the Luftwaffe attacked the city. The toll was horrendous: 900 people died, while another 1,500 were injured, and half the houses in the city were damaged or destroyed.

'I don't remember being afraid. Our neighbourhood wasn't hit, though the other side of the Falls Road was badly damaged. I remember the sirens going off. We would either hide under the stairs or assemble in a nearby park.'

His abiding memory of the war years is of his father, George, being forced to go to England to find work to support his family. 'He wasn't away all the time but it was very rough when he had to leave.'

McNally was introduced to boxing by a friend who told him about a new club which was opening near his home in Devonshire Street. The pair headed off one evening to the new Immaculata Club. Kitted out with their new boxing gloves, they were sent into battle against each other. 'I'd say we were about twelve at the time, and we proceeded to knock hell out of each other. My friend never came back but I was hooked from day one.'

Even though he was 5'9" in height and his chest measured forty inches, his waist was a mere twenty-seven inches so he was able to make the 54 kg bantamweight limit. His gruelling schedule kept his weight in check. He ran ten miles every morning, then enjoyed a breakfast which consisted of a big bap and a mug of tea. He did ninety minutes training in the club every night – and in between he served his time as a motor mechanic.

He was just nineteen when he won his first Irish title in 1952. Even though the victory put him on course for the Olympics, some selectors thought he was too fragile. As ever, the politics surrounding team selection was simmering underneath the surface. It was suggested that a more experienced bantam-weight, Dubliner Paddy Kelty – who won the Irish title in 1951 but didn't box in the championships the following year – would be a more suitable candidate. Furthermore, Kelty was a member of the Corinthians Boxing Club, a number of whose members were reputed to be influential figures in the higher echelons of the Irish Amateur Boxing Association (IABA).

According to McNally, his coach 'Wee' Sammy Wallace 'was years ahead of his time'. Together they set out to prove the pundits wrong. In the annual

Kuttner Shield international against Scotland, he beat an experienced opponent, Tom Beattie. Next up was a show between Ireland and the New York Golden Gloves champions.

His opponent was a first generation Italian-American, Jake Corvino. He had only taken up boxing the previous year when he heard that the winners of the New York Golden Gloves championship would be visiting Italy on a European tour in 1952. He figured it was the only chance he'd ever get to visit his grandparents. McNally remembers, 'He was a good-looking guy, but he was the hardest man I ever fought. Once I beat him, I wasn't afraid of anyone.'

Nevertheless, McNally still faced a box-off against Kelty. The Belfast boxer prevailed to secure his place on the team for Helsinki. He was joined by the Reddy brothers, Andrew 'Ando' (flyweight) and Tommy (featherweight); Kevin Martin (lightweight); Terry Milligan (light welterweight); Peter Crotty (welterweight); Willie Duggan (middleweight) and John Lyttle (heavyweight). Seventeen-year-old Harry Perry was left at home even though he had beaten Tommy Reddy in the Irish featherweight Elite final; he was considered too young.

There were no collective training camps in those days. 'I was working up until the day before I left,' recalls McNally. The journey to the Finnish capital proved something of an epic trip, lasting two days by trains and boats. 'A donkey and cart would have been faster.'

Listening to John McNally, it is evident that the Helsinki Games left an indelible mark on him. He loved athletics nearly as much as boxing and he spent every spare minute in the Olympic Stadium. Czech army officer Emil Zátopek dominated the Games. He fashioned an unprecedented treble, winning the 5,000 metres, the 10,000 metres, and the marathon – a feat which is unlikely to be ever attempted in modern times, never mind equalled. 'I saw him running,' says McNally, 'but didn't realise how good he was.' The presence of the first-ever team from the Soviet Union at the Olympic Games also caused a stir, though there was minimal contact with their athletes outside of the competition as they insisted on being housed separately.

The American boxing team, which included seventeen-year-old Floyd Patterson, who later became the youngest world professional heavyweight champion until Mike Tyson, took a shine to McNally and took him under their wing.

'The authorities wanted us to train at night. We kicked up hell and got a slot between the Americans and the Canadians. I always sparred with my teammate Terry Milligan from Belfast. Regardless of what the Americans were doing, they always came to watch and that's how they adopted me.'

McNally convincingly beat Alejandro Ortuoste from the Philippines in his first fight to earn a quarter-final clash against Italian Vincenzo Dall'osso.

Meanwhile, Milligan also advanced to the quarter-finals but lost to Italian Bruno Visintin. John McNally went on to make history in his quarter-final, beating the reigning European champion to secure Ireland's first ever Olympic medal in boxing and the country's first medal in any sport for twenty years.

Now the youngster was on a roll. He turned bronze to silver as he beat Korean Kang Joon-ho in the semi-final. Again, it was a unanimous 3-0 verdict, his third in a row.

'He was a nut case to fight but I won very easy,' remembers McNally. 'However, my back was a mess afterwards [from rope burns], and the Americans grabbed me and took me to their dressing room. Two of their boxers, Charles "Chuck" Adkins and Patterson were inside preparing for their fights. Their doctor asked them to hold my hands while he poured alcohol on my back. Boy, did it hurt.'

Adkins and Patterson later won the middleweight and light welterweight titles respectively, but their new Irish friend was not so fortunate. Ominously for the Irish camp, bantamweight Pentti Hämäläinen was the only Finnish boxer to reach the finals; four others bowed out in the semi-finals.

The dreams of the host nation rested on the slight frame of a twenty-three-year-old typewriter mechanic and, of course, the judges. So even before McNally stepped into the ring on 2 August 1952, the odds were stacked against the Irish teenager. 'I loved my first three fights. But in the final all Pentti did was to hang on. He even opened up a cut near my eye with his head. He was warned at least eight times but never lost a point,' says a wistful McNally. 'My own corner thought I had won; so did the Americans. It took the judges a long time to come to their decision. I was thinking if I won, why the hold up?'

When the decision was announced, the partisan crowd erupted. It mattered little that it was a split 2-1 decision. The British judge gave the nod to McNally, but the Austrian and American judges backed the local champion. McNally can afford to be philosophical about it all now. 'The result didn't bother me, it bothered other people.'

At the time, the newly-proclaimed Republic of Ireland was still something of an enigma to the outside world. McNally learned that the Olympic officials had planned to play the British army marching song 'It's a Long Way to Tipperary' as the Irish anthem at the medal ceremony.

Back in Ireland there was scant media coverage of the historic breakthrough, though it was a major talking point among the boxing fraternity, according to veteran commentator Jimmy Magee. 'It created a big stir, though the success didn't get a great deal of column inches.'

McNally was puzzled when his father insisted he stay in Dublin for a few days after the Irish team's arrival home. This was to allow his father time to organise a homecoming in Belfast, where, despite the pouring rain, thousands turned out to greet the boxer.

Politics, though, was to rear its ugly head. McNally was to be honoured by the civil authorities at a film premiere in the Ritz Cinema. He tells of how 'The Lord Mayor couldn't be bothered to come so I got the High Sheriff instead. I was wearing my Irish team blazer which had a tricolour emblem on it. The High Sheriff refused to join me on the stage unless I took off my jacket. My trainer didn't want a confrontation and I was so naïve that I took it off. I'd never do it again.'

The irony of the incident was lost on those who created the fuss. The film being premiered was *Jim Thorpe – All-American*, the dramatized story of the US athlete of mixed ancestry who won the pentathlon and decathlon at the 1912 Olympic Games. Later, he was shamefully disqualified and stripped of his titles when it was discovered he was paid a pittance for playing two seasons of semi-professional baseball. Thirty years after his death the International Olympic Committee (IOC) restored his medals.

At the 1953 European Championships in Warsaw, McNally, despite struggling to make the weight at bantam, won a bronze medal, while his sparring partner, light welterweight Terence Milligan, took silver. This effectively brought the curtain down on McNally's amateur career, in which he only lost 6 of his 314 fights. His last amateur fight was on a Corinthians show in the National Stadium on 29 January 1954 when he was outpointed by none other than Pentti Hämäläinen.

McNally recalls the build-up to the rematch. 'I had been ill with blood poisoning beforehand and was in hospital. I was urged by people around home not to take the fight, but a friend of mine, Colm Gallagher who was a TD in Dublin, arranged for Pentti to travel over so I agreed to it.'

Later that year, McNally turned professional, but he did not enjoy the pro-game and quit the ring in 1961 at the age of twenty-eight after just twenty-five fights. 'I hated every minute of professional boxing because of the gangsters who hung around the sport. All they wanted was money.'

John McNally went on to become a professional musician with the folk group 'The Freemen'. The esteem with which he is regarded in his native Belfast was underlined in 2013 when his Olympic medal was stolen. Following a public appeal, it was handed in to the UTV offices in the city.

At the 1955 European Championships in Berlin, six of the Irish team were defeated in the first round. Light middleweight Peter Burke advanced to the quarter-final, where he lost to the eventual bronze medallist Rolf Caroli from East Germany. So there were few reasons for believing that the seven-man boxing team chosen to compete at the Melbourne Olympic Games in 1956 would go down in history as the most successful ever male team in the history of the sport.

Ireland was an austere place in the mid-fifties. It has been estimated that between 1956 and 1961 more than 40,000 people emigrated. Money was tight and sending a team of athletes to the other side of the world was not a top priority. Ronnie Delany, who won the 1500 metres in Melbourne, scraped through the selection process by one vote, while high jumper Brendan O'Reilly, though selected, did not travel due to a shortfall of £1,000 in the Olympic Council of Ireland's £8,000 budget. With his bags packed in Michigan where he was in college, he received a curt two-word telegram from the OCI, 'Trip cancelled'.

The people of Drogheda came together to organise a special collection to ensure that their local hero Tony 'Socks' Byrne could make the trip. 'Everyone in the town threw their weight behind the fund-raising effort,' recalled Byrne in an interview with author Barry Flynn in *Irish Boxing Legends*. A sum of £653 was raised.

Belfast bantamweight Freddie Gilroy, a late addition to the team, also had to depend on public donations. But it was his weight, rather than finance, which nearly derailed Gilroy's Olympic ambitions. Born in the Short Strand area of east Belfast, his family moved to Ardoyne in north Belfast, where he joined the St John Bosco Club in Corporation Street. In May 1956 he toured the US and Canada with an Irish boxing squad which fashioned a memorable 5-5 draw against a Golden Gloves squad in Chicago. In *Irish Boxing Legends* Gilroy recalled how he decided to weigh himself at New York airport on the way home, 'The scales showed I was heading for two stone overweight.' The word got back to the OCI and it looked as if he wouldn't be selected. In the ensuing controversy, Gilroy insisted that even if the scales were accurate, losing two stone wouldn't be an issue. Eventually, he was added to the squad.

The other team members were John Caldwell, Fred Tiedt, Harry Perry and Martin Smyth. Donegal native Pat Sharkey, a former Irish junior champion and Scottish senior champion, who was working on the Snowy Mountain hydro-electric dam project in New South Wales, was added to the team. Christy Murphy, who had managed the team in Helsinki, was in charge again. But he fell ill on the journey, was diagnosed with thrombosis and spent the duration of the Games in a Melbourne hospital. Former Australian profes-sional Snowy Sullivan, who had little knowledge of the Irish boxers, assumed Murphy's coaching duties, while Martin Power, a former Irish junior cham-pion, then working in Melbourne, assisted the team in a voluntary capac-ity. Nonetheless, the Irish boxers trained hard once they reached Australia, according to accounts by Fred Tiedt.

In *Irish Olympians* he explained their routine. 'We bloody well trained, I'll tell you. We'd go down to the beach for a run in the morning. Then in the afternoon we'd train again. Then we'd do loose sparring with some profes-sionals over there – we murdered them.' Even though China, Spain, Holland, Egypt, and Iraq withdrew their teams as a result of the Hungarian uprising and the Suez crisis, all the then leading boxing nations sent their pugilists to battle in the Western Melbourne Hall.

On the first day featherweight Martin Smyth lost to a familiar opponent.

Eight years after he had beaten McNally in the Olympic bantamweight final, Finland's Pentti Hämäläinen, now operating in the featherweight division, ended Smyth's ambitions. The Finn went on to capture a bronze medal. Heavyweight Pat Sharkey was knocked out in round three of his preliminary bout by a Swedish opponent, Thorner Ahsman, while light welterweight Harry Perry was beaten by Claude Saluden from France. Neither Ahsman nor Saluden medalled.

It was Gilroy, the late addition to the team, who grabbed the headlines when he knocked out gold-medal favourite and European silver medallist Boris Stepanov from the USSR.

'I caught him with a sweet left hook in the third round, over he went and I knew he was not getting up,' recalled Gilroy in *Legends of Irish Boxing*.

The reaction of the crowd and the subsequent unprecedented media coverage underlined how the Games and politics are intertwined. Throughout the Western world anti-Soviet sentiment was rife at the time, in the wake of the USSR's invasion and brutal suppression of the Hungarian uprising the previous month. Gilroy had no interest in politics but he understood the political significance of the win. 'This was one in the eye for the Russians,' he suggested.

There was an ironic twist to Gilroy's story before the end of the Games. He outpointed Italian Mario Sitri to guarantee himself a bronze medal and a semi-final clash against a highly rated East German bantamweight, Wolfgang Behrendt. The fight was refereed by a Russian official, Andrey Timoshin. Most observers felt Gilroy did enough to win. The judges were split evenly on the verdict which left the Irishman's fate in the hands of the Russian referee. He raised the arm of Behrendt, who later won the gold medal.

In the lightweight category, Tony Byrne's first opponent, Josef Chovanec from Czechoslovakia, was disqualified in the third round after receiving a third warning for his illegal tactic of charging headlong into the Irishman. In his bronze medal fight against American Luis Molina, Byrne – who had a reputation as a heavy puncher – delivered three devastating early punches, two to the head and one to the body, which effectively decided the fight in his favour. He won it on a unanimous decision: 60-58, 60-58, and 60-57. Ultimately, Byrne had to be content with a bronze medal – he lost on points to West Germany's Harry Kurschat, who was then defeated by Great Britain's Dick McTaggart in the final. The latter was awarded the prestigious Val Barker trophy after being adjudged the Best Boxer in the tournament. Sixty days later, Byrne stunned the audience in London's Royal Albert Hall when he outpointed McTaggart in an international between the two countries.

Caldwell also ended up with a bronze medal in the flyweight division. Having received a bye in the first round, the Belfast man knocked out Burmese boxer, Yai Shwe in the third round of their last sixteen contest. In the quarter-final he faced local hero Warren Batchelor, who was the favourite to win the gold medal. But Caldwell prevailed on a unanimous points decision. At eighteen years and 205 days he remains Ireland's youngest ever Olympic medallist – in any sport. The victory came at a cost, however. His eyes were badly swollen and he had only forty-eight hours to recover before the semi-final. Just over two hours before he was due in the ring, the doctor declared him unfit to fight for the silver medal.

'I'll never forget John's reaction,' recalled Martin Power in the Setanta documentary *Tales from a Neutral Corner*. 'There were tears coming out of his eyes even though they were closed.' Power grabbed Caldwell's towel and went outside where he found a street vendor selling bottles of Coca-Cola. 'I gave her fifty pence and she filled the towel with ice. I spent the next two hours applying the ice to John's face in an effort to reduce the swelling.'

Caldwell was passed fit to box but lost to the experienced Romanian Mircea

Dobrescu, who was subsequently defeated in the final.

But it is the name of another Romanian boxer, welterweight Nicolae Linca which remains etched in the Irish sporting psyche. Fred Tiedt dreamed about boxing in the Olympics from the age of eleven. He applied himself to the task with unusual diligence once he joined a boxing club in 1950. He would rise at 5am to do a six-mile run, followed by abdominal exercises, and then on to his job as a carpenter. His commitment paid off in Melbourne. Like his colleagues, Tiedt had no prior knowledge of any of his opponents. He went in 'cold' to all his contests. 'But if you see a lad who is not marked and he is champion of his country, you say to yourself, this guy can box,' Tiedt revealed in *Irish Olympians*.

He beat a Pole, Tadeusz Walasek, in the first round to earn a bronze medal bout against American Pearce Lane. Instead of using the double jab, which he deployed against the Pole, the Irishman rocked the American with hooks to the body and won comfortably. For the first and only time in the country's boxing history Ireland qualified four boxers for the Olympic semi-finals. Twenty-year-old Tiedt was the only one of the quartet to reach the final, though. His opponent, Kevin Hogarth was the last Australian boxer left in the tournament. Tiedt knew he needed to win well. In the event, Hogarth couldn't get near his elusive opponent, who had established his reputation in Ireland as a brilliant counter-puncher. Tiedt cruised to a comfortable points win. All the controversy was in the other semi-final, where Linca got a questionable decision over European champion Nicky Gargano from Great Britain.

Saturday, 1 December 1956 was a momentous day in Irish sport. At the Melbourne Cricket Ground twenty-one-year-old Ronnie Delany surprised everybody by winning the gold medal in the 1500 metres. A few hours later, the attention switched to the West Melbourne Stadium for the boxing finals.

A southpaw, Linca struggled to cope with Tiedt. As the fight progressed, the Romanian appeared to wilt and, noticeably, in the third round started to make mistakes. When the final bell sounded, everybody assumed that an Irishman would be crowned Olympic welterweight champion.

'I thought I was the clear winner. Everyone was jumping on me saying well done. I said to myself, wait, wait, wait,' recalled Tiedt in *Irish Olympians*. Likewise, the then president of the Olympic Council of Ireland (OCI) Lord Killanin was sounding caution when his fellow officials were urging him to go down to ringside to present the gold medal to his fellow Irishman. When it was announced, the decision shocked the majority of the 7,000 fans in the arena. Linca was awarded the fight on a 3-2 split decision. 'I couldn't believe it,' said Tiedt, and neither could the crowd, who greeted it with a chorus of boos and whistles.

It only emerged later how unfortunate the Irish boxer had been. Two of the judges, an Italian (A Gilardi) and an East German (H Hertel) gave Tiedt the verdict on a 60-58 score. This meant that in their view Tiedt won two of the rounds while the other was tied. However, the Polish judge (J Neuding) opted for his fellow Eastern European 60-59, which in layman's terms translated to two rounds drawn with Linca winning the other.

His decision would not have mattered but for the fact that the other two judges, a Korean (SJ Chuu) and a Brit (H Hedger) scored the fight 60-60 – essentially they judged that all three rounds were level. But both of them opted to give the nod to Linca which gave him a 3-2 majority. Overall, Tiedt secured three more points (229 to 226) than his opponent but still lost.

The verdict provoked an outcry in the international media. Nat Fleischer, the renowned boxing author and editor of *The Ring* – then the bible of the sport – described it as 'the most disgraceful decision I have ever witnessed.'

Boxing News reported: 'Linca was well beaten by Tiedt but received a verdict that looked like highway robbery. Tiedt boxed the head off Linca and absolutely skated home, only to see the judges give the most disgusting verdict in the whole of the Melbourne Games.'

Forty-eight hours later the story still featured in the Melbourne papers. *The Argus* reported: 'Went along to the Olympic boxing finals Saturday night to see another Irishman, F. Tiedt beaten rather surprisingly by N. Linca of Romania in the welterweight. I thought Tiedt won it. So did Peter Wilson, English sporting writer. He noted that two judges gave the points score 59 each [sic] but put a cross against Linca's name to indicate a preference for him. So Peter cabled to London that Tiedt was beaten by the double cross!'

Unusually, the International Olympic Committee's official report on the Games alluded to the controversy, albeit in oblique terms. 'Probably the most unlucky boxer was Tiedt (Ireland) who lost a close final to Linca (Romania). Tiedt had very hard fights in his division against Walasek (Poland), Lane (USA) and Hogarth (Australia). Linca was declared the winner on points in the final, and is the only Romanian to have gained a gold medal in boxing.'

Irish journalist AP McWeeney, who was at ringside, described it as 'travesty of justice' and the 'worst decision of the championships' in his dispatches to the *Irish Independent*. Later, in a four-part series on the Games, he questioned the impartiality of the Polish judge. 'Fair competition with the Communist world is hardly possible at present on the basis of pure judgment. The whole foundation of the Communist philosophy is that one is a communist first, and a Russian, a Romanian or a Czech afterwards. It was a Communist Pole who was the final arbitrator in that dreadful decision which a communist Romanian gained over Fred Tiedt in the welterweight final at Melbourne. It was he alone of five officials who thought that Linca deserved a points margin, albeit a single point one over the Irishman.'

Lord Killanin, who later served as President of the International Olympic Committee, suggested that the judging 'was better than at Helsinki but unfortunately, we got one of the worst decisions.'

Even though the Games ended on a bitterly disappointing note for the boxers, on reflection securing four medals – one silver and three bronze – was an unprecedented triumph, which was only surpassed at the London Olympics in 2012.

CHAPTER 2

THE FALLOW YEARS

*'We asked him if he knew anywhere in Moscow we could go to Mass.
He brought us to this out of the way place. We went back every morning and I
ended up serving Mass nine days in a row.'*

Jim McCourt

By the time the Moscow Olympics rolled around in 1980, Ireland had gone sixteen years without winning an Olympic medal of any hue. Indeed, in the previous twenty-four years Ireland had secured just a single Olympic medal: Jim McCourt's bronze in the lightweight category at the Tokyo Olympics in 1964. The heady days of the Melbourne Olympics were a distant memory. Fred Tiedt and John Caldwell boxed in the 1957 European Championships in Prague. The former won a bronze medal – he was unable to box in the semi-final due to a hand injury. Caldwell was beaten on a controversial 3-2 decision by eventual gold medallist Manfred Homberg from West Germany in the preliminary round. The pair, together with Gilroy, all turned professional afterwards.

Tiedt struggled to make an impact in the pro ranks and retired in 1964 after just twenty-one fights. By contrast, Caldwell enjoyed considerable success. In May 1961 he won the world bantamweight title, defeating French title holder, Alphonse Halimi, in London's Wembley Arena. Arguably his most memorable professional fight, however, was against his fellow Olympian Freddie Gilroy in October 1962.

The Cuban missile crisis was dominating world headlines, but it mattered little to the 15,000 spectators who jammed the King's Hall in Belfast to see the battle for the vacant Commonwealth and British bantamweight title. Once close friends, Fred Gilroy and John Caldwell battered each other to a pulp. Gilroy, the underdog, prevailed when Caldwell was forced to retire with a cut eye at the end of the ninth round. The winner never fought again; he couldn't make the weight as a bantam. Caldwell's susceptibility to eye injuries restricted him during the rest of his career. He finally hung up his gloves in 1965.

Ahead of the Rome Olympics in 1960, Harry Perry was Ireland's leading medal hope. From Harold's Cross on Dublin city's southside, he defeated future Olympic silver medallist Fred Tiedt in the 1956 Irish welterweight final, but the selectors opted to nominate the latter in the weight division for the Melbourne Games. Following representation from his club, British Railways, Perry was granted a box-off against Tiedt, which he lost. However, Perry still went to Melbourne, where he boxed in the light welterweight category. Tiedt's departure to the professional ranks in 1959 meant that Perry was the undisputed number one welterweight in amateur boxing in Ireland in subsequent years. The final showdown between Tiedt and Perry took place in the National Stadium in March 1958 in the Irish welterweight final. It was their third successive meeting in the decider and, having been controversially beaten in the 1957 decider, Perry won. It brought the curtain down on a rivalry which had enthralled boxing fans for five years and which Perry 'shaded' 4-3.

At the 1959 European championships in Lucerne, Perry was forced to concede a walkover in the semi-final to the eventual silver medallist Carmelo Bossi, after damaging ankle ligaments in the third round of his quarter-final win over Denmark's Benny Nielson. Two of his teammates, flyweight Adam McClean and middleweight Colm McCoy also secured bronze medals there.

However, a year later, against more exalted company in Rome's Sport Palace, the ten-man Irish team floundered at the Olympics. Perry lost a split 3-2 decision to a Korean Kim Ki-soo, who went on to become the country's first professional world champion in 1966. Perry's teammates Adam McClean (flyweight), Colm McCoy (heavyweight) and Joe Casey (super heavyweight) were also beaten in their first-round bouts.

The other six boxers, Patrick 'Paddy' Kenny (bantamweight), Andrew 'Ando' Reddy (featherweight), Danny O'Brien (lightweight), Bernard 'Bernie' Meli (light welterweight), Michael 'Mickser' Reid (light middleweight) and Eamonn McKeon (middleweight) – a brother of 1948 Olympian Mick – won their opening bouts but lost next time out.

Ireland's failure to win a medal at the next two European Championships in Belgrade and Moscow led one Irish boxing journalist to question the wisdom of sending a team to Tokyo for the 1964 Olympics. In the event, the five-member squad performed credibly, even though Chris Rafter (bantamweight) – who had lost in a box-off to John Caldwell for a place on the Olympic team in 1956 – Paddy Fitzsimmons (featherweight) and Brian Anderson (light welterweight) all failed to get past the first round. Belfast flyweight Sean McCaffrey caused a big upset when he fashioned a unanimous 5-0 win over Cuban Rafael Carbonell. He then beat a Ghanaian boxer, Sulley Shittu, to reach the last eight. However, in his medal bout he was out-boxed by the eventual gold medallist, Italian Fernando Atzori.

Another Belfast native, twenty-year-old Jim McCourt emerged as the Irish hero. He had been immersed in Belfast's rich boxing culture virtually from the time of his birth. His parents were boxing fanatics. In post-war Belfast both amateur and professional boxing thrived. The pin-up pugilist on the professional circuit was Derry native Billy 'Spider' Kelly, who emulated his father Jimmy by winning the Empire and British bantamweight titles in 1954 and 1955 respectively. 'Spider' had an indirect link with the McCourt family.

'My mother gave him sweets after his first fight in Belfast, and when he won the British title he came down to the front row to greet her, and she had sweets for him again. My father took me to see one of his fights when I was very young and he was my inspiration,' remembers McCourt.

Jim McCourt walked through the doors of Immaculata Boxing Club for the first time on Monday, 24 January 1955. In those days youngsters could not join a boxing club until they were eleven. He was chuffed to discover that the Immaculata boxers trained on a Monday night – the day of his eleventh birthday. He joined the club during a momentous period in their history. Another member John Caldwell – who lived nearby – was heading to the Melbourne Olympics later in the year, as was another Belfast boy, Freddie Gilroy. McCourt often watched them spar each other before they left, and when he reached the Elite level himself he sparred against them.

McCourt was trained by Jack McCusker who had also nurtured Caldwell's career. Two years after winning his first Irish vest, he followed in the footsteps of John McNally and Caldwell to become the third member of the club to represent Ireland at the Olympics. McCourt got his first taste of international boxing in the featherweight division at the European Championships in Moscow in 1963. Having beaten British boxer Tony Riley in the first round, he bowed out in the quarter-final to the eventual silver medallist Italian Giovanni Girgenti. However, it was what happened away from the ring that left a lasting impression on the Belfast teenager.

The seventeen visiting teams were each assigned an official interpreter; the four-man Irish team immediately bonded with their official, christening him 'Paddy'. 'We asked him if he knew anywhere in Moscow we could go to Mass. He brought us to this out of the way place where Mass was being celebrated. There were 'look-outs' standing outside the church in case the security services turned up. We went back every morning for the duration of the stay, and I ended up serving Mass nine days in a row,' McCourt recalls.

Having moved up to the lightweight division, McCourt went on to underline his class at the Tokyo Olympics. At face value, it looked as if he breezed through the tournament, fashioning majority 4-1 wins over Suh Bun Nam (Korea), Ghulam Sarwar (Pakistan) and Domingo Barrera (Spain) to secure the bronze medal.

The reality was altogether different. 'I busted my left hand in my first fight but managed to get through the other two. Once I had the bronze medal secured, the team management didn't want me to fight the Russian in the semi-final. I begged Paddy Carroll who was in charge of the team to let me fight. I was close to tears because if I was going to lose I wanted it to happen inside the ring.'

He did have his way and was considered unlucky to drop a split 3-2 decision to the Soviet Union's Vilikton Barannikov. The Irishman felt he had done enough to win the fight, as did many ringside observers. It was a desperately close call. The Ghanaian and French judges sided with McCourt 59-58 and 60-59 respectively, but their three colleagues from West and East Germany and the Netherlands gave the nod to the Soviet fighter 60-59, 60-58 and 60-58. Barannikov was surprisingly beaten in the gold medal bout by Józef Grudzień, from Poland. The Cold War was at its height, and McCourt got a glimpse of the mood of the world at the time when he bumped into the US judge RJ Surkein before the final. 'He said to me, "The Russian robbed you in

the semi-final, but if this Pole stays standing I will vote for him in the final."'
Three of the other judges from Korea, Hungary and the Netherlands also gave
the nod to the Pole, while the British judge called the fight a draw.

As Ireland's only medal winner at the Games, McCourt was fêted on his
return home – especially in his native Belfast. He was puzzled when he met his
parents at Dublin Airport and they insisted that he travel home on the train
accompanied by his father. 'As we pulled into the station in Belfast I saw the
St Patrick's brass band there and I remarked to my father that they must be
going somewhere.'

They had assembled, of course, to honour McCourt, who was carried shoulder high from the station on to a waiting lorry. 'I was very surprised. I thought
I had let the people down by losing the semi-final.'

He lost again to the eventual gold medallist Barannikov in the semi-final
of the 1965 European Championships in east Berlin, but delighted boxing
fans in Dublin earlier that year at the National Stadium, when he achieved a
majority 2-1 decision over the 1964 Olympic champion Józef Grudzień, who
lost to Barannikov in the European final. He was Ireland's only medal winner
at those championships in which the Soviet Union team won eight of the ten
titles. Later that year, he won the gold medal in the light welterweight division
at the Commonwealth Games in Kingston, Jamaica.

Despite McCourt's personal efforts, Ireland's slide continued. At the 1967
European Championships in Rome, Ireland's seven-man team won just two
fights between them. There was a significant improvement in form, however,
at the Mexico Olympics in 1968. But the Games turned into a nightmare for
McCourt who had the honour of carrying the Irish flag during the opening
ceremony. He was so adversely affected by the oppressive heat in Mexico City
that he became ill and shed nearly half a stone in weight. 'I could have boxed
as a lightweight in Mexico. I was only weighing 9 st 5 lbs. I was able to eat my

breakfast before I went for the weigh-in.'

However, the weight loss left him completely devoid of strength for the 63.5 kg (10 st 0 lbs) light welterweight division, and his confidence was brittle as well. Five months before the games he had comfortably outpointed West Germany's Gert Puzicha in an international at the National Stadium. When they clashed again in the first round of the Olympics the outcome was very different, and the fight itself was a strange affair. The two boxers were repeatedly warned by the referee about their inactivity in the ring; neither was willing to come forward. The German did score enough points in the third round to get the verdict from four of the judges – the fifth marked the fight a draw. Puzicha exited in the next round. There was no consolation for McCourt, who still harbours pangs of regret about the experience. 'It was the biggest disappointment of my career. I wasn't myself in Mexico.'

Flyweight Brendan McCarthy, featherweight Edward 'Eddie' Tracey and lightweight Martin 'Marty' Quinn were unlucky in the draw. McCarthy lost to gold medallist Ricardo Delgado from the host nation; Tracey won his first round bout against Errol West from Jamaica but then lost to gold medallist Antonio Roldán from Mexico. Quinn, after knocking out Inoua Bodia from Cameroon in the first round, lost to defending Olympic champion and eventual silver medallist Józef Grudzień from Poland. Eighteen-year-old Quinn was unlucky not to eliminate the legendary Polish lightweight. He had him on the canvas in the third round. But he was slow to retreat to the neutral corner which delayed the start of the mandatory count. There was a break for thirty-eight seconds, which gave Grudzień sufficient time to recover and win the bout 4-1.

The Irish boxing hero in Mexico was twenty-one-year-old Castlecomer native Mick Dowling, who had arrived in Dublin five years earlier to train as a waiter in the Gresham Hotel. He enjoyed an eventful Olympics knocking out an East German, Bernd Juterzenka, in the first round of the bantamweight category, after catching him with successive right hooks. His second-round opponent, Australian John Rakowski was disqualified for illegal use of his head. Rakowski had been on the back foot from early in the second round when Dowling had caught him with a perfect right hand.

But Dowling's quarter-final bout against Eiji Morioka from Japan proved anticlimactic. He received two formal warnings which effectively scuppered his chances of securing the bronze medal. Nonetheless, he still became the poster boy of Irish boxing for the next decade.

In Europe though, the Eastern bloc dominated. At the eighteenth European Championships, held in the Romanian capital Bucharest in 1969, all but one of the gold medals were captured by boxers from the Eastern bloc countries. West German welterweight Günther Meier was the only boxer from a western nation to capture a title. This dominance extended to the full rostrum. Seven of the available eleven silver medals and twelve of the twenty-two bronze medals awarded in Bucharest were to boxers from communist countries. Dowling was one of the ten bronze medallists from the West. He won it the hard way – beating Russian Igor Kulagin in the first round before outpointing East Germany's Reinhard Schulz in the quarter-final. He was beaten on a split 4-1 decision by silver medallist Aldo Cosentino from France.

Two years later, in 1971, at the next European Championships staged in Madrid, Dowling – who competed in the bantamweight division throughout his career – was one of three Irish boxers who claimed bronze medals. Flyweight Neil McLaughlin and Brendan McCarthy – who had moved up to featherweight – also medalled. Again the championship was dominated by Eastern bloc countries, who between them won ten gold, ten silver and eleven bronze medals. Ireland did remarkably well – their three-medal haul left them ninth in the medal table and the third best non-communist country behind the hosts Spain and West Germany.

After beating home-town favourite Jose Luis Otero in the quarter-final, Dowling was confident ahead of his semi-final clash against Aleksandr Meinikov from the Soviet Union. 'He never hit me with anything in that fight,' declared Dowling in *Legends of Irish Boxing*. But Meinikov got the verdict 5-0. He was beaten in the final by Tibor Badari from Hungary. According to former IABA President Breandán Ó Conaire, there was an ideological war going on at the time. 'It was called the cold war because there were no battles. The Eastern bloc countries, particularly the Russians, inculcated into their boxers and, indeed, all their athletes the idea that they were representing their system in a battle against the capitalists. And the same applied to the officials,' suggests Ó Conaire, who served as chairman of the powerful Refereeing and Judging Commission in Europe during the latter half of the nineties.

Back at the coalface, neither Ireland's nor Dowling's luck changed at the Munich Olympics in 1972. There was controversy before the team departed when Jim McCourt's dream of being the first Irish boxer to compete at three Olympics Games became unstuck after he refused to undertake collective training with the Irish squad ahead of the Games. It was a bitter end to McCourt's career and it still rankles. 'Obviously I was very disappointed at how it ended. Collective training just didn't suit me for some reason. I had tried it previously and I couldn't lose the half stone. Whereas if I stayed in Belfast and followed my normal routine, the weight just fell off me. So, even though I had beaten him in the National Finals [in April 1972], Jim Montague went instead.'

While Ireland's six-man team failed to garner a medal, it was the country's best team performance in the Olympics since Melbourne, with all six winning at least one fight. Montague lost to gold medallist Ray Seales from the United States in the second round, welterweight John Rodgers bowed out at the same stage to Anatoily Khokhlov (USSR), while light middleweight Christy Elliott was stopped by Mexican Emeterio Villanueva in round three. Mick Dowling experienced rotten luck again, beaten on a split 3-2 decision by Orlando Martinez from Cuba in the second round. Martinez breezed through his two remaining two bouts on his way to being crowned bantamweight champion. Derry natives Neil McLaughlin (flyweight) and Charlie Nash (lightweight) also came tantalizingly close to capturing medals.

The latter's performance was all the more noteworthy, given the trauma his family had experienced just months earlier. Charlie Nash's nineteen-year-old brother William was one of thirteen civilians shot dead by British paratroopers during a civil rights march in his native Derry on 30 January 1972, while his father, Alex, was wounded. The boxing ring gave the twenty-one-year-old, who was raised on the city's Creggan Estate, some respite. Wins over Erik Madsen (Denmark) and Antonio Gin (Mexico) left him nine minutes away from an Olympic medal. But in the quarter-final he proved no match for gold medallist Jan Szczepanski from Poland. The referee stopped the contest in the third round.

From the Bogside in Derry, Neil McLaughlin had established his credentials at the European Championships in Madrid a year earlier when he won a bronze medal. At the Olympics the flyweight beat two African boxers, Abaker Saed Mohamed (Sudan) and Mohamed Selim (Egypt) to reach the quarter-finals. Another African boxer, silver medallist Leo Rwabwogo (Uganda) ended McLaughlin's medal ambitions when the referee stopped the contest in the third round.

The retirement of Dowling from international duty following the 1973 European Championships, and the decision of McLaughlin and Nash to turn professional left a void in the higher echelons of Irish amateur boxing for the remainder of the decade.

The 1973 Europeans followed a now-predictable pattern. Boxers from Eastern Europe dominated, winning ten of the eleven titles on offer. Apart from dubious judging decisions, all the Eastern-bloc boxers were full time which gave them a decided advantage over their opponents. Super heavyweight Peter Mullen did reach the quarter-finals in Belgrade, before running into gold medallist Viktor Ulyanich from the Soviet Union. However, even the best full-time boxers from Eastern Europe proved no match for the Cubans, who dominated the inaugural World Championships in Havana in 1974. The hosts won five of the eleven gold medals.

Ireland's two-man team, Commonwealth Games gold medallist Davy Larmour, who hailed from Belfast's Shankill Road, and Lisburn native John Rodgers met Cuban President Fidel Castro. In the ring Larmour lost in the first round of his flyweight contest to bronze medallist Constantin Gruiescu from Romania. Rodgers had a more eventful time in the welterweight category. His second-round clash against Reginald Forde of Guyana ended prematurely. Forde headbutted the Irishman; Rodgers retaliated but got caught and was disqualified in the third round.

Eastern bloc countries won an astonishing thirty-six of the forty-two medals presented at the twenty-first European Championships in Poland in 1975. The eastern haul consisted of ten gold, ten silver and sixteen bronze. Ireland returned empty-handed, an ominous sign just a year out from the Montreal Olympics.

Davy Larmour performed best of the five-man Irish team, reaching the quarter-finals of the flyweight division, where he lost to future professional world champion Charlie Magri from Great Britain.

A member of Albert Foundry Boxing Club, Larmour also came closest to securing a medal at the Montreal Olympics. The Games were boycotted by twenty-eight countries – mostly African – because the International Olympic

Committee (IOC) refused to ban New Zealand after the All Blacks toured South Africa earlier in 1976. However, the draw for the boxing was made on the assumption that the threatened boycott would not go ahead. It brought mixed blessings for Larmour who went straight through to the quarter-finals, after receiving byes in the first two rounds. By then, his scheduled opponents Robert Musuku (Sudan) and Agustin Martinez (Niger) were on their way home.

So his first bout in the Maurice Richard Arena was for an Olympic medal. But he lost a majority 4-1 decision to an eighteen-year-old American, Leo Randolph, who went on to win the gold medal.

As for the other Irish boxers: light flyweight Brendan Dunne – father of future world champion Bernard Dunne – was stopped by bronze medallist Orlando Maldonado from Puerto Rico in the first round; lightweight Gerry Hamill was beaten by bronze medallist Ace Rusevski from Yugoslavia in the first round, while welterweight Christy McLoughlin and light middleweight Brian Byrne both bowed out in round two.

Philip Sutcliffe, a seventeen-year-old teenager from Crumlin in Dublin, finally ended Ireland's medal famine at major championships when he won a bronze medal in the light flyweight category at the 1977 European Championships in Halle. In only his fifth senior fight Sutcliffe – the eldest of seven brothers from a family of eleven – outclassed gold-medal favourite Paul Fletcher from Liverpool, earning himself a five-minute standing ovation. He was stopped in the semi-final by the defending title holder and eventual gold medallist, Poland's Henryk Średnicki.

Two years later, Sutcliffe captured another bronze medal at European level – this time in the bantamweight category in Cologne. He broke his right hand in the first round of the semi-final, which he lost to the eventual champion, Nikolay Khraptsov from Russia. It was an injury which dogged him for the rest of his career. 'It just kept swelling up regardless of what I did. I couldn't lift a cup of tea or turn a screwdriver,' he recalls.

Meanwhile, renowned Belfast coach Gerry Storey had taken charge of an exceptionally talented group of boxers who swept the boards for Northern Ireland at the Commonwealth Games in Edmonton, Canada, in August 1978. Arguably the most talented of the bunch was Barry McGuigan from Clones, County Monaghan. Even though he had only recently celebrated his seventeenth birthday, he underlined his potential when he won the gold medal in the bantamweight category.

Olympian Gerry Hamill also took gold in the lightweight class; welterweight Kenny Beattie won a silver medal; while Hugh Russell captured a bronze in the flyweight category. McGuigan's victory compensated for the bitter disappointment he experienced months earlier when he was too young to compete in the European Junior Championships, hosted in Dublin. He was already training with the squad in Drogheda when one of his teammates showed him a newspaper article stating that he was ineligible for the championships. Just to rub salt in his wounds, his replacement, Mick Holmes – whom he had previously beaten, won a silver medal in the 54 kg category.

McGuigan's lifelong ambition was to win a gold medal at the Moscow Olympics. While still at school, he made a small T-square in woodwork class and inscribed on it: 'Please God let me win the gold in 1980.' And, despite his tender years, he looked bang on course to fulfil his dreams in Moscow. Moving up to the 57 kg featherweight in division in 1979, McGuigan beat two East Germans, Torsten Koch and Mario Behrendt – whose father, Wolfgang, won the gold medal at the Melbourne Olympics, having defeated Ireland's Freddie Gilroy en route – as well as securing a gold medal at a tournament in Constanta, Romania.

McGuigan was capable of competing on equal terms with featherweights from behind the Iron Curtain because, like them, he was a full-time boxer. 'My parents allowed me the luxury of being able to train full time. I gave them as much help as I could in their grocery shop. I'm proud to say that even when I was a kid I worked harder in the shop that anybody else in the family.' In-between packing the shelves, he was able to do his road work in the morning and train again in the afternoon.

Unbeknownst to McGuigan, however, his Olympic dream began to unravel in bizarre circumstances early in 1980. He arrived at the National Stadium to box Richie Foster in an Ulster *v* Leinster match, but an official took exception to a piece of sticky tape which McGuigan had used to secure the bandages protecting his hand. He ordered him back to the dressing room to change it, but an irate McGuigan refused. Instead, the boxer ripped off the bandages, pulled the gloves on to his bare hands and knocked Foster down three times. Unfortunately, in the process, he chipped a bone on one of the knuckles in his left hand. He missed the Ulster Senior Championships as a result but recovered in time for the National Seniors, where he damaged the knuckle again during his semi-final win over Damien Fryers, forcing him to concede a walkover to Mick Holmes in the final.

Next stop for McGuigan was the European Junior Championships in Rimini, Italy. He claimed a bronze medal after dropping a controversial 3-2 decision in the semi-final against the then world junior champion, Yuriy Gladyshev from the Soviet Union, who won the gold. It was of little consolation to McGuigan that all seven members of a jury panel who were overseeing the judging at the tournament gave him the decision. They didn't have the authority to overturn the decision. Ireland's seven-man team assembled in the Rosnaree Hotel in Drogheda to begin collective training ahead of the Moscow Olympics. However, three national champions were missing. The decision of the Christle brothers, Terry (middleweight), Joe (heavyweight), and Mel (super heavyweight), not to attend the camp effectively ruled them out of the team for Moscow. They wanted to remain training in Dublin under the direction of Olympic silver medallist Fred Tiedt. Ironically, Joe is now the chairman of the Irish Amateur Boxing Association's (IABA) Board of Directors.

McGuigan was captain of the team, and the nation expected him to deliver a medal. Unfortunately, at the squad's final sparring session, disaster struck. He was caught by a left hook delivered by Tommy Davitt, a professional boxer who was sparring with the squad. The force of the blow broke one of McGuigan's ribs. 'As a result I couldn't do any sparring when I arrived in Moscow, and my timing was definitely affected in my first fight against a Tanzanian, Issack Mabushi.'

Despite McGuigan's lack of practice he overcame the challenge of Mabushi; the referee stopped the contest in round three. But the victory came at a price; he had damaged his left hand again. McGuigan's injured hand was frozen with a local anaesthetic for his next fight against Zambian Winfred Kabunda. McGuigan believed he had done enough to win it, but was beaten on a majority 4-1 decision. It was only one of six fights he ever lost at senior level in his amateur and professional career.

'It was a bad decision, I clearly beat him. I was so, so disappointed. The funny thing is Kabunda was robbed in his next fight against the East German Rudi Fink, who ended up with the gold medal,' recalls McGuigan.

Double European bronze medallist Philip Sutcliffe made it to Moscow despite his hand injury but crashed out in the first round to a then unheralded Daniel Zaragoza. The Mexican didn't win a medal in Moscow but proved his calibre in the professional ranks, dominating the super bantamweight for more than a decade. Indeed, in January 1997 in Boston, he inflicted a first ever pro-defeat on Ireland's 1992 Olympic silver medallist Wayne McCullough when successfully defending his super bantamweight crown.

So it was left to McGuigan's room-mate Hugh Russell to carry Ireland's ambitions, not just in the Olympiski Sports Complex but for the entire Irish entourage as the country's other medal contenders fell by the wayside: John Treacy collapsed in the heats of the 10,000 metres; Eamonn Coghlan finished fourth in the 5,000 metres, and the Irish rowers were struck down with illness. David Wilkins and Jamie Wilkinson won a silver medal in the Flying Dutchman class in yachting. This competition was held 870 kilometres away in the Estonian capital of Tallinn and so it didn't have quite the immediate impact back at camp base.

Born and raised on the New Lodge Road in north Belfast, Hugh Russell developed a habit of saying, 'I was lucky'. 'Maybe "fortunate" might be a better description,' he later suggested – fortunate in that none of his immediate family became embroiled in the violence that raged in Belfast for close on three decades, fortunate that the Holy Family Boxing Club was three hundred metres from his front door, and fortunate that his coach was Gerry Storey.

'He was probably the best trainer in Ireland. One time he threw us a load of tennis balls to bounce, an exercise designed to improve our co-ordination. Everybody was laughing at what we were doing. Ten years later, when the Cubans came to Ireland they were doing the same thing with tennis balls.

'Lads that I went to school with are dead now while others were in jail for long periods. Without a shadow of a doubt boxing kept me and lots of other kids away from all that. I'm sure my parents were horrified every time any of us went out, but I never got any hassle. Boxing is a very personal endeavour. I hate to say this, but every time I stepped into the ring in Moscow, I promised God that I would never ask another favour in my life so long as I won this fight. Of course, I just had to ask him a bigger favour the next time I got into the ring.'

Russell sacrificed everything for boxing. 'I got selected for the Olympics and then I got the sack,' he recalls. At the time he was working in Belfast docks, driving a small tugboat. 'I couldn't get the time off to train so I left. My parents were very supportive, they said: "Follow your dream." I couldn't have done it without their support. It's the same in all sports: the more successful you are, the more you need your families. It gets lonely at times; your life is spent in the gym or in the house. There is no social life. I have always described being at the Olympics as like being in heaven. You're cocooned in this false environment in which everybody around you is healthy and beautiful.'

Sixty-five countries heeded the US-led boycott of the Moscow Olympics and did not compete. As a result, the numbers competing in the tournament were significantly reduced, with only twenty-two boxers in the flyweight category. Twenty-year-old Russell fashioned unanimous 5-0 wins over Samir Khiniab from Iraq and Emmanuel Mlundwa from Tanzania to reach the quarter-finals. For once Ireland got a favourable decision in an Olympic medal bout. Russell rode his luck against North Korean Yo Ryon-sik, getting the verdict on a split 3-2 decision. Ireland had secured its first Olympic boxing medal since 1964.

'By now most of the other Irish team members had finished their involvement in the Games and they came to see my medal fight. The place was buzzing. The first thing Storey wanted to do was to take the wind out of my sails. I had a semi-final coming up and he was adamant that I had to start focussing on it.'

The eventual gold medallist Petar Lesov ended Russell's involvement in the Games with a unanimous 5-0 win over the Irishman in the semi-final.

'There was probably more of a celebration that night than when I won the quarter-final to guarantee myself a bronze medal,' Russell remembers. 'I've always said it: "Winning an Olympic medal changes your life." I still get letters asking for my autograph.'

'I had never touched an Olympic medal until I received my own. No sooner had I stepped off the rostrum than an official insisted on taking it away to have my name engraved on it. I'll always remember going to collect it the next day. I couldn't help but notice a bin in the office, half-full of discarded Olympic medals which had been incorrectly inscribed. I would have loved to get my hands on them.'

The youngster was overwhelmed by the reception he received in his home city. There was an anecdotal story told that rioting on the New Lodge Road stopped during Russell's fights. 'I was only a kid. I didn't realise at the time what I had done and I kept wondering why everybody wanted to meet me.'

The Moscow Olympics influenced Russell's ultimate career choice when he retired from boxing. He became a professional photographer with *The Irish News* and is now picture editor of the paper. 'Being Paddys, we changed our money on the streets, where the exchange rate was more favourable. I ended up with a lot of rubles but little to spend them on. So I bought this very large Zenith camera. I don't remember exactly how much it cost. I guess it was forty or fifty quid, which was a lot of dough back then.'

After failing to medal at the European Championships in Finland 1981, Russell linked up with promoter Barney Eastwood and made his professional debut in the Ulster Hall in December of that year. He was driven by one ambition – to win a Lonsdale Belt outright. The belt, which is made partly from gold and porcelain, is presented to the British champion in each weight division in professional boxing.

The rules have since changed, but in Russell's day a boxer had to success-fully defend his title on two consecutive occasions to secure the belt outright. Having initially won the British bantamweight title, Russell then claimed the flyweight crown in January 1984, against Kelvin Smart, and successfully defended it the following November against Danny Flynn.

On 23 February 1985, in the King's Hall, Belfast, he stopped Charlie Brown in the twelfth and final round of their title fight; Russell was trailing on points at the time. With his Lonsdale Belt secured, Hugh Russell retired.

Barry McGuigan had an altogether more spectacular professional career. It too culminated in 1985. On 8 June, in London, the 'Clones Cyclone' dismantled the defences of the defending Panamanian title holder, Eusebio Pedroza to capture the WBA featherweight championship of the world. The victory sent the entire island of Ireland into a celebratory frenzy.

Ultimately, Hugh Russell's Olympic medal did not significantly alter the fortunes of Irish boxing. Another three Olympic cycles passed before Irish amateur boxers hit the front pages again. When the breakthrough came in Barcelona in 1992 it was nothing short of sensational.

CHAPTER 3

REVOLUTIONARY ROAD

'The Irish guys were great fighters. They were courageous, fearless and loved to
fight. It went back to the warrior tradition of Cúchulainn.'
Breandán Ó Conaire

B reandán Ó Conaire is not your archetypal boxing aficionado. A brilliant academic, Irish scholar, historian and author, he is the retired head of the Irish Department in St Patrick's College, Dublin City University. Arguably, he has also been the most influential administrator in Irish boxing during the last half century. And, at international level, he was at the forefront of attempts to reform judging and refereeing.

Ó Conaire was born in Dublin but lived in different parts of the country due to the transient nature of his father's work in the forestry industry. After completing his primary education, he won a scholarship to the newly-opened Gormanston College in County Meath, run by the Franciscans. Among his class mates were Joe Lee, currently Professor of History at New York University, and journalist and author Séamus Martin.

He has an abiding lifelong interest in boxing. 'I used to get *Ring* magazine delivered to the college,' he recalls. Such was his passion for the sport that he once attempted to organise an in-house boxing tournament in Gormanston. 'I matched up everybody in my class. I had been paired against a student who is now the rector of the college. It was complete nutcase stuff, but when you're sixteen or seventeen you are entitled to be a nutcase.' Fearful for the students' welfare, the college refused permission for the tournament.

On completion of his third-level studies Ó Conaire secured a post in the Irish Department in St Patrick's College. He continued to compete for Arbour Hill Boxing Club, though he didn't advertise it to his employers. But he was inadvertently rumbled by his former classmate Séamus Martin, then working as a sports journalist with *The Irish Press*. 'One night I was boxing a British army champion in the Stadium. Séamus and the late Tom Cryan, the boxing correspondent of the *Irish Independent*, were there. The following day there was a picture of me in action in one of the papers. Luckily, the college authorities didn't frown on it.'

After helping to establish a new club, Bay City Boxing Club, in the newly developed northside suburb of Bayside in 1978, Ó Conaire was encouraged to get involved in the administrative side of boxing.

Initially, he was reluctant – essentially because of his existing workload, allied to the fact that he was more interested in coaching. Despite his misgivings, Ó Conaire became secretary of the Dublin Boxing Board. He quickly discovered that the most effective way of getting things done was to do it yourself. And by the end of the 1970s Irish boxing was ripe for a revolution.

In the previous quarter of a century international boxing had changed irrevocably, but Ireland had not kept pace. The halcyon days of the 1950s, when Ireland had won five medals in successive Olympic Games, was a fading memory. The odds were now stacked against small nations ever competing on an equal footing with the Eastern bloc countries and Cuba, whose top amateur boxers were full-time athletes.

The Soviet Union first sent a boxing team to the Helsinki Olympics in 1952. They won six medals – two silver and four bronze – and were ranked seventh. Four years later, in Melbourne, they won three titles and were ranked number one. In two of the next three Olympics they were again ranked number one, before being upstaged in 1972 by Cuba, the new superpower whose coaches had been trained by their Soviet counterparts. In the 1976 Olympics in Montreal, the USA boxing team – which included future world professional champions, Sugar Ray Leonard, the Spinks brothers Michael and Leon, and Leo Randolph – topped the rankings with five gold medals. All but nine of the remaining thirty-nine medals went to boxers from Communist states. The only western European countries to win medals were Great Britain and West Germany who each won a bronze.

In his academic career Ó Conaire was used to analysing texts. He applied the same skills to his chosen sport, to ascertain the reasons Irish boxers struggled to make an impact in major international competitions. 'The Irish guys were great fighters. They were courageous, fearless and loved to fight. It went back to the warrior tradition of Cúchulainn, Fionn Mac Cumhaill, and local heroes in Irish folklore. Many writers in the Irish language have documented examples of local fighters. While some of it is fiction, much of it is based on local characters. The great Irish-American fighters of the late-nineteenth and twentieth century are modern examples of this tradition.

'I came to the realisation that we were boxing in a different realm to the gold medallists. In the Soviet Union, Cuba, and nearly all the Eastern bloc countries their boxers were full-time fighters. They were university students or soldiers in the army, so technically they were amateurs. Our guys could fight. They'd fight until they died, but they were running into punches and lacking some of the more technically advanced skills and expert conditioning of the "professional amateurs".'

Things move slowly within the corridors of power in Irish sport, and more particularly in the Irish Amateur Boxing Association. It wasn't until he was elected vice-president of the IABA in 1987, defeating incumbent Tom Muldowney, and became the association's Director of Coaching that he was in a position to initiate change. It didn't come easy.

'I was an outsider. There is a lot of politics in boxing. There was a group in the IABA Central Council that weren't going to be pushed. They backed each other up, and the same guys got elected every year. A general feeling became prevalent that new blood was required to drive the association forward.

'Boxing is a very special type of sport that requires a special mentality. People who attended schools such as Glenstal, Rockwell, Clongowes, Belvedere or Blackrock rarely turn up in boxing rings. Unlike the experience of rugby players, the boxer's "team mates" are always outside the field of combat, looking in.

'The association needed new faces, new energies, people with a boxing mentality, and a total commitment to the needs and welfare of the boxer. In subsequent years, individuals such as Joe Kirwan, Martin Power and Seán Horkan were elected to the officer board and made significant and enduring contributions,' says Ó Conaire.

Due to the absence of strict conditions regarding the establishment of boxing clubs at the time, anybody could set up a club. 'An ex-boxer could say, "I know about boxing", and open a club. This presented a dangerous situation for the association,' according to Ó Conaire. 'After being elected vice-president, I proposed a number of regulations to close this loophole and to commence the reform of the coaching sector. As a consequence, coaches had to be qualified and registered with the association.'

Ó Conaire's primary ambition, however, was to persuade his colleagues on the Central Council to adopt a new national coaching plan. 'There was almost internecine warfare to see who the chief national coach would be, even though it was a largely low-impact role. Before my election, I had done a lot of coaching work in Dublin and Leinster. There was huge support from the grass roots. I produced a national plan and coaching strategy and distributed it in advance to all the members of the Central Council so nobody could turn around and say they knew nothing about it.

'But it still took me two meetings to get it through, not because there was anything wrong with the plan, but I was the wrong person presenting it. As it turned out the president of the Ulster Boxing Council at that time was an archetypal straight-talking former British army [North Irish Horse which was part of the Royal Armoured Corp] man called Albert Uprichard. He wiped out all opposition by declaring that this was the way we were going to do things. So the plan became official IABA policy in February 1988,' recalls Ó Conaire.

The leading coaches in the country at the time, including Gerry Storey, Michael Hawkins and Austin Carruth as members of the National Coaching Committee chaired by Ó Conaire, spearheaded the practical implementation of the new strategy. They were joined by strength and conditioning coach Eugene Traynor and double European bronze medallist and nine times Elite champion Mick Dowling. Every aspect of boxing was covered: techniques, tactics, conditioning, nutrition, psychology, and the legal aspects of the sport. 'We went all over the country. It was really a full-time job; we were completely dedicated, though we were volunteers,' recalls Ó Conaire. One of the most striking outcomes of the 'crusade' was the increase in the number of national titles, at all levels, being won by boxers from outside the major centres – a trend that has continued.

This new strategy challenged long-standing practices within boxing clubs.

Traditionally sparring was regarded as a straight-forward fight rather than a learning process. 'This was diabolically wrong,' maintains Ó Conaire, 'because the guys in the ring knew how to fight and they learned nothing from battering each other. It was entertainment but it wasn't coaching.'

So when Ó Conaire and his colleagues organised sparring sessions, the boxers' coaches could come along and watch, provided they didn't issue instructions from the corner. 'I wasn't popular as a result with some coaches. While most coaches would sit down and watch, the more aggressive ones wanted to get involved. So we had to restrain them. Once we did, the rest followed suit.'

Learning defensive strategies was a key element of the new approach. 'You can fire all the shots you like, but if you are getting hit all the time you are not going to win, so we initially concentrated on defensive techniques.' Ó Conaire's core beliefs about the importance of learning how to avoid being hit were reinforced when Cuban coach Nicolás Cruz Hernández arrived in Ireland in 1988. As Ó Conaire adds, 'I recall him watching a light heavyweight contest in the stadium, and he remarked that neither boxer should have been allowed into the ring because they didn't know how to defend themselves correctly.'

In many respects the IABA was ahead of the other sporting organisations in Ireland in terms of their coaching strategy. It wasn't until 1991 that the government established the National Coaching and Teaching Centre (NCTC) on the campus of the University of Limerick. The NCTC produced a five-year plan called the National Coaching and Development Programme (1993–1998), with the aim of modernising, co-ordinating, supporting and developing coaches in all sports throughout Ireland. The establishment of a central accreditation system and a national register for all coaches was also included. Over sixty sporting organisations, including the IABA, took part.

By then the IABA had moved on and recruited a Cuban coach, following negotiations with the Cuban authorities in London. His primary task was to assist with the preparation of the international teams. An American coach, Luis Camacho, also spent a short time in the country. The boxers didn't quite gel with the first Cuban, Trotman Daley. But his successor, Nicolás Cruz Hernández, had a profound influence on Irish boxing for the next decade. Apart from his work with the international squad, Cruz was also involved in the coaching teaching programme.

'We brought him to the various clubs where he did specific workshops on specific topics such as pad work and 'school boxing,' remembers Ó Conaire. 'I still have the notes from a series of lectures he did in the National Stadium for Leinster-based coaches. We also brought over an East German coach, Karl-Heinz Nitzsche, for two weeks and he gave valuable practical seminars for the coaches.'

Even though finance or more correctly the lack of it was a perennial problem, Ó Conaire's vision was to imbue the coaches with a professional ethic. 'We needed to persuade the coaches that even though they weren't being paid, they needed to have a professional approach and mentality.'

Furthermore, it was crucial that youngsters coming into the sport were coached correctly from day one. 'Although we had very talented boxers and dedicated coaches at all levels, we found that some of the senior boxers had technical weaknesses. This arose because their coaches hadn't been trained how to build up their foundation and basic skills. So a lot of them would be defeated when they came up against the very best guys at international level. These faults were like memory muscle – they were ingrained,' Ó Conaire suggests.

But for Ireland to achieve success again at international level, the judging system at major championship events had to be reformed. Ó Conaire played a key role in implementing the requisite changes. All judged sport is subject to controversy, but none have come close to generating as much tumult as boxing.

Ireland had been on the receiving end of more than a fair share of dubious decisions over the decades. The failure to give Fred Tiedt the decision in the welterweight final in Melbourne in 1956 was the most controversial, though virtually every Irish boxer had a tale of woe, particularly from their clashes against Eastern bloc opponents.

Internationally, the issue crystalized at the Seoul Olympics in 1988. Four years earlier, in Los Angeles, the Koreans were upset by what they perceived as biased judging against their boxers in favour of US fighters. Hosting the Games seemed to empower South Korea to literally take the law into their own hands. After bantamweight Byun Jong-il was beaten by Aleksandar Hristov from Bulgaria, the Korean boxing trainer Lee Heung-soo charged into the ring and attacked referee Keith Walker. The referee's decision to instruct the judges to deduct two points from Byun for headbutting cost the Korean boxer the fight.

A full-scale riot ensued. One security guard took off his uniform jacket before going after the referee. He disclosed later: 'I acted instinctively for the love of my fatherland.' Fellow referees came to Walker's aid and he was eventually escorted from the arena to his hotel. He packed his bags and took the next flight home to New Zealand.

Interestingly, renowned Olympic historian David Wallechinsky claimed in *The Complete Book of the Summer Olympics 1996 Edition* that Walker had been criticised by Irish officials for *not* penalising another Korean boxer Song Kyung-sup for headbutting Billy Walsh in an earlier contest.

But this controversy paled into the shadows compared to the fall-out following the light middleweight final, in which American Roy Jones dropped a majority 3-2 decision to another Korean, Park Si-hun. Even allowing for the vagaries of the system, it was an outrageous decision. Jones landed eighty-six punches to Park's thirty-two. The Korean took two standing eight counts and was twice warned by the referee. Nonetheless, three of the judges, Bob Kasule of Uganda, Uruguay's Alberto Durán and Hiouad Larbi of Morocco, gave the Korean the decision. Even Park was embarrassed. At the medal ceremony he held the American's fist aloft. Though he didn't win the gold medal, Jones was awarded the Val Barker Trophy as the best boxer at the Games.

The fall-out continued for months. Confronted by the media, the Moroccan judge claimed that he was so convinced that his four colleagues would vote for Jones he gave the verdict to the Korean to ensure the host country wasn't embarrassed. The sport's governing body, the International Amateur Boxing Association (AIBA), whose president, Anwar Chowdhry, was a controversial figure, had little option but to launch a formal investigation. The outcome was announced in Nairobi the following spring. The three judges who favoured Park were suspended for two years; bizarrely so was Sándor Payer from Hungary who had voted 60-56 for Jones. A further thirteen officials were suspended from officiating at the next world championships, and among them was Zaut Gvadjava from the Soviet Union who also voted 60-56 for Jones. As investigative author Andrew Jennings wrote in *The New Lord of the Rings: Olympic Corruption and How to Buy Gold Medals*: 'So the two honest judges in the Jones bout were given the same treatment as the crooks!'

There the matter rested until after the reunification of Germany when the files of the Stasi, the East German state security service during the Communist reign, were released. It transpired that Karl-Heinz Wehr, the then general secretary of the AIBA, worked as a Stasi agent. Andrew Jennings discovered that Wehr had written a detailed – and presumably true – account of what happened in Seoul and the subsequent investigation. Extracts from his report were published in *The New Lord of the Rings*.

Wehr wrote: 'They [the host nation] repeatedly attempted to persuade me to take back my decisions, punishing judges they seemed to have an interest in.' He went on to allege that bribes were paid to several unnamed judges, including three from Africa and one from South America, with the instruction to vote for the Korean boxer in the bouts they officiated at. Wehr told his spy masters that he felt the 'manipulation' went high up into the executive of the AIBA and he added: 'I am not sure if those who have knowledge of these events will keep their mouth shut.'

In the event they did. Nonetheless, faced with the possibility of boxing being dropped from the Olympics, which would have effectively spelled the sport's death-knell at amateur level, the AIBA introduced a computerised scoring system. Each of the five judges had two consoles in front of them – coloured red and blue to correspond with the colour of the singlets worn by the boxers. Whenever a boxer connected with a punch, the judge pressed the corresponding coloured button. If three of the five judges pushed their button within a second of each other, the boxer automatically received a point. The boxer who accumulated most points at the end of the fight was declared the winner.

This supposedly foolproof system was nothing of the sort. It was discovered that judges had different motor reaction times. There was also a strong suspicion that on occasions they pressed the wrong button. Furthermore, if a boxer landed a flurry of punches it was very difficult to record them all, and sometimes judges were influenced by the reaction of the crowd. Worst of all, it didn't address the underlying issue of corruption as Gary Keegan and Billy Walsh discovered to their cost in the run-up to the Athens Olympics in 2004.

The final qualifying tournament for European boxers was held in Baku. The Azerbaijan capital is now one of the most cosmopolitan cities in the region but back then it was very different. 'We were eaten alive by mosquitos and fleas,' recalls Billy Walsh, though it was events at ringside which truly sickened them.

'Once we got involved in the international scene we realised how broken the judging system was,' says Keegan. 'In fact, I would use the word "corrupt". I don't mind using that word because I think it was that bad. We had developed a mindset around controlling the controllables. But this was something which we believed was very much outside our control.'

A bizarre regulation meant that in their individual scoring judges could be one hundred and fifty percent above the official score and escape any reprimand, whereas if they were one percent below the score they were sanctioned.

'I remember James Moore fought a Turk; the first round was very tight. Then suddenly the bell went in the second round to signal the fight was over under the twenty-point rule,* even though James was giving him loads. They [the judges] had obviously decided to give the fight to the Turk so they were all pressing his button to ensure that they were one hundred and fifty percent above the score,' says Walsh. (*If a boxer had a twenty-point advantage over his opponent, the referee was obliged to stop the fight except in the last round.)

Boxers from the smaller nations were being denied any sense of fair play in the ring. 'We were losing fights twenty nil in the first round; it wasn't just us, all the smaller nations were being destroyed. Azerbaijan was where the game changed for us. We could see the judges' practices; the pulling of the ear, the nods. We called it tic-tacing,' explains Keegan.

The High Performance Unit (HPU) was still in its embryonic state and hadn't yet employed Alan Swanton as their video analyst. However, they brought a video camera to international tournaments. One afternoon after the four Irish boxers had been eliminated, Keegan, sitting high up in the bleachers, had an idea. Instead of focusing on the action in the ring Keegan pointed his camera at the five judges. 'We zoned in on them and could clearly see some of their practices. We came away from of the tournament wondering how we could influence change.'

Keegan and Walsh opted for a twin-track approach. The former navigated his way on to the Coaching Commission of the European Amateur Boxing Association (EABA), while back in Dublin they prepared a detailed dossier on what they had witnessed in Baku and drew up a package of reforms. 'Once I got on to the Commission,' says Keegan. 'I argued that this practice had to change; it was affecting us as coaches and also our boxers.'

The Commission agreed to consider the dossier prepared by the HPU. 'We didn't submit the videos but indicated we had video evidence. I'm not saying that our submission had any impact or was a catalyst for change but things did change afterwards,' maintains Keegan.

It was against this background that Ó Conaire was elected chairman of the Referees and Judges Commission (R & J Commission) by the European Amateur Boxing Association at its congress in Moscow in 2006. (The organisation is now called the European Boxing Confederation.) This is a powerful committee as it controls the appointment of referees and judges at championship events on the continent. By then he was a respected international official; he was secretary of the Technical and Rules Committee on the world-governing body AIBA and had been elected as vice-president of the EABA at the Moscow congress.

Nonetheless, Ó Conaire was surprised by his elevation to the R & J Commission position. The then Russian president of the EABA, Eduard Khusainov, favoured the outgoing chairman from Azerbaijan who was challenged by the Armenian representative. However, Ó Conaire was proposed by the then president of the Romanian Boxing Federation, Rudel Obreja, who said, 'We want somebody who is straight and honest and knows his business.'

'I had no prior knowledge of notice of this development. I had neither expressed an interest in nor been approached regarding such a position. When the president announced the names of the three nominated candidates he added, "unless Mr Ó Conaire would like to withdraw". This perceived arrogance was a red rag to an Irishman so, I, not wanting to embarrass Obreja, stubbornly left my name in the bag, knowing full well that the chance of success was less than minimal.'

Unbeknownst to Ó Conaire, a sizeable number of EABA executive members who were dissatisfied with the performance of the previous incumbent had planned a coup d'état. The Irishman topped the poll with fourteen votes, the Armenian candidate received eight votes, while the outgoing chairman and chairman's nominee received four votes including his own. 'The result took me completely by surprise, as it also patently did my incredulous opponents, who were none too congratulatory, needless to say.'

Ó Conaire was thrown straight into the maelstrom as the 2006 European Championships were scheduled for Bulgaria two and a half weeks later. 'There were guys on the R & J Commission that I had to try and control. I took them all on. I'm a fundamentalist about honesty. With me, it is completely black and white.'

The election in November 2006 of Dr Wu Ching-kuo as the new president of the AIBA (Association Internationale de Boxe Amateur, now renamed the International Boxing Association but known by its original acronym of AIBA) was also a seminal moment in the reform campaign. Ó Conaire welcomed the changing of the guard. 'Chowdhry [the then President of the AIBA] was always saying, "If I am corrupt, then why are boxers from my own country, Pakistan, not winning?"

'The simple answer was that they were no good,' says Ó Conaire. 'He [Chowdry] seemed to consider himself as some kind of ancient Pasha chieftain. He was enormous [in size] and he had no shortage of acolytes. Obsequiousness is a huge thing in the boxing business.'

The Wu camp feared the election would be rigged. In any event, a member of the International Olympic Committee (IOC) oversaw the vote which was held at the AIBA Convention in Santo Domingo, capital of the Dominican Republic. Wu prevailed over Chowdhry by four votes, 83 to 79. In 2007 Chowdhry was banned for life from the AIBA for alleged mismanagement of their funds. He died three years later at the age of eighty-seven. Meanwhile, the pugnacious Khusainov was replaced as the Russian president in 2007 and lost his positions in Europe and on the AIBA executive.

'Dr Wu came in with a mandate to change the sport and that's what he did. He was an agent for change,' suggests Keegan. Under Wu's leadership, the AIBA adopted many of the changes proposed by Keegan and Walsh. Today judges and referees are formally assessed and rated as in other international sports. Only officials who are awarded a three-star rating by the AIBA can officiate at international tournaments. National Federations no longer have the power to nominate referees for these events. The R & J Commission are obliged to appoint neutral judges and, where possible, not to allow officials from countries adjoining those of the boxers officiate at their fights. Furthermore, they do not allow the same group of judges officiate at bouts involving boxers from specific countries.

Judges and referees are no longer allowed to mingle with team officials at the venue. They are sequestered away from the competition site, use a different transport system to coaches and boxers, and do not know in advance what bout they are judging or refereeing. There is even a draw to determine where they will sit around the ring.

However, suggestions that the judges wear ear muffs and be seated in individual booths were not accepted. 'But what was accepted suddenly levelled the field for everybody. Obviously we had to up our game so that we could compete and then beat the best,' says Keegan.

Over time, more changes have been introduced. Even though five judges officiate at each fight, only three randomly selected scorecards are counted.

This was further refined in 2012; then only the scorecards of the three judges whose markings most closely aligned counted. The scores from the remaining two judges were discarded; this was designed to eliminate 'rogue scoring'.

While the system is now more transparent and less susceptible to corruption, it is still far from perfect, acknowledges Ó Conaire. 'Judges aim for collective uniformity; they don't want to be seen to be diverging from their colleagues in how they score fights.'

While Ó Conaire has no specific evidence to back up his suspicions, he fears that some judges still signal to each other who they favour in a particular fight. 'I'm not saying it is happening, but it could happen. I've noticed, however, that by the end of the second round in many fights a pattern has developed in terms of the judging. A boxer who is winning after two rounds rarely loses.'

The so called 'home town' phenomenon also remains a feature of boxing. Ireland benefitted from it at the 2001 World Championships, when six team members qualified for the quarter-finals, a feat which they have never matched since. At the most recent Olympics in London the host nation Great Britain, which was not rated as a superpower in the sport, topped the medals table with five medals: three gold, one silver and one bronze. Similarly China headed the table four years earlier, when Beijing hosted the Games.

More fundamental changes were introduced prior to the 2013 European Championships in Belarus. In the longer term the AIBA has ambitions to become a significant player in professional boxing. With this strategy in mind, they have now replaced the computer scoring system with the judging regime used in professional boxing. Each boxer begins each round with ten points; the boxer that the judges deem to have lost the round is deducted at least one point. So typically a three-round contest could be scored 30-27 if the winner is deemed to have won all three rounds. In the new professional APB series and the semi-professional WSB series, three judges officiate but at European and

World Championships and the Olympics five judges score the fight, though only three randomly selected are counted. The end result is that for the first time since the Seoul Olympics in 1988 majority (2-1) decisions can decide a boxer's fate. This new scoring method faces its first acid test at the 2016 Olympics in Rio.

CHAPTER 4

FRIEND AND FOE

'Billy Walsh was affectionately known in our house as the seventh son.'
Michael Carruth

There is a striking bond between Michael Carruth and Billy Walsh, two of the most recognisable names in Irish boxing. Michael Carruth is Ireland's only male Olympic boxing gold medallist, while Billy Walsh, in his capacity as Head Coach of the High Performance Unit (HPU), is working to secure more Olympic titles for Irish boxers. The late-night phone call between the pair on the eve of Olympic finals involving Irish boxers has become a ritual.

'I was taking off my shoes and getting ready for bed when he called me in Beijing [2008 Olympics],' recalls Walsh. 'I still remember what he said: "This is my last night as Ireland's only Olympic boxing gold medallist."' Twenty-four hours later, Carruth was still Ireland's only Olympic gold medallist. 'I've told him since that he put the f… blight on us by saying that,' laughs Walsh.

Carruth again rang Walsh on the eve of John Joe Nevin's gold medal fight at the London Olympics. As was the case with Kenny Egan four years earlier, Nevin had to be content with the silver medal. 'I'm saying now I will have to stop ringing him because the lads keep losing these finals,' suggests Carruth.

The irony is that it could have been Walsh who fought for the 231 grams of precious metal on offer that famous Saturday morning in Barcelona in 1992. Instead, he accepted an invitation from RTÉ to watch the Olympic welterweight final in the sitting room of Carruth's parents' home in Greenhills, Dublin. 'I didn't think Michael had a hope; he was facing Juan Hernández, who I had seen win the world title in Sydney the previous year.

'Michael was ahead after the first round; he received a warning in the second, and the scores were level (8-8) at the end of the round. Then it hit me: Michael is going to win this. I was standing beside the late Noel Humpston, who was Michael's uncle and Kenny Egan's first coach. I remember saying to Noel, "I can't believe it; he is going to win this Olympic gold medal." I could see the legendary Cuban coach Alcides Sagarra chewing the balls off his protégé who had fallen into the trap of running after Carruth.

'We had soldiered together; it was great that one of us came out with a gold medal. There is always going to be "it could have been me." I would have loved the chance. But there are no guarantees that I would have done what Michael did. Possibly not! I think it was something that was mapped out for him in that moment in time. I just felt that medal was there in me somewhere but I never got to it,' acknowledges Walsh, who nearly a quarter of a century later is still chasing that elusive Olympic gold medal, albeit now as a coach.

Michael Carruth, the last of triplet boys, was born on 9 July 1967 and grew up in the south Dublin suburb of Walkinstown. His was a boxing family; his father Austin has been interested in boxing since the 1940s, while Michael's maternal grandfather, Martin Humpston, was secretary of St Francis, once one of the biggest boxing clubs in Dublin. Michael's parents first met when Austin called around to the Humpston house with a birth certificate.

Later, Austin Carruth was involved in the formation of Greenhills Boxing

Club based in a newly built community centre in the area. After having to vacate the centre, the club members moved to Drimnagh Boxing Club, and ultimately they decide to merge with them in 1982. The triplets, Martin, William and Michael all boxed, but ultimately it was the latter who fashioned a glittering career in the sport.

By the time Carruth was called into the Irish senior boxing squad for the 1987 European championships in Turin, Walsh was an established international boxer, having won his first Irish Elite title in 1983. 'Michael's father knew that I was a half-decent lad and would keep his son on the straight and narrow. He arranged that we room together and we continued to do so afterwards on all our trips abroad.'

The friendship developed over time: they sparred each other, Carruth would travel down to Walsh's home in Wexford, where they would train together, and the Carruth's home became Walsh's base in Dublin. 'Billy was affectionately known in our house as the seventh son,' remembers Carruth.

Walsh has fond memories of Michael's late mother, Joan. 'She was my "Dublin Mammy". She was a great woman for baking and after I stayed with her for a weekend I'd go home to Wexford half a stone heavier after eating all the cakes she made.' Joan's husband, Austin, who was Michael's coach, was less enthusiastic about the way his wife fed the two boxers.

It was at those European Championships in Turin that Carruth underlined his potential; for Walsh, though, it was another case of what might have been – beaten 5-0 by eventual welterweight bronze medallist Angel Stoyanov from Bulgaria. Very often Irish boxers went into major championships undercooked, but there are valid reasons for suggesting that on this occasion Walsh, in particular, had over-trained.

The IABA had broken with tradition in 1987 and recruited a Cuban coach to assist in the preparations for the championships. RTÉ boxing commentator

Jimmy Magee recalls having dinner with the late Felix Jones and Dermot Sherlock, the then respective president and secretary of the IABA, during the World Amateur Championships in Reno, Nevada in 1986. The Cubans dominated that World Amateur Boxing Championships, winning seven gold medals: four more than the USA, their closest rivals. 'Felix was adamant that the Association would have to recruit a Cuban coach if Irish boxers were to have any chance of competing for medals at this level,' recalls Magee.

There was agitation also within the ranks of the IABA for a foreign coach. Breandán Ó Conaire, who would later play a pivotal role in the overhaul of coaching structures in Irish boxing, was the Dublin Boxing Board's representative on the IABA's Central Council at the time. 'I kept saying we want coaches whose boxers have won gold medals. I wanted them to bring in a Russian or a Cuban -- preferably one who spoke some English.' The first Cuban coach to arrive in Ireland was Trotman Daley. 'We called him a doozy. He was old school,' remembers Carruth. 'He wasn't very good,' acknowledges Ó Conaire.

In another break with tradition, the Irish training camp for the 1987 European Championships was relocated to Staigue Fort House near Castlecove on the Iveragh Peninsula in south-west Kerry. Felix Jones, the then president of the IABA, had a holiday home nearby. 'Don't get me wrong it is a beautiful part of the country. But it wasn't the location to bring six or seven young lads to. Remember there were no mobile phones or iPads around in those days. All we had was a hotel ballroom in which a makeshift ring was erected and a few bags,' comments Carruth.

Daley was a tough taskmaster. 'He instilled discipline. It was his way or the highway; there was no compromise. He had us wearing sixteen-ounce boxing gloves for three hours while we were training. We were losing six or seven pounds in weight at each session. I was a cute little fecker despite my age. When I knew I was getting close to peak fitness, I would back off. Luckily my dad was with me in the camp. Daley was calling the shots, but my dad was an assistant coach and he told me to take my foot off the pedal.'

There were clashes between Austin Carruth and Trotman Daley. 'It's not so much that my dad lost the rag with him but he would question what Daley was doing. When it gets to the stage where your feet and knuckles are blistering, you know there is something wrong. But we couldn't question Trotman.' Billy Walsh found himself in an invidious position. 'Billy was made captain so he was the one who kinda had to impress the general. I'm convinced to this day that he was over-trained,' says Carruth.

On his European Championship debut, nineteen-year-old Carruth comfortably outpointed a Spaniard, Santiago Galan. Next up was a Soviet boxer, Orzubek Nazarov, who had won a bronze medal at the World Championships in Reno the previous year and later held the WBC lightweight title for almost five years. The winner was guaranteed a place on the podium.

Carruth has painful memories of that fight. 'I felt I beat him, though I didn't get the verdict. He looked at me afterwards and winked as if to say your time will come. He went on to win the gold medal. I know John Joe Nevin was the first Irish male boxer to win medals at European, World, and Olympic level. I keep telling him I was the first; it's just that I didn't get the medal I deserved at those championships.'

Twelve months later, the Irish squad were back in Castlecove for a six-week training camp ahead of the 1988 Olympics. Welterweight Walsh was the squad's elder statesman and captain, while the country's new light flyweight sensation Wayne McCullough, who had just celebrated his eighteenth birthday, was the rookie. The other members of the Seoul-bound team were Carruth (lightweight), Joe Lawlor (flyweight), John Lowey (bantamweight), Paul Fitzgerald (featherweight), and Kieran Joyce (middleweight).

It was a bitter-sweet moment in Walsh's career, as he had been controversially overlooked four years earlier. His dream had been to celebrate his twenty-first birthday at the 1984 Olympics in LA. 'I had serious aspirations of making the team. I had the second-best record on the team. The only guy who had a better record was Kieran Joyce, a welterweight, and I had beaten him. Ireland had seven internationals that year and I had won five of them.'

The Central Council of the IABA submitted the name of eight boxers, including Walsh, for selection to the Olympic Council of Ireland's (OCI) standing committee, which would make the final recommendation to its Executive Committee. The OCI were struggling to raise the £300,000 needed to send the Irish team to the LA Games. They had spent £2,000 on an advertising campaign seeking public donations. It had raised £740!

The Soviet Union-led boycott of the LA Games resulted in the withdrawal not just of the Soviets but other top boxing nations, including Cuba, East Germany and Bulgaria. This encouraged the notion that the OCI would send an eight-man squad. But it was not to be; the two boxers at the bottom of the IABA's original order of merit, Paul Larkin and Billy Walsh, were axed.

Walsh heard the team announcement on RTÉ radio while running on a treadmill in a gym in Wexford. 'I walked out of the gym that day and didn't step inside a boxing ring again until the following October. I was a country boy. I had no say in the corridors of power.'

He went back playing hurling and football; his club Faythe Harriers were beaten by Buffers Alley in the Wexford Senior Hurling Championship final later that year. However, he won a Wexford Senior Football Championship medal with Sarsfields. Though he temporarily fell out of love with boxing, his interest never waned. He tuned into all the fights from the Los Angeles Memorial Sports Arena and can still recall the minute detail of all the action. 'Even though boxing was my passion, I thought about it for a long time before I went back into the ring. I was gutted for many years afterwards.'

Walsh had celebrated his twenty-fifth birthday before he finally realised his Olympic dream. Once he was selected for the pre-Olympic tournament in the South Korean capital of Seoul in the spring of 1988, where he knocked out the local favourite Song Kyung-sup, he knew his place was secure. 'So I headed off to Castlecove in Kerry, in preparation for the humidity and time difference in South Korea,' he says with a wry smile.

It was actually costing him money to fulfil his dream. 'There were no grants in those days. I took unpaid leave from my job as a fitter. In fairness to the people of Wexford they did some fundraising for me at the time.' The seven boxers who checked into Staigue Fort House had a totally different experience from those who had attended the training camp in preparation for the European Championships the previous year. The arrival of Nicolás Cruz made all the difference, according to Carruth.

'Nicolás had just stopped boxing but still had the mentality of a boxer rather than a coach. Sometimes coaches forget what it's like to be a boxer. He understood that better than Daley. He told us in advance what sessions we were doing and how long they would last. He was more approachable and was more craic, for want of a better word. He did torture us in terms of the training, but there were no hidden agendas. Nicolás was everything; coach, masseur, psychologist,' remembers Walsh. 'He made a big impact.'

Curiously, the IABA opted not to bring Cruz or Austin Carruth – who had worked alongside the Cuban at the camp in Kerry – to Seoul. The two Irish coaches were Michael 'Mickey' Hawkins and the late Albie Murphy, a legendary figure in Cork boxing. While Cuba, together with Albania, Ethiopia, Madagascar, Nicaragua, North Korea and the Seychelles, boycotted the 1988 Olympics, Cuban coaches working with other countries travelled to Seoul. However, according to Cruz, 'The president of the IABA at the time, Felix Jones, decided not to take me for safety reasons. The boys were as fit as fiddles but they needed me there. Having worked with them for six weeks in Ireland, they were used to me and they trusted me.'

For Walsh, the highlight of the Seoul Olympics was the opening ceremony. But even before the Olympic flame was lit, he suspected that the omens were stacking up against him. 'As the host nation, the South Koreans were the last to march into the stadium. I was standing beside Michael Carruth and I remember saying to him, "I can't believe it; there's the guy I beat in the pre-Olympic tournament [Song Kyung-sup] marching in."

'Then it hit me. This guy must be good; he's still on the team. And guess what: I was drawn against him in my first fight. If I had the experience of being at a previous Olympics, I would have dealt with it differently. I was thinking about my family and friends and the support they had given me; about representing my country and the millions who were watching on TV. I thought I was going well and normally I never cut. But on this occasion, and despite wearing a head-guard, I got cuts above and below my eye. The referee stopped the fight in the second round. It was a cruel blow to take.' Before the tournament was over, the referee, Keith Walker, became the best-known boxing official in the world.

Walsh was so devastated that he couldn't bring himself to phone home. Eventually, he got a three-word telegraph from his mother: 'Please ring home.'

'I had waited so long to get to the Olympics, and as it I turned out it was my only shot. Maybe I sensed that at the time. My wife, Caroline, was pregnant; we had a mortgage, and I was thinking I might not get back to the Olympics in four years' time. I was gutted.'

Billy Walsh carried around the scars of the defeat for the bones of two decades. 'It took me that long to come to terms with it. Every time I spoke about it, I cried. Thankfully I'm not crying now. I was never debriefed; the defeat was never put away in a box. When I started working with the HPU, Gary Keegan [the founder and first performance director of the HPU] asked me to talk to the boys about my Olympic Games experience. I broke down in front of the lads. I realised then that I had wanted to win so much that I didn't control my emotions.'

Carruth fared only marginally better than his closest friend. After a comfortable win over a Japanese boxer, Satoru Higashi, his next opponent was Swede George Cramme, whom he had comfortably beaten the previous year, as he ruefully recalls. 'I had leathered him in Copenhagen in a multi-nation tournament. For two and half minutes in Seoul everything was going to plan and then I walked into a sledge hammer.'

Going forward, Carruth momentarily dropped his right hand, and the Swede caught him perfectly on the chin with a left hook. For the first time ever in a boxing ring, Carruth found himself on the seat of his pants listening to the referee counting one, two, three, four … By the time he got back on his feet there were only five seconds left in the round.

Carruth was looking forward to getting back to his corner, knowing he would then have a minute to recover. But the referee had other ideas; he took one long look at the twenty-one-year-old Drimnagh lightweight and signalled that his Olympic dream was over. Cramme ended up winning a silver medal.

'I was absolutely disgusted with myself. Hindsight is a wonderful thing. I had been struggling to make the nine stone, six pound lightweight limit in Seoul. I could have competed as a light welterweight as there was no Irish boxer in that category. I'm convinced I would have won a medal in Seoul had I moved up to the ten stone category.'

Overall it was a forgettable Olympics for the boxers. John Lowey won two fights, while Fitzgerald, Joyce and Lawlor won one bout each – the latter was beaten by the eventual bronze medallist, Timofey Skryabin from the Soviet Union.

Ireland's first Olympic-boxing medallist John McNally, pictured here in 1954, two years after his controversial defeat in the Olympic bantamweight final, and soon after he turned professional at the age of twenty-one.

A sprightly eighty-two-year-old John McNally relaxes in his native Belfast in the grounds of City Hall.

Left: Hugh Russell, an Olympic bronze medallist in Moscow, is congratulated by his mother, Eileen, having defeated another Irish Olympian, Davy Larmour, in Belfast's Ulster Hall in 1982 in a final eliminator for the British bantamweight professional title.

Olympic silver medallist Fred Tiedt **(left)** in action in the 1958 Irish welterweight fight in the National Stadium against his great rival Harry Perry, who won the contest to bring his overall record against Tiedt to 4-3.

Above: Breandán Ó Conaire, arguably the most influential official in Irish amateur boxing during the past half-century.

Below: Billy Walsh, a Seoul Olympian, was the first head coach of the IABA's Irish Performance Unit and now heads up the 'Medal Factory'.

Above left: Michael Carruth on his way to his fifteenth victory in the professional ranks in the National Basketball Arena in Tallaght in September 1998.

Above right: The late Austin Carruth, pictured in Barcelona with his son Michael, the newly crowned 1992 Olympic welterweight champion.

Below: Michael Carruth, flanked by his wife, Paula, and coach, Nicolás Cruz, shows off his Olympic gold medal to his fellow Dubliners after his return from Barcelona during an open-bus tour.

Above: 'The Pocket Rocket', Wayne McCullough, in action in the 1992 Olympic bantamweight final against the eventual gold medallist Joel Casamayor from Cuba.

Below: Barcelona Olympic medallists Wayne McCullough (**left**) and Michael Carruth reunite on the border at Carrickarnon, County Louth, in June 2012, during the Olympic torch run prior to the London Games.

Above: Cork light middleweight Michael Roche, who was the only Irish boxer to qualify for the Sydney Olympics in 2000, is put through his paces by coach Nicolás Cruz.

Below: Nine years after failing to qualify for the Sydney Olympics, Bernard Dunne celebrates as he is crowned WBA super bantamweight champion of the world in the O_2 Arena in Dublin.

Above: Andy Lee, who turned professional after boxing for Ireland at the Athens Olympics, shows off the WBO world middleweight belt outside Limerick City Hall after his sensational title win in Las Vegas in 2014.

Below: Barry McGuigan with his prodigy Carl Frampton prior to his IBF World Super Bantamweight title fight against Kiko Martinez at the *Titanic* Quarter in Belfast, September 2014, which the former Irish amateur champion won.

An emotional John Joe Joyce is congratulated by his club coach and then president of the IABA Dominic O'Rourke after qualifying for the Beijing Olympics at the final pre-qualifying tournament in Athens.

The boxers did earn the wrath, however, of disgraced 100-metre champion Ben Johnson for unwittingly blocking his path on the training track and then imitating his stammer when he chided them for not stepping out of his way. There was a protest from the Canadian, but the matter stayed within the boxing camp as the issue never came across the desk of Pat Hickey, who was Ireland's chef de mission in Seoul.

Hickey was, however, centrally involved in the decision to ask Wayne McCullough, a Protestant from the staunchly loyalist Shankill area of Belfast, to carry the tricolour at the opening ceremony.

Suggestions were made that the honour was bestowed on McCullough because he was Ireland's youngest competitor in Seoul. But the reality is that, while the gesture was designed to portray the unity of sport, it could have had serious personal repercussions for McCullough. According to Hickey, the boxer got clearance from his parents to carry the flag, and as far as McCullough was concerned, he was honoured to be fighting for Ireland and that honour meant he respected the country's anthem and flag. 'Boxing has always been apolitical in Ireland. I agreed to carry the flag, without thinking too much about it, and nobody ever said anything to me about it when I came home.'

McCullough was a child of the Northern Ireland conflict. Born at home on 7 July 1970, his parents' house, located between the Belfast Shankill Road and the Falls Road, was at the epicentre of the sectarian violence that erupted in the city the previous August. The infamous 'Peace Wall', erected in 1969, was one hundred metres from his house. The McCullough family, consisting of three brothers and four sisters, later moved to an estate at the top of the Shankill Road.

Over time, McCullough became immune to the violence. 'At that time, regardless of whether you were a Protestant or a Catholic growing up in Belfast's working-class neighbourhoods, the sounds of bombs going off and soldiers walking down the street seemed quite normal. Until I started travel-ling abroad, I thought this happened all around the world.'

McCullough's first overseas trip was to Korea for the Seoul Olympics. Boxing wasn't always his first sporting love. Like most Belfast-born young-sters of his age, he dreamed about being the next George Best, but when one of his older brothers won a boxing trophy, McCullough decided to join him in the nearby Albert Foundry Boxing Club. 'When I was fifteen, I knew boxing was the sport I wanted to make a career out of. I was a decent soccer player, but not good enough.'

Under the tutelage of Harry Robinson, the boxer set about achieving his goals. Ultimately, he wanted to win a world title as a professional, but even as he was starting out he understood the significance of securing an Olympic medal on that journey. Notwithstanding the clarity of his goal, his meteoric rise was sensational.

He was just seventeen when he secured his first Irish Elite title at light fly-weight – he also won Boxer of the Tournament. There were lingering doubts over the wisdom of sending the youngster to Seoul, but after winning twelve fights in a row, including three internationals by knock-out, the selectors' hands were forced. His eye-catching, all-action style caught the attention of boxing aficionadas in Seoul – including Commonwealth champion Scotty Olson, who beat the teenager in the second round. The Canadian predicted that he would win a medal in four years' time in Barcelona.

Walsh's foreboding that his Olympic dream would end in Seoul's Jamsil Students' Gymnasium proved prophetic. What he couldn't have foreseen was that it would be his closest buddy in boxing, Michael Carruth, who would shatter those Olympic dreams four years down the road. Initially their paths didn't cross. Carruth underlined his potential when he won a bronze medal at the World Championships in Moscow in 1989, in the light welterweight category, though he was now struggling to make that weight limit as well.

Meanwhile, the luckless Walsh lost in the quarter-finals of the middle-weight category to an unheralded Egyptian, Salem Karim Kabbary. 'He was unlucky; he picked up a bug just before his bronze medal fight against the Egyptian. We were never beaten by an Egyptian. I felt dreadfully sorry for him,' remembers Breandán Ó Conaire.

Walsh boxed again in the middleweight division in 1990, winning the Irish title, but he wasn't comfortable at the weight. 'Once I got into serious training I noticed that I was only a pound and a half over the welterweight limit. I remember beating a guy called Robin Reid [a future WBC super-middle-weight champion] in an Ireland *v* England international in the National Stadium, just before Christmas 1990, but I was very sore afterwards. I decided then that, if I was serious about going to the Olympics in Barcelona, I would have to box at my proper weight, which was welterweight. The Elite Championships were coming, so I knew I had to get down to 67 kg. What I didn't know was that Michael was planning to come up from 64 kg.'

As always, prior to the start of the Elite Championships, there were rumours about boxers switching categories. Carruth had decided he was moving up to the welterweight division when he heard stories about Walsh coming down to the same category. 'On Valentine's Day in 1991 I knew that Billy was coming into my weight category. We were scheduled to meet in an exhibition down in Portlaoise, but Billy never turned up. I said it to 'Aussie' [his father, Austin], and all he said in reply was "let's get ready for Walsh then." In the end, three Irish title holders, Carruth, Walsh and the defending champion, Eddie Fisher, entered the welterweight division at the 1991 Elite Championships, along with five other hopefuls. There was no seeding; Carruth and Walsh were drawn to meet each other in the first round.

For the first time in nearly a decade Walsh had to find new accommodation in Dublin ahead of the National Championships. 'Obviously he wasn't staying in our house because he was now my enemy,' remembers Carruth.

So, in front of a handful of spectators, two of Ireland's leading boxers at the time traded punches in competition for the first time ever. Walsh got the verdict, but Carruth still believes he was unjustly treated by both the referee and the judges.

Carruth disputes the decision of respected referee Jack Poucher to issue him with a public warning for dropping his shoulder in the third round. This decision was compounded, he argues, because three of the judges erred by not taking into account a rule change under which the punishment for a public warning was the loss of the round and not the fight itself, as was previously the case. In the Walsh-Carruth contest, two of the judges totally disregarded the public warning and voted 60-57 in favour of Carruth; the other three scored the fight 58-58, which effectively meant they gave Carruth the first two rounds but still gave their casting vote to Walsh.

'I got penalised twice. Those three judges ballsed it up. And just to make matters worse, the new computer scoring system, which was being used on an experimental basis that night, gave me the verdict by six points,' insists Carruth.

Walsh went on to be crowned welterweight champion – in fact, he received a walkover in the final. He subsequently represented Ireland at the 1991 European Championships in Gothenburg. Carruth was ruled out after having eight stitches inserted in a facial wound near his eye, which he sustained in an international against Spain. Again Walsh's quarter-final jinx struck – losing by two points to Mujo Bajrović from Yugoslavia. 'I thought I had done enough, but I didn't get the verdict.'

Meanwhile, Carruth's Drimnagh clubmate Paul Griffin claimed the headlines in Sweden, winning the gold medal in the featherweight category. He was Ireland's first European champion since Maxie McCullagh in 1949.

A year out from the Barcelona Olympics, Walsh looked in pole position to make the team as Carruth's woes continued. Six years after joining the Irish army, he was stationed in Cathal Brugha barracks in Dublin. Thinking that gymnastics might improve his flexibility, he tried out some moves in the barracks' gymnasium. All was going well until he mistimed a vault and ended up taking the full weight of his fall on his right arm, snapping a bone in his elbow.

The next major ranking tournament, the World Championships in Sydney, was four months away. Due to the cost involved, Ireland was always likely to send a small squad. In the end, four boxers were selected; newly crowned European champion Paul Griffin was an automatic choice. He was joined by Irish middleweight champion Denis Galvin. But eyebrows were raised when Michael Carruth – who had assured the selectors that he had fully recovered from the broken bone in his elbow – and bantamweight Wayne McCullough were nominated. While both had boxed at the Seoul Olympics, neither competed at the subsequent European Championships in Gothenburg, nor were they Irish champions in their respective weight divisions. Billy Walsh and Joe Lawlor, the reigning bantamweight champion, could only look on with wry amusement at the latest selection machinations by the IABA.

Six days before they were due to fly to Sydney, Carruth's career hit another speed bump; he broke his left hand. It was common practice in those days to bring in other boxers for sparring sessions with the Irish team. On this particular Saturday, in the Holy Family Boxing Club in Drogheda, Carruth was trading leather with Martin McBride from Edenderry.

'I hit him with a left hook. It hurt so much that I couldn't do anything for the rest of the session. I was walking the wall with the pain afterwards and spent most of the night with my hand under a cold tap. Eventually, at 5am, I knocked on Nicolás Cruz's door and said I needed to go to hospital. Christy

McKenna drove me to Our Lady's Hospital in Drogheda where my hand was x-rayed,' remembers Carruth.

A few minutes later came the devastating prognosis. Carruth had broken the scaphoid bone in his left wrist. 'Half an hour later my hand was in plaster, my arm was in a sling and I was waiting for my dad to come from Dublin to collect me. I remember telling Christy McKenna to make sure to get somebody to ring Billy Walsh straight away. Otherwise these f... eejits won't do it for a day or too and he will have even less time to prepare.'

Walsh was coming through Dublin Airport the next morning – he had just won the gold medal at a tournament in Belgium – when he met the vice-president of the IABA, Breandán Ó Conaire, who asked whether he could travel to Australia as Carruth's replacement. 'I said, hang on a second, I have to go back to Mick Millar, my boss in Pearse Engineering and ask him can I go.'

By now there was a formal qualification system in place for the Olympics, and the die was rolling at an incredibly high speed for the two Irish protagonists in the welterweight division. 'I was sweating buckets,' admits Carruth, who could only sit at home and nurse his injured hand as Walsh made his second bid to secure the coveted Olympic spot. His only consolation was the fact that unless Walsh won the gold medal in Sydney he wasn't guaranteed a place in Barcelona. The silver and bronze medallists only secured a place for their country rather than as individuals in their weight category.

Walsh made the perfect start in Sydney by avenging the quarter-final defeat he suffered to Mujo Bajrović from Yugoslavia at the European Championships, winning 21-17. But he lost in the next round to local favourite Stephen Scriggins (16-6), who went on to win the bronze medal. In terms of the welterweight spot on the Irish Olympic team it was still all to play for. But Carruth faced a desperate race against time to be fit to box in the Elite Championships, which were scheduled to begin in early January.

He finally got the plaster off three days before Christmas. 'I trained on Christmas Eve, along with Paul Griffin; Dad gave us Christmas Day off, and we trained again on St Stephen's Day and right through the rest of December and into January.'

For the first time ever in his career, he began to focus on mental preparation. Due primarily to the prompting of Ó Conaire, the Elite boxers could now avail of the services of a psychologist. Finding a suitable psychologist proved a major headache, however. 'I interviewed them all and observed them interacting with the boxers. The big problem with some of them was their lack of boxing knowledge.' recalls Ó Conaire. Carruth availed of the services of sports psychologist Felicity Heathcote. 'She had interesting ideas about visualising situations in the boxing ring. So though my body mightn't have been ready for battle, my mind was.'

The IABA did not repeat the mistake of the previous year when they left Carruth and Walsh unseeded. They were on opposite sides of the draw, as were the two high profile boxers in the bantamweight category, Wayne McCullough and Joe Lawlor. Everybody knew what was at stake.

Carruth was drawn against Martin McBride, against whom he had broken his scaphoid bone while sparring the previous November. Ignoring his doctors, who had warned him that he risked doing further damage by returning to action just nineteen days after having the plaster removed, Carruth stepped into the ring in the National Stadium. He outclassed McBride, winning 24-3. 'My dad said he'd never seen me throw so many punches.' So incensed was one of McBride's supporters with the scoring, that he lifted a computer and flung it into the ring after the decision was announced and hit Carruth on the leg.

Meanwhile, on the other side of the draw, the defending title holder, Walsh, comfortably advanced and so the scene was set for the showdown on finals' night. Carruth got the verdict 12-9 and felt he deserved it. 'I felt my luck had finally changed,' he says.

Walsh remembers the final differently. 'It was very close, a lot of people thought I had done enough. I retired again [he had also briefly retired after the Seoul Olympics], kissed goodbye to everybody. It was my tenth senior final, and I had won seven of them. I felt I'd had enough; I wanted to go off and have a real life.'

So Walsh returned to Wexford, resumed his GAA club career and enjoyed having a few pints again with his mates. Carruth, meanwhile, was selected to box for Ireland against the US in an international. Given the fragile state of his hand, there was a long debate in the Carruth camp as to whether he would actually participate. However, the IABA had yet to name the team to box in the pre-Olympic qualifiers; the days of automatic selection for the Olympics were over.

Carruth boxed against the US and won his bout comfortably. Finally, he could relax prior to departing to San Pellegrino in Italy for the Olympic qualifying tournament in late March. Austin Carruth was now a member of the IABA Central Council who would select the teams for the pre-qualifying tournaments. He had mentioned to his son that there was talk of a couple of trials being ordered. 'Honestly, I never saw what was coming next. I had just bought my first house with Paula [his future wife] in Tallaght. We were planning to get married after the qualification tournament.

'The Central Council meeting at which the team was being selected took place on a Saturday, and I arranged to ring my dad at five o'clock to hear the news. I hadn't taken a drink for months, so I bought a flagon of cider with the intention of drinking it that night to celebrate my selection. We had no phone in the house; so I walked two hundred metres to the nearest telephone box and dialled his number.

'I knew there was something up immediately. He came straight out with it. "You will have to fight Billy Walsh next Friday." I lit up the phone box with every swear word I knew. My dad simply said, "If you don't fight Billy, they will pick him for the qualifiers and you can forget about the Olympics. I'll see you in the club in the morning."

'I went home and drank the flagon of cider in the company of Paula and my brother Fergal (who became chief executive of the IABA in 2013).' When he weighed himself the following morning in Drimnagh Boxing Club, Carruth was four hundred grams under the limit.

Meanwhile, down in Wexford, Billy Walsh was coming to terms with the fact that he was six kilograms over the limit. 'I had to lose a stone. I starved myself. I was dehydrated. I did everything I shouldn't do just to make the weight.'

Astonishingly, when they officially weighed in the following Friday, Walsh was actually lighter than his rival, but he looked gaunt. The pair exchanged some banter under their breaths about what weight they should be fighting at before stepping into the ring for the bout – the third on the programme. Not surprisingly, it turned into an anti-climax. 'The first round was pretty close,' recalls Walsh. 'But I just blew up after that.'

Carruth cruised home 24-3, winning the last round 11-1. Carruth's brothers labelled it the 'Valentine's Day Massacre'. Carruth still regrets that he didn't accept Walsh's invitation afterwards to go for a drink. 'His Olympic dream was over and he wanted to go for a pint. I couldn't go. It was Valentine's Day and I hadn't got a present for Paula. I ended up buying her a bloody box of chocolates. I felt terrible leaving the Ringside Club because, despite the rivalry, we were great pals.'

When Carruth sat down a couple of weeks later to compile a guest list for his wedding, the first name he wrote down was Billy Walsh. 'I didn't know whether he'd come, but of course he came. One of my army mates got a picture of me jumping off my feet after beating Billy in the senior final and stuck it up on a pillar beside Billy's table. I ripped it off and vowed that if I discovered who the culprit was I'd kill him. Needless to say, nobody owned up. Billy didn't need that. I was going to the Olympics; he wasn't.'

Carruth still had one more barrier to negotiate before securing his ticket to Barcelona – and it almost cost him everything.

CHAPTER 5

GOLD AND SILVER

'I grew up listening to stories about Ronnie Delany winning the 1500 metres at the Melbourne Olympics. Irish boxers had come close before in the Olympics; we had bronze and silver, but we didn't have the big one.' I said to my dad; "Delany's time is up; I'm going to win this fight."'

Michael Carruth

One wall in the office of Drimnagh Boxing Club is entirely devoted to the memory of Austin Carruth. His son Michael is Ireland's only male Olympic boxing gold medallist. But it is the framed certificates, pictures and memorabilia from his father's coaching career that grabs the attention of anyone who walks into the office. Sitting in the chair once occupied by his father, Carruth reflects on the unique relationship he had with his father, who died in February 2011. There were three strands to it: father, coach and sometimes a friend he called 'Aussie'.

'All my life, even as an Olympic champion, I have tried to live up to his mark. It may sound daft but I still admire him: his dignity, coolness and knowledge.

It's funny to be sitting here now, because when we were younger the only time we were in this office was when we were in trouble with him.' Austin laid down the rules and Michael followed them – not out of fear but respect. 'We were more like brothers than father and son. I knew the boundaries I couldn't cross. So when he told me to be in at eleven o'clock I made sure I was coming in the door at five to. That's the way we did things. But he knew not to push too far. I suppose I had my late mother's fiery temper. My way of getting at him was to be silent which drove him absolutely barmy.'

Cuban native Nicolás Cruz Hernández stepped into this unique partnership in 1988. Like an arranged marriage it had the potential to self-destruct. Instead, it gelled perfectly – particularly during sixteen scorching days in Barcelona in the summer of 1992.

But Carruth almost didn't make it to the Spanish city. No blame could be attached to either Austin Carruth or Cruz; they were thousands of miles away. This was the moment Carruth had to face and conquer his own self-doubts, aided by a dollop of 'tough love' administered by his fellow boxers, Neil Gough and Joe Lowe, together with Irish coach Mickey Hawkins.

Leonardo da Vinci is reputed to have visited the Italian commune of San Pellegrino in 1509 to sample the town's 'miraculous' mineral water. In March 1992, four centuries later, it was the venue for the final qualifying tournament in three weight divisions: light welter, welter and light middle for European boxers bidding to compete at the Barcelona Olympics.

By now five other Irish boxers had secured their Olympic tickets. Reigning European featherweight champion Paul Griffin qualified automatically; flyweight Paul Buttimer and super heavyweight Kevin McBride secured their spots at a tournament in Copenhagen in February, while bantamweight Wayne McCullough and heavyweight Paul Douglas got through in early March at the Chemistry Cup tournament in Halle, Germany.

By the time Carruth stepped into the ring against his first opponent, German-born welterweight Jürgen König – who was representing Austria – the Irishman was running low on reserves and struggled to a 7-4 win. Next up was Polish boxer Wiesław Małyszko. Carruth had bad memories of Polish competitors, having being worked over by one at the World Junior Championships years previously. Carruth lost 12-3 to Małyszko, who, ironically, was beaten 6-1 by César Ramos from the Dominican Republic in his first bout in Barcelona. Fortunately, Carruth was given a reprieve through the since discontinued repechage system, in which boxers eliminated in the quarter-final got a second shot.

'Jesus, I was brutal,' recalls Carruth. 'My hands were sore; parts of me I didn't know existed were sore. I was feeling sorry for myself. I wanted my mammy.' Instead, he had to make do with Hawkins and his teammates Gough and Lowe, both of whom had seen their Olympic ambitions flounder earlier in the tournament. They were waiting for him in the changing room after his defeat. 'Let's just say there was a lot of the "f" word used. And together with Mickey Hawkins they convinced me I wasn't a quitter.'

Carruth's next opponent, a Lithuanian, cried off with flu, which meant that if the Irishman could beat a French boxer, Saïd Bennajem – who also received a walk-over in the previous round – he was Barcelona-bound. 'He was a slick southpaw. I was delighted because I know what southpaws do; I'm one myself.'

Leading 4-2 at the end of the second round, Carruth went for the kill in the first half minute of the final round, much to the consternation of Hawkins. 'I always had this thing with my father; I started the third round fast. But I was under instruction from Mickey to box on the back foot, so when I went forward in the first twenty seconds, Mickey was hyperventilating in the corner. I caught Bennajem with a hook to the jaw and dropped him. I knew then I was going to qualify. I was feeling relief, joy, agony and ecstasy rolled into one. I was selected for my first Olympic Games, but I had qualified for this one which meant even more to me.'

Carruth knew the result in advance – 11-6 in his favour; Lowe was strategically seated so that he could 'spy' on the scoring computer and he was relaying the information to Hawkins in the Irish corner. Once the decision was announced, Carruth had only one thing on his mind; he wanted to phone home.

'I was due to stay and receive a medal, but I ran out into the corridor to find a phone. My family had kept a bottle of champagne in the fridge since before the Seoul Olympics. My father's first word was "Well?" "Well, I replied, "you know that bottle of champagne in the fridge. I think you should open it. I'm after beating the crap out of that French guy." Bearing in mind I was twenty-four and getting married in three weeks' time, I will never forget what he said in reply: "Don't act the eejit tonight."'

Carruth's qualification scarcely raised a murmur outside the boxing community. Ahead of the Olympics, the focus was on Wayne McCullough, now operating in the bantamweight division. Dissuaded by his coach Harry Robinson from turning professional after he returned from the Seoul Olympics, McCullough – nicknamed the 'Pocket Rocket' – was the hottest property in Irish amateur boxing at the time.

Breandán Ó Conaire agrees that McCullough was Ireland's main hope for a medal in Barcelona. 'I knew him from a very young age; he was one hundred and fifty percent dedicated to boxing. I remember bringing a team to Tenerife one time. Even before the others got out of bed in the morning, Wayne would be out running up the mountains. He had unbelievable dedication.'

Five months out from the opening ceremony in Barcelona, Nicolás Cruz was assuring his Irish boss that McCullough would win gold. 'Felix Jones [then President of the IABA] invited me and my ex-wife, who was visiting from Cuba, down to Kerry for dinner. I remember saying to him, "We are going to bring the big medal home."

'Later we had a media day in Drogheda. I told the press, "We are not going to let the Irish people down. We will bring the big medal home." I was confident; all my hopes were on Wayne; he was amazing. And the training we did was savage.'

Virtually from the moment they met at the pre-1988 Olympic training camp in Kerry, Cruz and McCullough gelled. 'I thought he was unbelievable; he was responsible for getting me my Olympic medal. He was like a pro-coach,' says McCullough. 'I remember I used to do the mitts with Nicolás every day. A lot of the guys didn't like doing it, but I absolutely loved it. He doesn't get the credit for what he did for us. I was shocked that he wasn't the national coach for all the years he was in Ireland.'

On 4 May 1988, when Cruz disembarked from an Aeroflot flight at Shannon Airport he could never have envisaged how stepping on Irish soil would have such a profound impact on his life. Havana's hosting of the inaugural World Championships in 1974 had initially stimulated Cruz's interest in boxing.

His first love was basketball, but he switched to boxing while studying to become a physical education teacher. By 1981, he was the number two ranked light heavyweight in Cuba, but any ambitions he harboured of representing his country at the Olympics were dashed when Cuba boycotted the Los Angeles Games in 1984. After doing three years compulsory army service, he returned to teach at the Higher Institute of Physical Culture in Havana. Then, totally out of the blue, the Cuban Boxing Federation contacted him in 1988 and asked him to go to Ireland.

Cruz travelled to Ireland with a Cuban team, which was meeting Ireland in an international in the National Stadium before travelling to Glasgow for an international against Scotland. The party travelled by bus to Dublin and stayed in the old Power's Hotel near Trinity College.

'Ten days later, the team went back to Cuba and I was left alone, which I found a bit strange as it was the first time I had been abroad by myself for any lengthy period. I was very uptight and reluctant to go out. I eventually walked up O'Connell Street, went into a bar and sat by myself, just like you see in America. It wasn't long before somebody came up and asked me where I was from and would I like a drink. I then started to relax and realised that Ireland is just like Cuba in terms of culture, history and idiosyncrasies, though there are two marked differences: language and weather.'

Breandán Ó Conaire was instantly impressed when he saw Cruz working the corner during the international between Cuba and Ireland. 'I said, "This is the guy", because he was very technical; he was a trained coach, so he knew all the Cuban techniques – such as the proper way to do a warm-up, which is all standard now. He was an educationalist as well and he knew about the mental preparation.'

Two years after the Seoul Olympics, McCullough embellished his burgeoning reputation when he won the gold medal in the flyweight division at the Commonwealth Games in Auckland – a first for Northern Ireland since the Barry McGuigan (bantamweight) and Gerry Hamill (lightweight) wins in Edmonton in 1978. The drama came after the fight. During McCullough's medal presentation there was a technical glitch and only the sound of silence emanated from the tape recorder which was due to play the team anthem, 'Danny Boy'. A Northern Ireland expatriate, Bob Gibson, who was working at the Games, climbed into the ring, grabbed a microphone and sang the song.

The Kiwis loved McCullough; so much so that he was offered the chance to stay in the country and become a citizen, provided he boxed for them at the Barcelona Olympics. 'I thought about it for about one second. Back home was where my heart was, and I wanted to fight for my country at the Olympics.'

His next stop was the now-discontinued World Cup tournament in Bombay in November 1990. He switched to bantamweight and captured the bronze medal, to become the first and only Irishman ever to medal at the event. 'To this day, I believe it was a tougher tournament than the Olympics because there is only one bronze medal presented.'

Having lost to the eventual silver medallist and future world champion and 1996 Olympic silver medallist Serafim Todorov from Bulgaria in the semi-final, he faced a familiar foe in the box-off for the bronze medal – Fred Muteweta, who he had beaten on his Olympic debut in Seoul. The Irishman maintained his unbeaten record against the Ugandan bantamweight and confirmed his status as Ireland's best medal prospect in Barcelona. At the 1996 Olympics Todorov defeated a nineteen-year-old American, Floyd Mayweather Jnr, by one point (9-8) in the featherweight semi-final. Mayweather – who has never lost a fight since – is now the highest paid athlete in the world while the Bulgarian lives on a monthly pension of €387.

In a break with tradition, the IABA opted to send the squad, including Mark Winters, who had been nominated as a reserve in the lightweight category, abroad to fine-tune their Olympic preparations. They chose a sports complex in Cottbus, a university city in Brandenburg, just over two hundred kilometres south of Berlin. The Irish shared the camp with the Thai boxers.

'I think somebody saw it in a brochure and went for it. I doubt if anybody went to Germany and actually checked the place out; if they did they're blind,' suggests Carruth. 'The boxing facilities were excellent, and so was the sparring, but away from the gym it was a different story.'

'All of us had to share one shower and one toilet. There were no laundry facilities and there were fleas jumping out of the beds,' according to McCullough, who cringed when offered Coca-Cola to drink with his dinner. The Irish envied the Thai squad who had the foresight to bring their own provisions.

'We were getting chicken to eat three times a day,' recalls Carruth. The camp was due to last four weeks, and boredom set in quickly in the stifling heat. 'We didn't have a television to look at; we didn't have a newspaper; we couldn't get cold drinks. I rang my wife three times a day. She was wondering what was wrong because, according to her, I'd usually only ring about three times a month when I was away in camp.'

The revolt fermented for ten days. Cruz acknowledges that judged by Irish standards, the accommodation facilities were poor, but he contends that the food was more than adequate. 'There was yogurt and fruit on the tables every morning. What I tried to do was convince the boys that they were preparing for the Olympics, which happen once every four years. They might never get the chance again.'

'I wasn't the first to complain; everybody complained,' says McCullough. 'We had a meeting and all agreed that whatever we were going to do we would all do.' Overcome with frustration and feeling his medal chances were slipping away, he decided to leave and went to summon his teammates. 'I'll always remember they were sitting on their beds. I asked them, "Are you ready to go?" Nobody moved!

'I remember walking out and banging the door behind me. I went to see the team manager, Seán Horkan, and told him that I couldn't stay any longer.' Harry Robinson faxed McCullough an airline ticket and he took a taxi to Berlin airport and boarded a plane for home. 'It cost me money to leave, but it was the best thing I ever did.' He completed his Olympic preparations in Belfast.

Carruth had sympathy for his teammate, but he couldn't join him on the protest. 'If any of the other boxers – including myself, and I was team captain –walked out of the camp, we would have been thrown off the team. Wayne was our fancy for a medal so he got away with it.

'The proof of the pudding is in the eating; Wayne failed at the last hurdle in Barcelona. I stayed in Cottbus; I even had my birthday there. What we didn't realise at the time was that the experience toughened us up mentally.'

The squad were reunited in Drogheda on the eve of their departure to Barcelona, though there was no late call-up for Mark Winters. The other boxers clubbed together and bought him an airline ticket for Barcelona. At least he would see the Olympics. At the World Championships the following year in Tampere in Finland, Winters was unlucky again as he was narrowly beaten by gold medallist Damian Austin in the quarter-finals.

On their first morning in Barcelona, Cruz had the boxers out of bed at 6.15am for a pre-breakfast training run. They made such a commotion in the apartment block that the rest of the Irish team complained about their nocturnal habits.

For the remainder of the Games they were allowed a lie-in until eight-thirty. Being different never worried Cruz. To avoid the hassle of travelling into the city by bus for training every day, he developed a series of exercises which the boxers performed on the pavement outside their apartment, which meant they could rest for longer.

Keeping them out of mischief proved problematic. Early in the tournament some of the team amused themselves by launching water bombs from the balcony of their apartment and drowning not just Irish athletes but competitors from other countries. This time the complaints did reach the desk of the chef de mission, Pat Hickey. They were summoned to appear before him and warned that if they didn't desist they would be removed from the village. Things quietened down afterwards.

As in all major championships much depended on the draw. Carruth got a lucky break. The names of thirty welterweight boxers went into the drum;

there would be fourteen first round ties, while the two boxers left in the drum would receive a bye and meet in round two.

Eventually there were four names left: Carruth, Saïd Bennajem – the Frenchman that Carruth had beaten in the qualifiers had made it as a late replacement – Maselino Tuifao from Western Samoa and the world champion and gold medal favourite Juan Hernández Sierra from Cuba.

Carruth's luck held; first out was the Frenchman followed by the Cuban. It was a triple boost for the Irish camp. Carruth got a bye into the second round; his first fight was against the unheralded Western Samoan and he was in a different side of the draw to Hernández.

'As soon as I saw the draw I said to my dad, "I'll get to the final and he'll [Hernández] get to the final, and I'll beat him there." We shook hands on it. I won't lie. I didn't think I'd win the gold medal, but I believed I could win a medal.'

Carruth had urged his older brother Austin to back him at odds of 100/1 to win the gold medal. 'I wanted him to put a hundred quid on me. He wasn't too keen, so I suggested he put it on for me instead. Of course, he never did, and I remember telling him on the day before the final that he would owe me £10,000.'

For McCullough, the draw brought mixed emotions. At least he was familiar with his first opponent. Incredibly, he was drawn against Ugandan Fred Muteweta – the same boxer he faced on his Olympic debut in Seoul and whom he had also beaten two years later at the World Cup in Bombay.

Inside the ring Ireland initially hit the headlines for all the wrong reasons. Paul Griffin experienced a meltdown. The European featherweight champion struggled to find his rhythm against Steven Chungu from Zambia. He took two counts before the ringside doctor, Italian Antonio Franconi, jumped to his feet and ordered the referee to stop the contest.

Frustrated by his indifferent performance and the unorthodox end to the fight, Griffin reacted badly. He kicked his gum shield into the third row of the press area and had to be physically restrained as he confronted officials. Initially, he was banned for two years, later reduced to six months. He made a triumphant return the following year by winning a bronze medal at the European Championships in Turkey.

Paul Buttimer lost to a Nigerian opponent; he succeeded McCullough as Irish bantamweight champion in January 1993. He retired two months later after suffering a brain aneurysm on 13 March, on the morning of an international against the United States in San Jose. Kevin McBride was also beaten in his first bout. Paul Douglas, however, came within touching distance of a bronze medal, before being stopped by Dutch heavyweight Arnold Vanderlyde in the first round of their quarter-final bout.

McCullough sailed serenely through the early rounds, despite damaging ligaments in his arm. He overwhelmed Muteweta; his twenty-one point victory (28-7) was the second biggest in the tournament. He then beat Iranian Ahmad Ghanim (10-2), before amassing a remarkable thirty-one points – the highest tally recorded at the Games – in his eighteen-point demolition of Mohamed Sabo from Nigeria, to secure a bronze medal.

Carruth experienced a lot more anxiety on his way to the semi-final. He beat Tuifao 11-2, but broke a small bone in his right hand midway through the second round. At the time the x-ray was inconclusive. Anyway, he had other things on his mind; twenty-four hours later he was facing his nemesis, Andreas Otto. The East German had won a silver medal at the World Championships in Sydney the previous year and had beaten the Irishman 18-1 in the silver medal bout in the light welterweight category at the World Championships in Moscow in 1989. Otto was boxing for a united German team at the Barcelona Games.

The Irish camp thought the scoring in the first Carruth-Otto fight was ludicrous. Carruth had waited five years to exact revenge. He did so, though not before giving the growing number of Irish fans a scare in the third round. Leading 5-3 after round two, Carruth's exuberance got the better of him in the final round. He was fortunate not to receive a public warning for wrestling the German to the ground, which would have cost him the fight. The judges scored the round 3-1 in Otto's favour, which tied the aggregate score 6-6. However, Carruth won the contest 35-22 on a countback of punches. He was now guaranteed a bronze medal.

So, on the eve of the Olympic semi-finals an unthinkable scenario had evolved. Carruth and McCullough were in the last four in the welterweight and bantamweight categories respectively along with the Cuban pair, Juan Hernández Sierra and Joel Casamayor Johnson. Cruz would now be obliged to plot the downfall of his native country's boxers if the Cubans and the Irish reached their respective finals.

Carruth needed no introduction to his opponent Arkom Chenglai from Thailand; they had sparred each other the previous month at the training camp in Cottbus. McCullough had never shared a ring with North Korean Li Gwang-sik, but he had watched him beat World champion Serafim Todorov from Bulgaria in the quarter-final.

The welterweight semi-final was relatively straight forward; Carruth controlled the contest, winning as comfortably as the 11-4 score suggests. Meanwhile, McCullough and Li went to war. 'Some people thought it might have been the best fight in the Olympics,' recalls the Belfast boxer. 'The guy hit me with everything, and I hit him with everything and I beat him.'

McCullough's ringside craft allied to his incredible work rate enabled him to accumulate the scores, and he was five points ahead at the end. Unfortunately, the victory came at a cost. 'The Korean cracked my cheekbone in three places and burst a nerve on the left side of my face.' And after they left the ring, he tried to inflict more damage on his opponent. 'I went to the back of the arena afterwards to shake his hand. I think Pat McCrory was with me. Li tried to kick me, and of course once he raised his foot I went towards him and Pat pulled me back.

'I remember afterwards at the medal ceremony as soon as he was presented with the bronze medal he took it off again. Maybe he was facing punishment back in North Korea for not winning the gold. Funnily enough, I never heard of him again,' says McCullough. Indeed, there is no record of him competing again at international level.

Predictably, Juan Hernández Sierra and Joel Casamayor Johnson together with seven of their teammates also qualified for the finals. So on Saturday, 8 July 1992 the Irish nation came to a standstill when, for the first time in the history of the Olympics, two Irishmen fought for gold medals within an hour of each other. There were actually three Irishmen involved in the finals that day; Jackie Poucher from Newry – who is also a FIFA-accredited soccer referee – refereed the middleweight final.

The bantamweight final was second on the programme; the welterweight decider was fifth. The then Cuban president Fidel Castro later praised Cruz for his dedication to his professional duties in preparing the two Irishmen for their clashes against his fellow countrymen. The legendary Cuban coach Alcides Sagarra and his colleagues in the Cuban Boxing Federation were less enamoured. Ultimately they exacted their retribution.

In truth, Cruz was a tortured soul in Barcelona, torn between the love of his native place and his allegiance to the Irish boxers. He found it particularly difficult to plot the downfall of Hernández. 'We're both from the same province of Artemisa in western Cuba; we carry the same surname so our families are connected, and when I was teaching in the Institute in Havana he was one of my students. In fact, I was his tutor for his thesis.'

McCullough passed the perfunctory medical ahead of the final. 'Basically, the doctor took a look at my hands and never glanced at my face. My cheek was numb, but as I said in a BBC interview afterwards, "Do you really think I was going to pull out of an Olympic final because my cheek felt numb?"'

He had to warm up twice for the final; he forgot that there was a medal presentation after each contest. Just before he climbed into the ring, the enormity of the moment dawned on him. 'I started to think about things happening back home, my religion, winning the gold, and all that crap. Those things had never crossed my mind before.

'I felt the first round was pretty even, but I was 6-1 down at the end of it, which I thought was ridiculous. Early in the second Casamayor caught me on the face and the punch did more damage to my cheekbone which was now hanging by a thread.'

Trailing 10-2, McCullough would have been entirely justified had he retired. As a result of the damage to his cheekbone, there was blood seeping out of the corner of his eye. Incredibly, the Pocket Rocket went out and took the fight to the champion elect. It was arguably the bravest three minutes of boxing fashioned by an Irishman in Olympic history. Nearly a quarter of a century later there is justifiable pride in his voice when he recalls how he took that final round 6-4, though it could have cost him his career. He will carry the scars of the injury to his grave. 'I don't have any feeling in an area on the left side of my nose.'

Carruth watched from the tunnel as McCullough's bid for gold ended in a gallant 14-8 defeat. Now it was Carruth's time to prepare for his date with destiny.

His father took the lead role. 'My dad grabbed me by the legs, hitting them hard, and said, "Your legs. Your legs, they're going to win this fight for you." I just lost it and said, "Aussie, will you f... off and get out of my face for a minute and calm down.'"

Then it was his father's turn to be startled as his son grabbed him and declared, 'Delany's time is up; I'm going to win this fight.' Carruth says, 'I grew up listening to stories about Ronnie Delany winning the 1500 metres at the Melbourne Olympics. Irish boxers had come close before in the Olympics; we had bronze and silver, but we didn't have the big one.'

Cruz had spelled out to Carruth what he needed to do to secure the gold. The game plan was deceptively simple, but to carry it through required iron discipline from Carruth. 'I said to him, "Juan Hernández hasn't been beaten for three and a half years; the only medal he doesn't have is an Olympic gold. We can take it from him, but you mustn't take a step forward. If you go forward, he will top you. You must do what he does best rather than what he expects you to do.'

Carruth stuck to the game plan in the first three minutes and deserved his 4-3 lead at the end of the round. Cruz remembers how unnerved the Cuban coaches were. 'The Cubans didn't expect Michael to fight like he did, so Juan found himself behind. The senior Cuban coach was losing his temper and wanted Hernández to go forward.'

In an effort to nullify the impact of Hernández's devastating left hook, Cruz devised a specific strategy to frustrate him. As soon as Carruth threw a punch, he had to reposition his arms in such a way so as to prevent his opponent from getting his left hook off and making it look like the Cuban was holding him. 'We rehearsed the move the day before. Unfortunately in the second round the referee realised what was really happening and gave Michael a public warning [for holding],' remembers Cruz.

Even though Carruth had three points deducted as a result, the scores were level 8-8 with one round remaining. 'The normal reaction after getting a warning would be to panic, but I nailed him with three crackers before the bell. I looked at him and he knew I had it; he knew he had to come on to me, and when a southpaw comes on to a southpaw there can only be one outcome.'

'My hands were quicker than his and I nailed him with three right hooks early in the last round. Then I did what the old Liverpool team used to do: I closed up shop. I was a master at doing it. He panicked. His natural instincts would have been to counterpunch and catch me when I was coming in. When the bell sounded, I knew I had won the fight and more importantly he knew he'd lost. Just look back on the tape and see our reactions: boxers know.'

Carruth won the round 5-3 to take the fight and the Olympic title 13-10. What he didn't realise was that his father had tried in vain to signal to him to keep away from his opponent in the final twenty seconds. Austin Carruth had got the nod from an Irish official who was watching the computer score screen over the shoulder of one of the judges that Carruth was three points up.

Wayne McCullough watched Michael Carruth's final in the company of his Cuban conqueror Joel Casamayor on a tiny TV screen in the drug-testing room. 'You've got to pee, but it is very difficult because you're dehydrated after a fight. I remember after the decision was announced he gave me a look as if to say, "What's after happening there?" I just looked at him and smiled.'

Carruth had planned to go down on one knee and bless himself as Delany had done in Melbourne if he won the gold medal. Instead, the new Olympic welterweight champion jumped several feet off the ground, as did his dad. Poignantly, when he returned to his corner, his dad thanked him for keeping his eighteen-year-old promise to win an Olympic gold medal for him before warning him, 'Now you're to behave like a champion.'

As soon as they got back to the Olympic village, he took his son's gold medal and put it in his sock, pointing out that it was highly unlikely that any thief would bother stealing one of his smelly socks. And he poured cold water on Michael's plan to go out and get 'locked', advising him to have two or three beers, which would allow him to remember every second of his momentous day. 'This was when he became the father again. I liked it better when he was the "coach" or the "friend". But I still did what he asked; I had two bottles of beer that night.'

For Breandán Ó Conaire, the victory, together with Wayne McCullough's silver medal, was a vindication of his efforts to modernise amateur boxing in Ireland. 'Michael's win was a tactical victory which was down to the coaches, Austin and Nicolás. Most people in Ireland would have put their houses on him losing the final.'

On the flight home Michael sat alongside McCullough and Cheryl, Wayne's partner; directly across the aisle was Austin Carruth. The cabin crew handed out all the Irish daily papers which, of course, had extensive coverage of the boxers' exploits forty-eight hours earlier.

Michael Carruth's attention was drawn to another story. There had been a tragedy on Blessington Lake that weekend, in which four Dublin men, ranging in age from eighteen to twenty-one, had drowned. *The Star* had published a list of those who had previously drowned there. The last name was seven-year-old Gary Carruth, Austin's grandson and Michael's nephew, who had drowned on Sunday, 16 July 1989.

'I looked across at my dad and he was reading the same story. I remember saying to him, "Look at that medal; you can give it f… back." It was a very poignant moment, and it served as a grounding for me. I had just won the greatest prize in boxing, but as a family we had lost the greatest prize of all when my nephew died.'

Carruth had one more fight as an amateur – headlining a Drimnagh Boxing Club promotion fundraiser in the National Stadium in February 1993. Later, he turned professional, winning eighteen of his twenty-one fights and coming close to capturing a WBO welterweight world title in 1997. 'I lost on a split decision in Germany and the zest went out of it for me afterwards. My love of boxing had gone but not my love for boxing.'

Seven months after the Olympics, McCullough, then based in Las Vegas, made his professional debut in California. And just three years after his exploits in Barcelona he achieved his lifetime ambition. In the Japanese city of Nagoya he fashioned a unanimous points win over defending title holder and local hero Yasuei Yakushiji to secure the WBC world bantamweight title.

Even though McCullough didn't hang up his gloves until 2008, he never quite reached those dizzy heights again. 'I don't really care but I didn't get the credit for that win. No other Irish or British fighter has gone to Japan and come back with a belt. But I understand the politics of boxing; it's worse than real politics.'

Joel Casamayor Johnson defected to the USA on the eve of the 1996 Olympics Games. He turned professional and earned the moniker 'El Cepillo', which literally translates as 'the brush', referring to his ability to 'brush off' punches from opponents as well as his uppercut punch which raked them across the face. In 1999 he was crowned WBA super featherweight world champion.

Juan Hernández Sierra never won an Olympic gold medal, despite being crowned world champion on four different occasions. Four years after the Barcelona Olympics, he was beaten again in the welterweight final at the Atlanta Games.

By then, Nicolás Cruz was living permanently in Ireland, having defected from Cuba in February 1996, leaving his wife, Marie, his seven-year-old daughter, Laura, his one-year-old son, Nicolás Junior, and his parents behind. Five years and eight months passed before he was allowed back to visit them in Havana. By then, his marriage had disintegrated, his father had died, and he had contemplated taking his own life.

CHAPTER 6

DASHED DREAMS

'There was a lot of snow that year and I used to take it into my hand and feel it because I had never seen snow in Cuba. I was thinking, this is the first and last time I will be doing this. I had the rope ready.'

Nicolás Cruz

Ultimately, the breakthrough achieved at the Barcelona Olympics did not signal the dawn of a new era in Irish boxing, though flyweight Damaen Kelly won a bronze medal at the World Championships in Tampere, in Finland, in 1993.

Even though the government allocated a sizeable grant for the purchase of equipment by the boxing clubs after the 1992 Olympics, essentially the IABA did not have the financial resources to capitalise on the successes achieved by Michael Carruth and Wayne McCullough.

'We had limited means of fundraising other than regular bingo sessions in the National Stadium. We hosted the occasional concert or conference but that became less productive once other venues in the city opened up,' recalls Breandán Ó Conaire.

'This was a huge problem for us. We had top-class boxers and coaches but had no money to send squads abroad to training camps. They were working-class guys and they couldn't afford to take time off work. We were still able to send the younger guys abroad, and they were medalling at underage level in European competitions. Cathal O'Grady made a significant breakthrough in 1995 when he became the first Irish boxer to win a European junior title. However, some of these lads lived in disadvantaged areas, and they disappeared from the sport after juvenile level.'

The reality on the ground was that while clubs were inundated with youngsters dreaming of becoming the next Michael Carruth, the infrastructure wasn't in place at any level to cope with the spin-off. 'There was no full-time coaching; nothing to harness the interest. Complacency set in as well, and I'm not sure that the belief was there that we could do this all the time,' suggests Billy Walsh.

Cospóir, the predecessor of the Sports Council, provided limited financial support for the Elite boxers. However, coaches did not qualify for any payment, and overall there simply wasn't sufficient resources available to allow the boxers to train full time.

'Common sense dictated that both boxers and their coaches required adequate support and funding to be in a position to realistically compete for the major medals at international championships,' argues Ó Conaire.

Furthermore, the distribution of the grants caused rancour. The *Irish Independent* reported that the grants issue 'provoked a lengthy debate that at times became heated' at the IABA annual convention in Ballina in 1990. At the time, eight boxers were at a camp in Drogheda, preparing for a World Cup tournament in the National Stadium. But only one of them, Belfast's Eamon Magee was being grant-aided. He was receiving £4,000 following his silver medal success at the World Junior Championships in Puerto Rico the previous year.

At the meeting, Ó Conaire acknowledged that the grants issue was having a disruptive influence on the squad. 'There is unrest and it's not good for morale,' he told delegates.

Arguably, the country's most consistent boxer during the nineties was Waterford native Neil Gough. He competed in eleven consecutive national finals between 1991 and 2001. He won eight Elite titles – the first in the light welterweight category and the remainder in the welterweight division. Gough was unbeaten in domestic competition in the 67 kg category for six seasons. He surrendered his title in 2001 to James Moore, who went on to win a bronze medal at the World Championships in Belfast five months later.

Gough could be forgiven for thinking that he peaked in the wrong decade. His international career coincided with the break-up of both the Soviet Union and Yugoslavia, which necessitated the introduction of pre-Olympic qualifying tournaments. 'Instead of having one boxer representing the Soviet Union, there were fifteen coming from countries which broke away from the USSR. So my timing was all wrong,' he acknowledges.

He represented Ireland in seventy-five senior internationals, and his dream was to make the Olympics. He boxed at pre-qualifying tournaments prior to the Barcelona, Atlanta and Sydney Games. At times, the system seemed to conspire against him. In the run-up to the Barcelona Olympics, he fought at the same pre-qualifying tournament in Italy as Michael Carruth. They both won their initial bouts but lost in the next round. For Gough it meant elimination from the light welterweight category, but because Carruth's second fight was a quarter-final, he got a second chance. The rest is history.

'The biggest problem was, while we had a full-time coach [Nicolás Cruz], we weren't full-time boxers. I worked in an electrical wholesale company, initially in the stores and later in sales. I trained before and after work. Then before big international tournaments we had three or four weeks' full time training.

'Before Paul Griffin won his European title [the first since Maxie McCullagh's victory in Oslo in 1949] we could win bronze medals at major championships but struggled to land the gold. Nicolás Cruz could see that, with proper preparation and planning, we had the ability to perform at the highest level. I could see that myself. I had beaten fellows who had made it. It wasn't that we weren't good enough.

'It was difficult coming up against full-time performers. I was drawn on three different occasions – twice in Olympics qualifiers and once at the World Championships against the Russian Oleg Saitov, who won two Olympic, one world and two European titles. It was difficult to have the edge over him because I knew going into the ring he had the benefit of full-time training.'

Nonetheless, Gough fashioned a brave performance against Saitov, the then Olympic champion, in the quarter-finals of the World Championships in Budapest in 1997. The Irishman went down 6-2 to Saitov, who went on to win the gold medal. So effectively Gough finished fifth in the tournament. A year later, Gough became a full-time amateur boxer.

'I was married, and our two boys were aged three and one at the time; my wife Elaine was working which was a help. She knew I had this dream of making the Olympics, and I had spent a decade trying to achieve it. The two words I didn't want to hear when I retired were "what if". So I just went for it.'

There was an ironic twist to his decision to give up his full-time job in the Waterford-based company EWL, where he had worked since the age of sixteen. 'My boss told me he was putting me on the road as a salesman. All I could say in reply was that I had made a decision to give up work. I had eighteen months to achieve my dream.'

He secured financial support from the newly-established Irish Sports Council and the Olympic Council of Ireland, as well as sponsorship from three Waterford-based companies. 'For taxation purposes I classed myself as self-employed and paid tax on the income I was receiving.' But there were still practical issues which remained unresolved. While Cruz had returned to Ireland in 1996, having defected from Cuba, and was back in favour with the IABA, there were no structures in place to support him.

Nonetheless, Cruz had a seminal influence on Gough's career. 'I remember being interviewed by RTÉ's Jimmy Magee at the 1991 European Senior Championships. I pointed out that I would never have made it to Gothenburg but for the influence of my club coach John Finn who trained me from the age of six. Actually, I came home in tears after my first night but my mum knew John, and I returned the following week and stayed for the next twenty-five years.

'But John [Finn] had a job and couldn't work with me full time. Nicolás gave us all an extra dimension. He had a background in sports science and was with us from the time we got up at 6.30am until we went to bed at 9pm. He watched us training, what we ate, and how we lost weight. He had a fantastic skill in putting the combinations together, and because he was working with us day in, day out, these skills were cemented in our mind, and it became second nature to us to do them when we got into the ring.'

Gough and Cruz kept in touch by mail after the latter went back to live in Cuba in 1994. 'I really admired him, and we became very friendly. I always wanted to learn more about boxing and he would help me with things as much as he could.' Through their correspondence Gough knew that Cruz was anxious to return to Ireland, but the Cuban authorities were loath to allow him back. In their eyes he had been too successful. However, in March 1996, Cruz was sent to Puerto Rico with a Cuban boxing squad. Gough and Breandán Ó Conaire were aware of his desire to defect once he reached San Juan, the island's capital city.

Even now, nobody is willing to reveal the precise details of what happened next. However, it is believed that the Irish organised a plane ticket, while Cruz managed to secure possession of his passport – normally it is retained by the team manager on foreign trips. The visa on his Cuban passport allowed him to travel outside the country until the following January, and he had a visitor's visa to Ireland for six months. In the words of one of the parties involved, 'between the jigs and reels' he turned up unexpectedly at the Elite finals in the National Stadium on 8 March 1996. He was there in time to see Gough beat Sean 'Seanie' Barrett on his way to winning his fourth Irish senior title.

In any event, Neil Gough did not make it to the Sydney Olympics in 2000. His dream died six months earlier in Liverpool. As the *Irish Independent* reporter poetically put it: 'Neil Gough's dream died on Merseyside last night and it wasn't from natural causes.' He was on the wrong end of a controversial 4-2 decision against Danish boxer Reda Zam Zam. The verdict was described in the paper as 'sounding more bizarre than his exotic name'.

This view was echoed by Irish coach Christy McKenna, who was in the Irish corner with Nicolás Cruz. He told the *Irish Independent*, 'As far as we were concerned, Neil clearly won the fight, but we have found the judging very difficult to understand ... Neil boxed well and, if it was hard to comprehend how he could go into the last round one point behind, it's unbelievable that those final two minutes should have been 1-0 in Zam Zam's favour after Neil tagged him at least six times.'

Boxers have to accept the vagaries of the judging system. There was absolutely nothing Gough could do but accept this fate. What annoyed him most was the fact that he had previously beaten the two boxers that his Danish opponent – who ultimately didn't make it to Sydney either – faced in his next two fights in Liverpool.

'Had I won that fight, I probably would have made it. I was going on thirty-one, and that was it. I was glad I had given it everything. But it was hard not to have achieved what I set out to do. When I retired, I realised that up until then everything in our family had revolved around me. All of a sudden I was available to cut the grass, take the kids somewhere or go on a holiday.'

Gough's fellow Waterford man John Treacy – who was appointed the first chairman of the newly-established Irish Sports Council in 1997 – helped the boxer secure funds when he went full time. There was an element of serendipity that the Olympic silver medallist would ultimately play a pivotal role in the consolidation of boxing as Ireland's most successful Olympic sport. Twenty-four hours after Carruth's gold medal performance at the Barcelona Olympics, Treacy bade a low-key farewell to his own distinguished Olympic career when he finished fifty-first in the marathon.

In July 1999 the ISC became a statutory body and Treacy became its first chief executive. Once there was a statutory body in place, the state had a mechanism whereby they could invest in sport. 'The ISC was the vehicle for directing it,' explains Treacy.

Blessed with a better political antenna that his contemporaries, Breandán Ó Conaire, then president of the IABA, immediately recognised the significance of the new body. 'Right from the very beginning I believed that boxing would be the unique sport which, in the international arena, would justify the council's existence. At the time, we were going nowhere because we were boxing professionals and we were amateurs. We had talented boxers and coaches, and they needed financial support.'

The ISC's first initiative to support athletes was a carding system. According to Ó Conaire, the IABA was one of the first organisations to sign up. 'Now the boxers knew they had something to aim for besides a medal and this was approved year on year. Once it was established, it couldn't be de-established.'

He peppered Treacy with correspondence. 'I still have these long letters I sent to him explaining how we had looked after the disadvantaged groups in society who were interested in boxing, such as members of the travelling community. I eventually convinced him that a boxer cannot train himself. So the coaches would have to be looked after as well.'

The IABA's campaign for a bigger slice of the financial pie was boosted when the ISC employed a sports consultant to investigate how the sports organisations spent their money. 'We opened our books to him and he was astonished. We were the guys who were doing the business internationally but were getting minimal funding, whereas the bulk of the monies was going to organisations such as the GAA, the IRFU, and the FAI, because they had the best lobbyists.' Predictably Treacy has a different view. 'The IABA was never shy about asking for money but we could never meet their expectations.'

In January 2000 Ó Conaire called a press conference at Dublin's Wynn's Hotel to announce the appointment of two full-time professionals to oversee the development of boxing. Nicolás Cruz was appointed as the IABA's first national coaching administrator. He was one of six candidates interviewed for the position. Michael Carruth and Billy Walsh were among the other interviewees. The latter was named as Cruz's part-time assistant and remained in position while the funding lasted, according to Ó Conaire. The other appointment was that of Glasgow-born Don Stewart, who was elevated from the position of National Stadium manager, a role he had performed for the previous ten years, to administrative director of the IABA.

The *Irish Independent* reported at the time that the three positions would be funded by the IABA's own resources, with practical assistance from the Sports Council and the Olympic Council of Ireland. The IABA provided Cruz with a bedsit, including meals, and a personal office in the National Stadium, reimbursed his travelling expenses in Ireland, and assisted him in acquiring an Irish passport and citizenship.

During the previous four years Nicolás Cruz's life had struggled in his personal life. After defecting, he lived in the National Stadium. He recalls how a friend, Joe Lavelle, brought a bed on the back of a truck from Belmullet for his humble accommodation. Even though Cruz held a master's in sports science, he had to content himself with sweeping the floor of the National Stadium after bingo sessions, cleaning the nearby Ringside bar, and working nights with a security company to make ends meet.

Eventually he secured part-time teaching jobs in St Patrick's Institute and Portlaoise Prison but was told he would have to learn Irish to secure a full-time position. 'Breandán helped, and I tried, but in general Irish people don't speak Irish.' He felt isolated, his marriage broke up, and inexplicably the IABA did not appoint him team coach for the Atlanta Olympics. He reached breaking point in the winter of 1997.

'I felt I had nothing to look forward to,' he recalls. 'The idea of hanging myself came into my head as I watched the trees from the back door of the gym. There was a lot of snow that year and I used to take it into my hand and feel it because I had never seen snow in Cuba. I was thinking, this is the first and last time I will be doing this. I had the rope ready.

But a chance meeting with a Buddhist monk at a yoga seminar in the Little Flower Hall in Meath Street in Dublin changed his life. 'It was something from above,' he suggests. Slowly his acute feelings of fear and anxiety subsided. He recognised that he had something to live for. In a symbolic gesture he tore the rope into three pieces. He then tied the pieces together and used it as a boxing aid in the gym – the boxers had to bob and weave around it. 'I carried that rope around until it was no good.'

Initially Cruz was delighted to finally secure a full-time position in the IABA. However, he still believes he made one vital error when accepting the job. 'I concentrated on going for the job and I didn't ask about the pay. I did it the wrong way around. When I finally enquired, I was told the salary was £15,000 per year. 'Jesus with that I couldn't even save enough to go back home or bring my family over here on a visit.'

Furthermore, Cruz claims that, at the time, he was put on the wrong tax table. 'I wasn't used to the system, and I was taxed incorrectly for a good number of years. Eventually, it was sorted out in 2008, but I could only claim back tax for the four preceding years, and I lost a lot of money. Out of the £15,000 I was getting very little of it into my hand. I eventually asked for a raise and got £2,000.'

'We simply didn't have enough money to pay him any more. Whatever he was paid was money we got from the Sports Council, which we then probably had to match ourselves. We were penurious. What he got was all we could afford. The top Irish coaches continued to work on a voluntary basis,' explains Ó Conaire.

In 2000, after four years in office, Ó Conaire unexpectedly stepped down as president. Before leaving office, he set himself one final target – the renovation of the National Stadium, which had become old and dank.

'I approached Bertie Ahern, who was Taoiseach at the time, and, together with the then minister for sport Jim McDaid, we put together a comprehensive redevelopment plan for the Stadium. The government ear-marked £1.3 million for the refurbishment project; the IABA had to raise an additional £260,000 from the corporate and business sectors and fundraising projects organised by the association to avail of it.'

Ó Conaire took a leave of absence from his job to oversee the completion of the project. It wasn't all plain sailing. 'The government grants were slow in arriving and there was a danger of the builders pulling out at one stage. I personally met Bertie at the Community Games' finals in Mosney. He assured me he'd sort it out, and by Monday the builders had their money.'

Within two years of his departure, the High Performance Unit has been established. His dream had been realised. The next phase in the evolution of Irish boxing had begun.

CHAPTER 7

THREE WISE MEN

'My boxers had better food than my children. And I was happy. I swear to God this is true. I was so fanatical about boxing that I sacrificed everything. I wasn't sleeping. I was just thinking about the boxers.'

Zaur Antia

At first glance, they were an odd threesome. Gary Keegan, a Dubliner, Billy Walsh, a Wexford man and Georgian native Zaur Antia, whose English vocabulary consisted of six words when he arrived in Ireland twelve years ago. But this triumvirate changed the face of Irish amateur boxing forever. They all come from working-class backgrounds.

Born in Ballybough, in Dublin's north inner city, Gary Keegan walked past Croke Park on his way to school every day, though like most inner city kids in the sixties he never played in the stadium. Instead, after his family moved to Coolock, a friend, Michael Thompson – whose older brothers, Paul, Shay and Tommy were all noted pugilists – inveigled Keegan to join Transport Boxing Club, which, ironically, was based back in the inner city.

Walsh grew up in Wolfe Tone Villas, a corporation housing estate in the centre of Wexford town – within sight of the county's premier GAA ground. 'Every family on the estate seemed to have six or seven kids and I was a robust young fella. The gym for St Joseph's Boxing Club was in the grounds of the local Christian Brothers' school. The Brothers were heavily involved in the running of the club. I discovered years later that my late father, Liam, asked them to take me into the club to calm my ways.'

Initially, Walsh had no luck. 'In my first county championships I got a head-butt which left me with a closed left eye for a few days. Then when I went to the Leinster championships the eye swelled up again and I had to withdraw.' He also dabbled successfully in Gaelic football, hurling and soccer. By the time he was fourteen, he had won an All-Ireland boxing title and was a member of the Wexford U-14 soccer, Gaelic and hurling teams. 'I should have been a brain surgeon but I didn't have time to study,' he suggests with a wry smile.

Kilkenny were not as dominant in hurling in the 1980s as they are currently. Walsh entertained realistic ambitions of winning silverware with his mates, who included Martin Storey, Tom Dempsey and John O'Connor – all of whom played pivotal roles in the county's historic All-Ireland success in 1996. Another of Walsh's teammates on that U-14 team which won a Leinster title was Andy Ronan, who ran for Ireland in the Olympic marathon in Barcelona in 1992. In the 1981 Leinster Minor Hurling Final, Wexford, the defending title holders, looked set to capture back-to-back titles for the first time since 1967–1968 when they led by five points with six minutes left. Walsh vividly remembers what happened next.

'I was playing wing back, and being marked by John McDonald from Mullinavat. I was clearing a ball, but he got a touch to it and it went out over the side line. But the linesman gave them the decision. I remember glass milk bottles were still in use at the time and a few of them were thrown at the lines-man. From the side-line cut somebody doubled on the ball in the square and it finished up in the back of the net. Kilkenny won the match by a point. There and then I said f... this! I threw my hurley down and vowed that I was going to box in the Olympic Games. I didn't want to be relying on fourteen other fellas. I gave up hurling and football and set my sights on celebrating my twenty-first birthday in three years' time at the Los Angeles Games.'

The eldest in a family of three, Zaur Antia was born and raised in Poti, a port city in Georgia, located on the eastern Black Sea coast. On 14 March 1921, the city was occupied by the invading Russian army who installed a Soviet government in Georgia, which remained in place until the dissolution of the USSR in the early 1990s. Antia's father worked as a labourer in the thriving port. In common with the rest of the population Antia's family spoke Georgian, one of the oldest languages in the world. There have been suggestions that Jesus prayed in the Georgian language. 'When I was growing up we were under Russian occupation but it wasn't a big deal, though we all learned to speak their language.'

The local boxing club was housed inside the port area, a five-minute walk from his parents' apartment. Antia went along with his friends, but he also sampled soccer and wrestling. 'I was good at wrestling, which is a very traditional Georgian sport, but my boxing coach "poisoned" me. He made me love boxing by making a motivational speech before every training session. He was like a father to me; he was a very special coach. He was always reading the newspapers. Once he said to me, "Zaur, listen to me – this newspaper only cost two cent. Take it and read it."

'I did what he asked and as a result I started to read books, many books. When somebody speaks to you at a particular time in your life it can make a big difference.'

Unlike his two colleagues, Gary Keegan did not make his name inside the ring. Instead, he left home at the age of sixteen to join the merchant navy. By the time he returned three years later there was an embryonic drug problem in parts of Dublin, including Coolock. 'Drugs had just arrived in the area and concerned parents approached me to give them a hand at setting up a boxing club in order to get the kids off the streets. I set up Glin Boxing Club in the local community centre which was just across the road from where I lived.

'However, I quickly realised that I was neither qualified nor experienced enough at the age of nineteen to run a boxing club or coach the kids. I plugged into Tommy and Shay Thompson [who was Irish featherweight champion in 1982] as they had both just retired from boxing. I asked them to help out. They both came down; Shay didn't spend too long, but Tommy became the head coach of Glin Boxing Club.'

After he got married, Keegan moved to Blanchardstown. There he got involved in Corduff Boxing Club and set about acquiring his coaching badges under the tutelage of four of the legendary figures in Irish amateur boxing: Austin Carruth, Breandán Ó Conaire, Michael Hawkins and Mick Dowling.

Later, he set up a new club called St Mochta's on the Clonsilla Road in Blanchardstown. Initially, it was based in an old national school, and when that closed they moved to the St Brigid's Community Centre in the village and renamed the club St Brigid's Boxing Club. Keegan ran this club for seventeen years. Hundreds of kids passed through it, including an Irish-Jamaican youngster called Darren Sutherland. During this period Keegan also became increasingly immersed in the affairs of the Dublin County Boxing Board and the IABA.

Despite the heartbreak he endured when Wexford failed to win the Leinster minor title in 1981, Billy Walsh didn't give up entirely on the GAA. Indeed, at times, it proved an important outlet for his talents when issues inside the ring soured his love affair with boxing. He was a substitute on the Faythe Harriers team that won the Wexford senior hurling championship in 1981. Three years later when he was controversially left off the Irish boxing team for the Los Angeles Olympics he found refuge in the GAA.

Following his defeat by Michael Carruth in a box-off for a place on the team for the Barcelona Olympics in 1992, Walsh switched to coaching. Together with Tom Hayes, he ran St Joseph's/St Ibar's Boxing Club, turning it into one of the top clubs in the country. Once they had five national title holders on their books. A three-year drop in the upper-age limit meant that Walsh was ineligible to bid for a place on the Irish team to compete at the Atlanta Olympics in 1996. But a year out from the Games the age limit was restored to thirty-five. Walsh couldn't resist the urge for one last hurrah. 'I was working for a company called Snowcream, who were part of the Glanbia group. I went to them and they agreed to sponsor me.'

Two weeks before the Elite championships, Walsh busted his hand in a club bout against his namesake Billy Walsh, who was a native of Cork and had won an Elite title at welterweight in 1994. Then he got the worst possible draw – he was pitted against another Cork native, Michael Roche, who four years later was the only Irish boxer to qualify for the Sydney Olympics.

'There weren't too many punches thrown, but he ended up beating me. That put it to bed once and for all. Actually, RTÉ retired me! The late Noel Andrews, who was commentating on the fight, and Mick Dowling, his co-commentator, came into the ring afterwards and asked me such pertinent questions that I had no option but to announce my retirement on the spot. I knew I hadn't got it any more. I cried all the way home to Wexford.

'After I retired originally in 1992, I remember my dad saying to me, "Son, you don't come back." And when it was all over he said, "I told you so", and he was right. But I just felt that [Olympic] medal was in me somewhere but I never got to it. So I just went back coaching with my club.'

Now regarded as one of the best technical boxing coaches in the world,

Zaur Antia was anything but a stylist when he donned a pair of boxing gloves. 'At the beginning I was only a bronze medallist. I was a tough fighter but had no skill. I was not thinking. I was just physically trying to win. When I was sixteen or seventeen I learned more about boxing and came to understand that it is like chess; you need to think.'

Antia won five Georgian senior titles. He represented his native city, Poti, in the Spartakiad, a mass participation sports festival held every four years in Eastern bloc countries prior to the break-up of the Soviet Union. He qualified to compete in the Soviet Union championships – a rare achievement for any sportsperson who came from Poti – and won a bronze medal. In addition, he was awarded the title 'Master of Boxing' by the USSR.

However, his career within the ring left him unfulfilled. 'I felt I didn't achieve enough. Of course, my dream was to get to a major championship. But I always remember what my coach, who as a boxer didn't make it to the Olympics either, said, "Sometimes there are people whose possibility is bigger than their achievement." When I boxed, Georgia was part of the Soviet Union and it was very difficult to win a Soviet title.' The Soviet boycott of the 1984 Olympics meant that Antia would have missed out even if he qualified. But then his life took a different route. He got married when he was twenty-one; he became a father shortly afterwards when his wife, Nona, gave birth to their daughter, Natia.

Then, having completed two years' compulsory army service, he enrolled as a student at the Institute of Sport in the Georgian capital, Tbilisi, a five-hour, 344-kilometre drive across the Likhi mountain range from his home in Poti. He was a part-time student; he travelled to Tbilisi twice a year for five years, staying for a month attending lectures and sitting examinations. For the rest of the year he worked in Poti as an organiser of sports events and as a boxing coach. It quickly dawned on him that he had found his real vocation in life.

Back in Ireland, Gary Keegan was making progress through the labyrinthine governing structures of Irish amateur boxing. He served as vice-president of the Dublin Boxing County Board, but his abiding passion was coaching. He got his opportunity when he became involved in the coaching committee of the Dublin Board who ran squad sessions in Dublin clubs in the aftermath of Michael Carruth's historic gold medal win in Barcelona. Carruth's uncle, the late Noel Humpston – who was Kenny Egan's first coach – and the late Paddy Hyland from Tallaght worked alongside Keegan. They crossed paths with the late Austin Carruth, then arguably the most influential coach in Irish boxing in the wake of his success in Barcelona.

'I think Austin took a bit of a shine to me and took me under his wing. I always found him a great sounding board for my coaching ideas. Our relationship grew over time, and Austin co-opted me on to the IABA's National Coaching Committee. I was only thirty-three, which in terms of the age profile of the other members was very young. Dominic O'Rourke, who was the youngest coach on the committee until I arrived, was probably ten years older than me.

'I got involved in managing the structures around international squad sessions at youth, junior and senior levels. I set up the squad training programmes and put coaches in charge of them. This was my introduction to seeing how things were done and why Irish teams were not doing as well as expected. This got me thinking a lot about how we prepared our boxers for international tournaments.'

Keegan had first-hand experience of the preparations ahead of the Atlanta Olympics in 1996 when Ireland's ambitions were seriously undermined by an exodus of boxers to the professional ranks. In the wake of the Barcelona Olympics, Michael Carruth and Wayne McCullough turned pro, as did Paul Douglas and Kevin McBride. [McBride was to enjoy fifteen minutes of fame in 2005 when he beat former world heavyweight champion Mike Tyson, who quit on his stool before the start of the seventh round of an untitled fight in Washington DC.]

Worse still, seven of Ireland's leading Atlanta hopefuls, including former European gold medallist Paul Griffin as well as Danny Ryan, Jim Webb, Darren Corbett, Mark Winters, Martin Reneghan, and Neil Sinclair also joined the pay ranks in 1996. Sinclair had won a gold medal at the Commonwealth Games in Victoria, Canada, the previous year, as had Webb, while Winters and Reneghan both won silver.

The loss of Sinclair, who had also won medals at European and world level while a junior, cut deep within the IABA. It underlined the difficulties which the organisation faced, as its president Breandán Ó Conaire acknowledged at the time. 'It was known for some time that he [Sinclair] was unemployed, and professional managers were trying to sign him up. A bursary should have been put in place to make it financially viable for him to remain an amateur until after the Olympics at least. Now we have lost a great talent, which has weakened our Olympic hand considerably.'

Four boxers, flyweight Damaen Kelly (who had won a bronze medal at the European Championships in Denmark four months earlier, to add to the World bronze he captured in 1993), Francis 'Francie' Barrett, Brian Magee and Cathal O'Grady, qualified. Most of the attention was focused on Barrett, the first member of the Travelling community to represent Ireland in the Olympic Games.

Living on a halting site at Hillside, on the eastern edge of Galway city, Barrett's career was nurtured by barber Michael 'Chuck' Gillen in the Olympic Boxing Club, whose training base was a locked-up metal shipping container which had no electricity or running water. From these humble origins Barrett made it to Atlanta. He was given the honour of carrying the tricolour and leading the Irish contingent into Centennial Olympic Park for the opening ceremony.

Inside the ring, Barrett made a winning debut in the light welterweight division, hammering Brazilian Zely Fereira dos Santos 32-7, before losing 18-6 in the second round to eventual bronze medallist Fethi Missaoui from Tunisia. Heavyweight Cathal O'Grady was stopped in the first round by a New Zealander Garth de Silva, who exited the tournament in the next round. Belfast natives Damaen Kelly and Brian Magee made it through to the last eight. Kelly lost 13-6 to the eventual silver medallist in the flyweight category, Bulat Jumadilov from Kazakhstan, while Magee lost 12-9 to Algerian Mohamed Bahari who won a bronze medal in the middleweight division.

Occasionally an individual Irish boxer broke the mould, as evidenced by the performance of light heavyweight Stephen Kirk at the 1997 World Championships in Budapest. He captured a bronze medal, though was stopped by the eventual champion, Russia's Alexandr Lebziak in the semi-final. Unfortunately, on the eve of the 1998 Commonwealth Games in Kuala Lumpur, Kirk was forced to retire after failing a brain scan.

By then the world of amateur boxing had changed utterly. The former Soviet republics were now established boxing powers, and Ireland had slipped further down the ranking list. This was illustrated by the fact that for the first time ever, only one Irish boxer, Michael Roche, qualified for the Sydney Games in 2000.

Meanwhile, Gary Keegan had risen through the ranks of the IABA. He was chair of coach education and secretary of the National Coaching Committee. He had qualified as a coach tutor and was involved in developing a new coaching education programme for boxing. And he was also running his own business. 'I was doing all the boxing work on a voluntary basis. I was running a transport company, which I sold and moved into retail. Later, I went back into transport, but like all passionate sports people, whenever I was negotiating a work contract I checked out how it would impact on my involvement in sport.'

At the beginning of the new millennium, Walsh was working as a milkman in his native Wexford while continuing to coach at club level. Twelve days into the new century, Nicolás Cruz was named as the IABA's first ever full-time National Coaching Administrator. He was to have the support of two part-time staff – one of whom was Walsh. Walsh was an obvious choice for the position, according to Cruz, 'I used to get on very well with him and his late father Liam. He was always interested in coaching. While Billy was still boxing I remember telling him, "You are going to be one of the best coaches in Ireland."'

For Walsh it was a chance in a lifetime, though taking up the job involved significant sacrifices. He was self-employed and the position of assistant coach was voluntary. 'I thought it was a great opportunity for a young coach, even though there was no pay.'

Initially, the squad prepared in Athy for the qualifiers ahead of the Sydney Olympics. Walsh remembers, 'The set-up there wasn't good enough really, so we ended up going to the University of Limerick. There were three pre-qualifying tournaments for the Sydney Olympics in March/April 2000. Nicolás [Cruz] would have gone to the tournaments while I stayed behind with the boxers who weren't involved.'

Walsh had to turn down another opportunity to work with Cruz ahead of the European Championships in Tampere, Finland, in May 2000. 'I simply couldn't afford it. I had to pay somebody to look after the milk round when I was involved earlier in the year.' Nonetheless, a flame had been ignited in Walsh's soul which ultimately yielded spectacular results.

From the moment he started coaching school children in Poti, Zaur Antia used a different approach than his contemporaries. 'There were ten of us coaching in the schools, all of whom were trained by my first boxing coach, whom I loved very much and who was very famous. But I was completely different to the others. When I spoke about boxing, up to fifty children came to listen and they all came back to train. None of the others, including my original coach, had fifty coming to training. During my own career I had learned that boxing is better than fighting in the ring, so I coached boxers differently.'

Eventually, there was a stand-off between Antia and his former mentor. 'He called me something which wasn't nice. I was different. I loved the way I was teaching them how to box, and I told him I would prove that I had the best approach.'

Traditionally, Georgian boxers gathered in clubs at noon every Sunday for a sparring session. 'They came to Poti because they knew that's where they would find the best sparring. When the young boxers I trained matured and started sparring, they did well. Coaches found out that I didn't copy; I did my own thing. I have something that I never learned from anybody.'

His protégés began to make an impact, not just in Georgia but in the Soviet Union itself. In the latter half of the 1980s Georgian boxers coached by Antia garnered medals at the Soviet Union championships. 'This is how I became involved in the Soviet Union boxing squad. Now I was working alongside their head coach Nikolay Khromov. I was spending most of my time away from home, not just in Moscow, but at different training camps.'

However, everything changed with the collapse of the old Soviet state in 1991. Antia was offered a sweetheart deal by the Russians. 'They asked me and the two Georgian boxers, Koba Gogoladze and Zurab Sarsania – who were members of the Soviet Union squad at the time – to stay in Moscow. They said, "If you sign a contract, we will give you a club here. You will have good money. Your boys [boxers] will stay here and we will continue to work together." The boxers came to me looking for advice. But I was thinking, if I stay, my country will call me a traitor.'

Antia left Moscow and returned home to Poti with his two boxers, whom he now felt morally obliged to support. Having declared independence on 9 April 1991, Georgia rapidly descended into chaos. Just eight months later, a bloody coup d'état sparked a civil war which lasted four years.

'It was a terrible time; there was no electricity, water or fuel. The Russians cut off everything. People weren't being paid. There were mile-long queues for food. The boxers were from poor families and had nothing. I was trying to feed them in my own home, and I wasn't thinking about my own family. All I knew was I had food in my house and I had to feed the boxers.'

Eventually, his tearful wife Nona called a halt. 'She said, "I love when people eat with us, but we don't have enough food – the children have nothing to eat." I was so fanatical about boxing that I sacrificed everything. I wasn't sleeping. I was just thinking about the boxers.'

Antia deployed his ingenuity and friendships to see his boxers through the civil war. He persuaded the mayor of Poti to provide him with a letter urging restaurant owners to provide free meals for the boxers. Armed with the letter, he approached restaurateurs and appealed to their patriotism. The boxers got fed. 'My boxers had better food than my children. And I was happy. I swear to God this is true.'

Business acquaintances of Antia's provided them with pocket money; a physiotherapist friend looked after their injuries, and others provided them with vitamins. In time, normality returned to Georgia which enabled Antia to secure sponsorship for his boxing club from the company that ran Poti port. Under his guidance the club mushroomed into the biggest and most successful in the country, and Antia became head coach of the Georgian junior team.

The new independent state of Georgia made a sensational debut at the 1993 European Championships in Turkey, winning four medals. Antia coached super heavyweight Zurab Sarsania to a silver medal. Tragically, the boxer was later murdered at the age of twenty-one. Antia's other protégé, lightweight Koba Gogoladze, won a bronze medal at the 1997 World Championships in Budapest and a silver at the Europeans a year later, before leaving Georgia to pursue a professional career in the UK and the US.

Antia's dream was to coach a Georgian boxer to win an Olympic title. But a disagreement with the president of the Georgian Boxing Federation and a chance encounter with an Irish boxing referee changed the course of his life and that of Irish boxing.

CHAPTER 8

NEW BEGINNINGS

'I just cracked up when they went off on the piss. I had come from a generation that would have died to fight for their country. Incidents like this had been brushed under the carpet by previous managers. What happened in Poland was beyond a joke as far as I was concerned.'

Billy Walsh

S onia O'Sullivan's silver medal in the 5000 metres at the Sydney Olympics in 2000 camouflaged an otherwise indifferent Games for Ireland. Other sports, particularly boxing, failed to deliver. For the first time in seventeen Olympics an Irish boxer failed to win a single bout at the tournament.

Ireland's sole representative, Michael Roche, was beaten 17-4 by Fırat Karagöllü in the first round of the now discontinued light middleweight category. The Turk was eliminated in the next round.

Destiny played a big role in getting the Cork native there in the first place. Even though he had won four Elite titles on the spin between 1997 and 2000, he had limited international experience due to work commitments. The situation improved when he changed jobs in 1999. His new employers, Pfizer, were more accommodating and allowed him time off work. But other unforeseen events outside the ring nearly scuppered his chances.

The Chemistry Cup tournament in Halle, Germany, in early March was the designated Olympic qualifying event for European-based light middle-weights. But Roche almost didn't make it to Halle.

'I flew from Cork but the flight was late landing in Dublin. Luckily the plane that I was due to travel to Germany on was delayed as well so I made the connection.' The drama still wasn't over. He was given the wrong date for his fight.

'After the draw was made on Tuesday, I was assured by the team management that I wasn't fighting until Friday, which I found surprising due to the number of boxers in my weight category. On the Wednesday morning I was in the hotel lobby, having just returned from a run, when team coach Nicolás Cruz came running down the hall and said I had to weigh-in straight away. They had fucked up.'

Roche was due to fight later that day and faced immediate disqualification if he didn't weigh-in. The previous night he had eaten a couple of squares of chocolate and he was one and half pounds over the limit. 'Nicolás was on his knees begging the officials to give me a chance. They let me train for fifteen minutes and I just made the weight. It was a comedy of errors but I think it was just meant to be,' says Roche who won three fights in Halle to secure his spot in Sydney.

The smallest ever Irish Olympic boxing team, consisting of Roche, Bernard Dunne (who was first reserve in the featherweight category), coach Nicolás Cruz and team manager Martin Power left Ireland to complete their preparations in Newcastle, a coastal city one hundred and sixty kilometres north of Sydney. The camp was a shambles. 'It wasn't a proper training camp. I was sparring against youngsters,' recalls Roche.

Despite the disparity in their sizes, Bernard Dunne became his primary sparring partner. 'By God, he had power. I had never been as fit before in my career but from a boxing viewpoint it wasn't the ideal preparation.' And so it proved: Roche's Olympic dreams unravelled like a slow motion horror movie over nine forgettable minutes on 19 September. He was anxious to put on a show for the hundreds of Irish emigrants who had taken the day off work to see him make his Olympic debut. A classic counter-puncher, he decided to go forward and found himself in a scrap. 'The Turk was shocked when I went forward. I was surprised myself because it was the only time I did it in my career.' The outcome was inevitable.

At least Roche got the opportunity to box in the Olympics. Bernard Dunne's experience literally left him scarred for life. He fractured three metacarpals in his right hand when he caught Roche's elbow one day in the ring. Nevertheless, he wasn't giving up on his Olympic ambition; he secured a spar against Thai bantamweight Somluck Kamsing knowing that he needed to knock him out to have a chance of a late call-up. But Dunne sustained a nasty wound over his left eye in the spar which finally ended his Olympic dream.

Worse still, Dunne was cut adrift once the party arrived in Sydney. He wasn't an official competitor so he didn't have access to the Olympic village, and he was told that his travel arrangements couldn't be changed when he requested to be sent home.

The O'Driscolls, a Cork-born family living in Sydney who knew Roche, looked after Dunne, while RTÉ's Jimmy Magee secured him a media pass into the boxing. Eventually, he swapped plane tickets with Roche's wife, Yvonne, and flew home. In his autobiography *Bernard Dunne, My Story* he revealed his grandfather William died the night he got home. The experience ruptured his relationship with the IABA. Then aged twenty, he had originally planned to stay in the amateur ranks until after the Athens Olympics. Instead, he opted to pursue the professional route straight away. Nine years later, he was crowned

WBA super bantamweight champion of the world.

But boxing wasn't the only sport experiencing traumatic times at the start of the new millennium. Ireland was light years behind other countries in terms of their expenditure on high performance sport. The results were evidence of this. Ireland was ranked sixty-fourth in the medal table. Among the European countries that finished above them were Moldova, Belgium, Croatia, Estonia, Latvia, Slovakia, Switzerland, Slovenia, Lithuania, Austria, Finland, Denmark, Czech Republic, Turkey, Spain, Belarus, Ukraine, Norway, Sweden, Greece, Bulgaria, Poland, Hungary, Romania, and the Netherlands, together with the continent's superpowers: Russia, Germany, France, Italy, and the United Kingdom.

Scarcely a month after the closing ceremony, the then minister for sport, Jim McDaid, requested the Irish Sports Council carry out an in-depth review of Ireland's preparation for the Games. The report from the steering group was published in December 2001. Commonly known as the Sydney Review, it made twenty-nine recommendations. It led to the establishment of the Athens Enhancement Programme which resulted in the limited funds which were available for Olympic sports being targeted in a specific way by developing what was termed 'a High Performance strategy'.

'It became abundantly clear that we needed to pick the sports that we were going to invest in because you can't do a scatter gun approach when it comes to High Performance. So you have to select the horses you are going to back. What we did for the Athens Olympics was to ensure that we were backing our best sports and athletes,' recalls John Treacy, the then chief executive of the ISC. Four sports – equestrian, athletics, swimming, and boxing – were earmarked for the enhanced funding.

Notwithstanding their travails in Sydney, it was self-evident that, given its history, boxing would be one of the sports targeted ahead of the 2004 Games. It was a no-brainer as far as Treacy was concerned. 'Look at the significance of the sport in the country and the number of medals Irish boxers had won. 'We were not deterred by the fact that there was only one Irish boxer in Sydney. Instead, we looked at the success of the boxers in 1992. There was a tradition there, and we felt they could do a lot better. There were issues about the judging system. Let's put it this way: it mightn't have been the fairest in the world, but it looked like it was changing in terms of reaching fair decisions and becoming a bit more transparent,' says Treacy.

Meanwhile, the IABA had an ideal opportunity to showcase its organisational ability and the fact that it could still hold its own inside the ring when Belfast's Odyssey Arena hosted the eleventh edition of the World Boxing Championships in June 2001. While Nicolás Cruz was still employed as the association's national coaching director he had a peripheral role in preparing the team. Instead, the boxers brought their own coaches to the University of Limerick, where the final training camp was staged.

Bernard Dunne had departed but Michael Roche competed. 'I had planned to retire after the Olympics, but Jimmy Magee persuaded me to stay on for the Worlds.'

Among the other team members was nineteen-year-old Kenny Egan and super heavyweight Eanna Falvey, who was later to become the Irish rugby team doctor. Against the odds, the Irish boxers performed exceptionally well, though Roche bowed out in the first round. Half the team, John Paul Kinsella (light flyweight), Damien McKenna (bantamweight), Michael Kelly (light welterweight), James Moore (welterweight), Egan (middleweight), and Alan Reynolds (heavyweight) made it through to the quarter-finals. 'It was Ireland's best ever performance at a World Championships; it has never been surpassed, even since the High Performance Unit was set up. Getting to the last eight is one thing; making the next step on the podium is a different matter though,' says Kenny Egan.

The Irish skipper James Moore was the only one of the six boxers who managed to win his quarter-final bout and secure a bronze medal. He drew with his Turkish opponent Fırat Karagöllü 24-24 but won on a countback of punches 118-82, before losing to American Anthony Thompson 24-36 in the semi-final Coincidentally, the Turkish fighter that Moore beat to secure the bronze medal was the same boxer that had ended Roche's Olympic ambitions in Sydney.

However, any delusions of grandeur that the boxers' performances in Belfast engendered were rudely shattered a year later at the European Championships in Russia. The Russian city of Perm built on the banks of the Kama in the western foothills of the Ural Mountains hosted the event. The Irish boxers had plenty of time to view the scenery as they saw very little action inside the ring. Moore, John Paul Kinsella, Damien McKenna, and Michael Kelly, together with Cavan lightweight Andrew 'Andy' Murray and Derry light middleweight John Duddy, all failed to win a fight.

Murray and Duddy later had strong professional careers. Duddy, who now lives in Queens, New York, is also known for playing the role of Scottish professional boxer Ken Buchanan in the movie *Hands of Stone* about the life of legendary Panamanian middleweight Roberto Durán. The film which was released in 2015 starred Robert De Niro, who is friendly with Duddy.

Kenny Egan missed the tournament; he was suspended by the IABA at the time. Then a self-confessed 'messer', even he knew drastic action was required. 'It was lambs to the slaughter out there. Something had to be done. We were going nowhere. There was no leadership. There was still no full-time training. We were brought in at the weekends, but the National Stadium had only one ring. So you had to queue up and wait your turn before you got a chance to spar,' he recalls. Worse still, there was a worrying pattern developing as the five-man team sent to the previous European Championships in Tampere, Finland, in

2000 had failed to win a single bout.

Unbeknown to Egan, a revolution was fermenting in the boardroom of the IABA and more specifically the sitting room of Gary Keegan's home in Bettystown. John Treacy had identified the High Performance model used in the UK, and elsewhere, as the best means of delivering Olympic medals. As part of the Athens Enhancement Programme, finance was available from the ISC to fund the appointment of High Performance directors and coaches in specific sports.

In keeping with the kind of inertia which was to become the hallmark of the IABA, initially they didn't apply for funding under the new scheme. This odd situation might have continued but for Keegan. In his capacity as chair of coach education and secretary of the association's National Coaching Committee, he was present at a meeting with ISC officials and members of the Board of the IABA in 2002. 'I was there to give an update on coaching education. A guy from the Sports Council said at one point, "By the way, we still don't have an application in from the IABA for the High Performance Programme."'

Keegan volunteered to put one together. The deadline was five days away. He burned the midnight oil for much of the next week. He was nothing if not ambitious; he included plans for clubs and regions together with a national programme. When he totted up the figures, the cost amounted to €1.2m. The deadline for receipt of applications was 6pm on a Friday evening. Keegan stuffed the documentation into a brown envelope and pushed it through the letter box of the ISC at 5.50pm on deadline day.

The Sports Council was already bank-rolling the IABA. In 2002 they received €427,873 as well as an additional €80,000 for equipment. A further €260,420 was paid out to individual boxers under the Council's International Carding scheme grants which had been introduced in 1998. Seven boxers were the principal recipients: James Moore (€30,500), Kenny Egan, Alan Reynolds, John Paul Kinsella, Damien McKenna and Michael Kelly (€22,500 each), and John Paul Campbell (€19,500).

The Sports Council earmarked £207,000 for the new project. It was a far cry from the figure the IABA had sought but it was enough to launch a High Performance programme. Keegan, then aged thirty-eight, was the obvious candidate to head up the initiative. Before accepting the job, he consulted with his former coaching mentor Breandán Ó Conaire.

'I felt he had the mentality and the focus to do the job. He had a history behind him; he was extremely ambitious and driven,' says Ó Conaire. 'He had a background in running a business. I felt he had the personality traits to do it. I couldn't see anybody else who had the talent to grab hold of the thing and bring it to the next step.'

Keegan accepted the offer to head up the High Performance Unit (HPU) in November 2002. He got down to work straight away.

Andy Lee, fresh from winning a silver medal at the World Junior Championships in Cuba two months earlier, sensed that something was afoot when Keegan summoned the best young boxers to a training session in Drimnagh Boxing Club. 'No one knew what it was about. After we trained, he came to me and said he was putting together a programme called High Performance. For me it was if all my dreams had come true,' remembers the future WBO World middleweight champion.

Keegan then set about assembling a coaching team. He had definite views about how it should be structured. 'I wanted it to be Irish-led. I wanted it to have a sense of real legacy. I felt that an Irishman would have a greater sense of ownership in leaving a legacy behind.' Billy Walsh was an obvious front runner for the job.

Prior to the European Championships in Perm, Walsh was the team manager/

coach of an Irish squad that took part in a joint ten-day training camp with Poland. John Joe Nevin's coach, Brian McKeown, was Walsh's assistant. 'I was deeply honoured to be selected as coach to the national senior team for the first time,' recalled Walsh. The boxers were based in Wisla, whose claim to fame was that it was the home town of Poland's then iconic sports star Adam Malysz, a four times world ski-jump champion and Olympic medallist. It wasn't long into the trip that Walsh had more mundane issues to worry about than the Pole's prowess on the slopes.

Two internationals were included on the itinerary. The hosts won the first 6-2. Ireland's only winners on the night were flyweight Darren Campbell and light welterweight Michael Kelly. Kenny Egan was dropped by a body shot and received a standing count of eight. He got up and finished the fight but lost 21-10. Some of the squad later drowned their sorrows by going on a drinking binge. Walsh read them the riot act the next morning.

The second international was two days later. Egan claimed he injured his hand in the first fight and wouldn't be able to box forty-eight hours later. Together with two of his teammates, he scarpered ahead of the weigh-in for the second match.

'They went off on the piss,' recalls Walsh, who was enraged. 'I just cracked up. I had come from a generation that would have died to fight for their country.'

Egan's AWOL stunt was particularly embarrassing for the Irish camp as his opponent Robert Gniot had invited his sponsors to the fight. A furious Walsh decided to take matters into his own hands.

'I was disgusted and embarrassed when we couldn't find Kenny. So I went into the changing rooms and asked the lads did any of them have a size eight pair of boots they could lend me. I didn't have a gum shield so I stuffed some cotton wool in my mouth and taped up my hands. I wanted to go into the ring and take on Kenny's man. I remember saying to Brian McKeown, "If I don't knock him out in the first round, throw in the towel because I'll be fucked.'"

Walsh's Polish counterpart intervened and wouldn't allow him to box. So Ireland conceded a walkover in the middleweight bout and lost the tournament 6-1. Michael Kelly was the only Irish winner. Walsh was determined that it wouldn't be a case of 'what goes on tour stays on tour'. 'I wrote a report about it because I felt they had let their country down.'

The three boxers were suspended and Egan's funding was stopped for six months. 'I didn't find out until the day the envelopes were handed out, and there was none for me,' the boxer recalled in his autobiography, *Kenny Egan, My Story*.

'I wouldn't have been too popular at the time,' remarks Walsh. 'Incidents like this had been brushed under the carpet by previous managers. But this had got to a ridiculous stage. What happened in Poland was beyond a joke as far as I was concerned. I think it probably led me to getting the chance to coach in the High Performance Unit. Gary Keegan was secretary of the Coaching Board at the time and maybe he felt that discipline was an issue.'

Keegan believed a twin-track approach was needed to turn Ireland's fortunes around; an Irish coach would head up the programme but he would require international expertise to assist him. Furthermore, a change of attitude was needed among the boxing fraternity. The break-up of the Soviet Union was a game changer in terms of Olympic qualification.

'Geographically the majority of the countries that were part of the old Soviet Union were in Europe which made it the strongest boxing continent in the world,' explains Keegan. 'This had made life very difficult for Irish boxers and we hadn't responded. We were very insular and domestic in our thinking. We were sending out boxers in the hope that they would do the business. There was a feeling that the system was against us.'

Ireland needed to hire a world-class technical boxing coach. The choice was relatively straight forward: either go the Cuban route again or look east to Russia. 'I felt the Russian route was best. We needed to learn all we could in Europe and become competitive against European opponents.'

Cork businessman Dan O'Connell is a highly respected figure within the IABA. He qualified as a referee at the age of twenty; he was the youngest in Ireland at the time. Later, he acted as assistant coach to the Irish team that competed at the Montreal Olympics in 1976, before becoming an international judge and referee.

At the European Championships in 1993 O'Connell met and befriended Georgian native Zurab 'Rob' Tibua, who became an international referee at the championships which were held in the Turkish city of Bursa. [Georgia made its debut as an independent state at the championships, finishing fifth in the medal table]. Tibua and Zaur Antia are lifelong buddies; both are natives of Poti and share a common passion in boxing.

During the subsequent decade, O'Connell and Tibua – who is a fluent English speaker – would meet regularly at international tournaments. In September 2002 Tibua invited O'Connell to Poti, in Georgia, to work with the local boxing referees and judges. While working with them in a boxing gym in Poti, O'Connell spotted Antia doing a coaching session.

'I noticed a coach working with a group of boxers in the other half of the gym. The guy just caught my attention. I don't know how to explain it. It's a bit like seeing a golfer swing a club, a high jumper's run-up or a footballer taking a penalty. There was something there. I remember thinking "that guy looks good."'

O'Connell later had dinner with Antia, together with other coaches from Poti. According to Antia, his hosts made sure that their Cork visitor was left with a favourable impression of the country. 'Georgia is the home of hospitality so we had big hospitality for Daniel who is a very nice man. I told him what we were doing and how our boxing club was the number one in Georgia. Daniel asked me would I come to train the Irish boxers. I said, "Why not?" without any consciousness. I had big plans in Georgia; I had income, big sponsors and I was coaching European and world medallists,' recalls Antia.

'I had an inkling that something was afoot back home in terms of setting up new structures and looking for a national coach,' remembers O'Connell. 'So when I returned to Ireland, I spoke to Don Stewart, the CEO of the IABA and explained to him that I had seen this guy and I thought he was something else.' O'Connell's recommendation was passed to Gary Keegan, who did his own research and was astonished by what he discovered. 'He [Antia] was phenomenally successful, phenomenally entrepreneurial, a phenomenal relations builder and very creative in the way he did things. This was very obvious because he had more boxers on the old Soviet Union teams than any of the republics other than Russia. There was the language issue but this was counterbalanced by other factors.'

Antia spoke Russian but more importantly had worked inside the Soviet Union system. He had contacts with coaches all over Eastern Europe. Keegan was already thinking several years down the line. He might be the man who could get Irish boxers into a Russian training camp.

Meanwhile, back in Georgia, Antia was blissfully unaware that his career had been analysed in minute detail by the new guru in Irish boxing. His ambition was to secure his financial future by coaching one of his boxers to win an Olympic gold medal. In return, he would receive the equivalent of half a million euro together with a flat and pension. 'It would make my life.'

Dan O'Connell and Zurab Tibua stayed in touch. The upshot was that Antia was invited to come to Dublin in early 2003 to be interviewed for the position of head coach with the HPU. Antia had just been re-elected as the head coach in Georgia but was having what he describes as 'an on-going problem' with the president of the boxing federation. However, the issue was being resolved as the president had apologised. His friend Zurab Tibua was adamant that Antia should travel to Dublin. He kept saying, 'Come on, Zaur. Let's go to Dublin.'

Following representations from O'Connell, the IABA agreed to foot the bill for the flights and accommodation. Eventually, Antia agreed to travel. 'I said to Rob, "We will go and drink Guinness." It is true I tell you.' Tibua accompanied the coach and acted as his interpreter.

In late January 2003, ten days before the interview O'Connell drove from his home in Cork to Dublin Airport to pick up the Georgian pair. 'I brought them back to Cork, where they stayed until Zaur was due to be interviewed. The plan was to teach him a few words of English in preparation for his interview.' It was a futile exercise, as O'Connell acknowledges. 'Imagine going to Dublin for an interview and only being able to speak about ten words of English – all in a Cork accent. The interpreter helped, but I was actually brought into the interview because the interpreter was struggling a bit.'

The ace in Antia's armour was the quality of his coaching plan. 'He brought a most magnificent coaching plan with him. Unfortunately it was all written in Georgian. We spent most of the ten days trying to understand it and translate it into English as best we could. Given that I had a background in coaching I was able to present his plans better than the interpreter.' Twelve candidates were interviewed on a dank February day in 2003 for the position of head coach. Apart from the Irish applicants, who came from both sides of the border, there were British candidates, a New Zealander and of course, the Georgian.

On the eve of the interview, however, Antia began to have second thoughts. 'I was best coach in Georgia I was number one. I was best coach in Soviet Union because I had more boxers on the team than the other republics, but I had never done an interview. But if I don't get the job, people in Georgia will say, "If I'm such a strong coach, why I didn't get this job in Ireland?" I think, "This is terrible thing." So I went into pub and had too much Guinness. In the morning I had little headache.'

Antia did manage to learn one full English sentence: "'Where I am there is victory." That's what I told everybody,' he recalls with a characteristic hearty laugh.

The interview panel included Gary Keegan, the then president of the IABA Dominic O'Rourke, the current President Tommy Murphy, and the late Christy Kirwan, a former president of the Irish Congress of Trade Unions, who acted as chairman. Initially, there was a formal Q & A session, followed by a practical coaching session. Candidates were asked to design a six-week block of training in preparation for an international against a named country. Keegan reckoned this part of the process would allow a non-English speaking coach to demonstrate his ability.

'We brought the boardroom table down to the gym, and we had six boxers there for the candidates to work with. We wanted to get a sense of the appropriateness of their training plan. I also asked them to demonstrate what they would do with the boxers on the sixth day of the last week leading into the event. The fact that each of them was given a different country meant they had to consider what tactics to deploy,' says Keegan. Billy Walsh remembers he got Cuba.

Predictably, Antia struggled in the formal Q & A session. The language barrier was an obvious issue, according to Keegan. And the hangover didn't help either. 'He told me later he had his first pint of Guinness the previous night. I'm sure he had more than one because he was very nervous,' remembers Keegan.

But he wasn't too perturbed. For him the coaching plan Antia had submitted was a game changer. Keegan was blown away by the proposals made by Antia. 'It excited the hell out of me; the scientific way it was laid out, the clarity around his thinking. I wasn't expecting a whole lot from him in the Q & A session. I was asking some very strange questions because I was coming in from a position of starting to build a strategy. What I was expecting was to make a personal connection with the coaches I was interviewing and to see a bit of personality and character. Both Zaur and Billy have those things in spades. They have a lot of passion, character and humour. They complemented each other really.'

Still, Keegan wasn't sure whether he could convince the other members of the interview board that Antia was the man for the job. He knew the chairman, Christy Kirwan, had reservations about the Georgian's lack of English. 'When he came into the gym for the practical demonstration, I was sitting there with my fingers crossed, hoping he could do the business. He went on to the floor with six boxers. Using gestures and signals, he sent the boys off around the gym. Within five minutes he had them eating out of his hands. It was just phenomenal. I just looked at the chair of the board and knew he was happy.'

Future Olympian Darren O'Neill, then one of the country's talented junior boxers, was one of the 'guinea pigs', as was Andy Lee. 'He hadn't a word of English,' says O'Neill. 'The translator helped to a degree, though he didn't do justice to what Zaur was attempting to demonstrate. But Zaur is very good at showing boxers exactly what he wants and he was able to demonstrate this to the interview board.' Lee concurs. 'Zaur couldn't speak English but he could speak boxing. Every one of us could understand him. He can display technique and footwork better than any fighter.'

Walsh and Antia had their first discussion later that night over a few pints in the Ringside Boxing Club. Zurab Tibua translated. A few weeks later, Billy

Walsh was offered the full-time position of head coach. 'I didn't think at all about it; my wife would have thought about it. I was working with my brother at the time and sold the milk round to him.' Zaur Antia was appointed the technical coach. 'Sometimes I wonder why I came to Ireland. Maybe God see how I fed my boxers more than I fed my children in my own city. I am a very friendly person. For me friendship is number one, that's why this happened.'

Over the next decade, Dan O'Connell's instinctive views on Antia were to prove unerringly accurate. 'He is probably the most under-recognised coach in Europe. Due to the language barrier, he doesn't always portray himself terribly well and is not the best subject for an interview. So he prefers to stay in the background.

'But his contribution has been enormous. He's actually the best technical and tactical coach around in boxing. The other thing he brought to the table was his relationship and contacts with the Russian Boxing Federation. Were it not for Zaur, there is no way an Irish team would have got into a Russian training camp,' said O'Connell.

The HPU also employed a third coach, Cathal O'Grady, who had boxed for Ireland at the 1996 Atlanta Games. 'He blew us away: he was articulate, educated, smart and very charismatic. His programme was very strong as well and he had lots of ideas. I told the board, "We have to find a way to get this guy."

'I thought Zaur would only be with us for two years, which was the experience other countries had with foreign coaches. I needed somebody to be understudy with him and be a sponge and draw everything we could out of him. So we took on Cathal O'Grady,' says Keegan.

Initially, Antia's wife, Nona, shared Keegan's view that her husband would spend a short time in Ireland before returning home. At the time, the couple had two children, eight-year-old Natia and four-year-old David. 'It was difficult leaving my family behind,' says Antia.

Within two years, with the assistance of Keegan and the Irish government, his family had moved to Ireland. Their youngest son, George, was born here. All the family members are now Irish citizens. One suspects, however, there were times when Antia must have questioned his decision to come here. On a practical level, the language barrier was a huge irritant. Antia once spent half a day wandering around Dublin because he got off at the wrong bus stop, couldn't remember his address and was unable to contact a friend in Georgia who spoke English. On another occasion, a taxi driver misinterpreted his instructions and took him to the Zoo instead of DCU.

But the real culture shock came when he began his day job in the National Stadium two months after his interview. Verbal communication with the boxers was minimal. 'He didn't have a word of English, not a f… word. So we had this little fat man walking around the stadium with his head down. He'd say hello and nod his head, that's how bad it was,' remembers Egan.

Antia had other more pressing concerns, however. For starters, he was shocked that the elite boxers still only trained twice a week. Their counterparts in Georgia trained six times a week. 'There was a lack of skill and I say, "How can we make progress if we only train twice a week?"' And he wasn't particularly impressed with the standard of these top boxers. When he became more fluent in English and got to know them a bit better, he revealed his innermost thoughts, as Egan recalls: 'He told us this story later. He couldn't fathom how James Moore had won a bronze medal at the World Championships. Personally, I would have given myself an eight out of ten rating at the time. He told me I was a two! It was hilarious, but I was disgusted.'

According to Egan, Antia began his re-education of Irish boxers by teaching them what he had taught children back in Georgia years previously. 'He believed we didn't even know how to do a proper warm-up.'

Darren O'Neill recalls that the chasm between how Antia perceived the boxers and their view of themselves was addressed. 'It was a bit difficult at first because initially we went back to doing basic footwork movements. This was the kind of stuff we did as kids. We were wondering the reason for this. The funny thing was very few of us could do it. It's hilarious when you look back on it now. But getting the basic things right is so important in boxing.'

The first couple of months of the fledging High Performance programme was a bit chaotic according to Walsh, who worked with the boxers while Antia's visa application to work in Ireland was being processed. 'There was mayhem at times with lots of stuff going on. We didn't have the boxers full-time; they would come in at the weekends.'

The building adjacent to the National Stadium was transformed into the epicentre of the HPU. With finance from the ISC's capital-funding budget, the training area was transformed. Having started off with one boxing ring and seven bags, the HPU now had a modern gymnasium which included a treatment area, sauna, strength and conditioning area; two new boxing rings; sixteen hitting apparatuses and a recovery area. An administration unit was added later.

The next logical step was full-time training. It was like a train changing tracks, according to Keegan. There was resistance within the wider boxing community at the way this sea change in the sport was implemented. This evolved into a festering resentment about the entire programme among certain elements of the boxing fraternity which ultimately had serious consequences for the HPU.

CHAPTER 9

BEHIND CLOSED DOORS

'Forget about Athens. It's only eighteen months away. But, if we're allowed do the things we want to do the way we want to do them, we'll win medals in Beijing – I guarantee that!'

Gary Keegan

After the establishment of the High Performance Unit, the first controversial decision taken by Gary Keegan and Billy Walsh was to ban the boxers' coaches from training sessions. 'It was a tough one,' remembers Walsh, who made the shock announcement shortly after the programme was launched in February 2003.

Standing up one Saturday morning in the ring which had been used at the World Championships in Belfast Walsh remembers that he announced: '"Thanks very much for coming. I just have to ask all the coaches to leave now. We are going to start a High Performance coaching session." I didn't feel that great about doing it but I felt I had to. Normally, club coaches would stay for the sparring sessions. But that would have meant no change in how we did things. We had to set out our standards. It went down like a lead balloon with a lot of them. We had to decide on our culture; we needed to change the culture and have our own type of training.'

Kenny Egan remembers the moment Walsh made that game-changing announcement. 'It was the right decision. The last thing a boxer needs is the head coach telling him what to do and the club coach, who could be his father, telling him something different.'

It wasn't an issue either for Brian McKeown who coached Andy Murray and John Joe Nevin before they graduated to the HPU. 'Gary Keegan had an idea and had the balls to see it through.'

But McKeown's benevolent attitude was not universally shared. Excluding the coaches was a prelude to a three-month 'lock-down', as Gary Keegan explained, 'It meant the doors were locked and only the boxers, myself and the coaches were inside. Closing down the gym created a whole host of trouble. We were doing it from a very authentic place. We weren't looking to cause any trouble. But it did build resentment to the term "high performance". It was like, "Who do they think they are?" This wasn't our intention but it was the outcome.

'We were simply looking to do the right thing and get to know the boxers in a closed environment. So if we had to use bad language, shout, scream, or fall out with anybody, we could do it within the confines of those four walls. Although I got rancour, my main focus was on the boxers. From the very beginning I believed that the Athens Olympics wasn't going to be our time. In the first interview I did, with Gerry Callan from *The Star*, I set out my goals.'

The latter vividly recalls the conversation. 'I asked Gary what his targets were, and this was his answer: "Forget about Athens. It's only eighteen months away. But, if we're allowed do the things we want to do the way we want to do them, we'll win medals in Beijing – I guarantee that!" We often remind each other of that,' says Callan.

'It seemed a case of shooting for the stars,' Egan noted in his autobiography. He didn't know Keegan 'from Adam' prior to his appointment. 'So he comes in, a skinny man, and I felt straight away, "We have something here."'

Initially, the boxers only trained at the weekend, but they quickly moved to a full-time programme. 'If we were going to make a difference, we had to go full time. We went in from Monday to Thursday, had a break on Friday, and returned on Saturday,' recalls Walsh, who acknowledged that his relationship with Egan was strained at the outset. 'As a result of my report, his funding had been suspended. We weren't the greatest of buddies then, but we ended up having a very good relationship.' Indeed, Walsh wrote the foreword for Egan's autobiography in 2011.

Keegan agonised for days on the words he would use to convey the key message in his inaugural address to the boxers. More than a decade later, he can instantly recall that speech. 'I said our job is to remove all excuses for underperformance and replace them with reasons to perform.'

Andy Lee remembers other defining moment during the early months. 'Gary had to break down a lot of barriers. The older guys on the team, like Alan Reynolds and James Moore, had been used to doing things a certain way. Gary was still improving as a coach and had a lot to do to win the respect of these guys. But it was either his way or the highway.'

Not surprisingly, half the team were gone within a year. 'We lost some through indiscipline, some left because they couldn't stick the training, while others left because the programme was full time,' Walsh recalls.

There was a frontier feeling about the project from its inception. Individually the boxers were funded to the tune of €189,500 by the ISC. But, overall, money was woefully scarce, and for the first couple of months they slept on blow-up beds in the changing rooms. 'The guest-house owner wanted €25 a night, but when the budget was done we could only afford €20 and he wouldn't do a deal. So we bought blow-up beds instead,' recalls Keegan.

Andy Lee vividly remembers sleeping there on St Stephen's night 2003, along with Irish Elite lightweight titleholder, Andy Murray and light welter-weight champion Paul McCloskey from Dungiven. [McCluskey later won British, European and Inter-Continental titles as a light welterweight in the professional ranks but was beaten by defending title holder Amir Khan in a WBA world title contest in 2011.] 'We had Christmas Day off, but we were back training the next morning for the European Championships in February,' recalls Lee.

Later, they purchased bunk beds and transformed the gym's attic, which was once the gunroom of Griffith Barracks, into living quarters. 'There was no heating and you could see your breath at night during the winter time,' recalls Walsh.

Keegan told the team that the Spartan-like living accommodation was designed to replicate what they would experience at training camps and competitions in Eastern Europe.

There was a set pattern to the day's programme. After breakfast, which consisted of cereal, tea and toast, the boxers and coaching staff went for a walk along the banks of the nearby Grand Canal. The first formal training session of the day was at eleven. Initially, they used the gym in City West for weight training. There was a second training session in the afternoon. They did their speed work in the Éamonn Ceannt Stadium in Crumlin and travelled to the Dublin Mountains for basic endurance work. Lunch and dinner was served in the stadium canteen.

Keegan created a flip chart which he displayed on the gym floor. Bad habits were written in red; good ones in green. Top of his hit list were the boxers' beloved sweatsuits. They wore them during training in order to sweat more which, in theory, helped control their weight. But it was a crude form of weight-management. Instead, the boxers were encouraged to drink more water: for every kilo of weight lost they needed to consume one and a half litres of water to prevent dehydration. Initially, the boxers simply ignored the coaches' instructions.

'They thought it was stone mad to be drinking all this water,' remembers Keegan. They didn't bother filling up their water bottles before they came into a session. So the coaches taped their names onto the bottles. And anyone found with an empty bottle during training had to leave the floor. 'We started to link behaviour to improvement,' explains Keegan.

The boxers weighed themselves before and after every training session. Urine samples were taken and measured every day, with the results posted on a hydration chart. 'We had to reinforce the simple things; attention to detail was drilled to the fine letter,' says Keegan.

In some respects, they were ahead of the pack, though they didn't know it at the time. For example, the boxers wore heart monitors during all their sessions. 'We wanted to see what their hearts were doing. It was an obvious thing. Heart monitors were out there; other sports were using them long before us. We were going outside our sport and seeing what was happening elsewhere and looking for ideas.'

With the coaching staff in place, Keegan began to build a team around the boxers. John Cleary, the strength and conditioning coach, was joined by sports psychologist Gerry Hussey. Later, Alan Swanton a sports performance analyst was recruited. A medical team and a nutritionist were appointed. 'We had to knock out all the usual stuff: bread, sweets, chocolates, Coca-Cola, Fanta, all sparkling drinks and all the junk,' recalls Egan.

Ostensibly, there was a no-alcohol policy. 'It wasn't that we were anti-alcohol,' says Keegan. 'We discussed it with the boxers. We talked about alcohol reversing the effect of training. So why would you train five days a week and then go on the piss at the weekend?'

Being a boxer in the HPU was the equivalent of having a regular nine-to-five job according to Egan. 'We were funded so you had to get off your arse and be there. If you couldn't turn up, you had to send in a sick note. Obviously the team changed every year, depending on the results in the Elite Championships,' explains Egan, who was the longest-serving boxer on the programme.

At the end of the 'lock-down', Keegan organised a symbolic passing-out ceremony. He stuck a strip of red insulation tape which he found in his office drawer on to the floor of the gym. 'We had spent three months with the guys drilling down where the excuses were and what we needed to do. I wanted to close out that period. So I said to them, "We now have a definition of what we believe is world class. None of us are there yet, but if anybody wants to join us on the journey they have to make the choice and cross this taped line now."'

'It was a very significant moment for all of us. It was like a red line in the sand.' 'I remember it like it was yesterday,' says Egan. 'I was the first to step across and everybody followed.'

Meanwhile, Walsh became Zaur Antia's unofficial English language teacher. Walsh recalls rooming with him at the European Junior Championships in Warsaw four months after his arrival in Ireland. 'I'm teaching him and he is writing stuff down. But his English was still really bad. He was trying to tell me a joke in English, but it went on for so long that I fell asleep in the middle of it and he cracked up.'

But there were few difficulties on the floor of the gym according to Walsh. 'Boxing is a universal language. I understood everything he was doing in terms of boxing technique.'

From the boxers' point of view, the changes initiated by Antia were revolutionary. Egan recalls: 'Normally we would come into the gym do a warm-up followed by a bit of sparring. There was no real thought put into the training.

But Zaur explained why he wanted something done during sessions.

'Coaches can read stuff out of a book and tell boxers to jab, slip, right hand, left hook, and so on. But they can't actually show you how to do it. Zaur was able to do this. It was a whole different approach. We'd start with half an hour of basics and fundamentals. We'd be sweating like pigs, and we hadn't even started sparring. This was serious stuff.'

Everybody involved knew that ultimately the survival of the HPU depended on results. The new team made a promising start in April 2003, winning the Four Nations (Ireland, England, Scotland and Wales) in Cardiff. Eric Donovan (bantamweight), Paul McCloskey (light welterweight), James Moore (welterweight), Andy Lee (middleweight) and Alan Reynolds (heavyweight) all won their respective finals while Stephen Ormond (featherweight) and Egan (light heavyweight) were runners-up. It was an experienced squad. Moore had won a bronze medal at the World Championships in Belfast in 2001; Egan and Reynolds had contested the quarter-finals in Belfast; Lee had captured a silver medal at the World Junior Championships in Cuba in 2002, while Ormond and McCluskey were Irish Elite title holders. Eric Donovan, a precocious seventeen-year-old from Athy was the only rookie on the team. 'We still had a lot of work to do. But we can look back on it now and say we were kings of that dungheap' says Walsh.

But the coaches had grander ideas. For meaningful progress to be made Keegan believed it was essential for the Irish boxers go to international training camps. 'We called our programme High Performance. But we were way off being high performance. While we had a title and an ambition now we had to earn it.' The first port of call was Great Britain. Their 'world class' boxing programme, which was based in Crystal Palace, had an annual budget of £1.3 million, dwarfing the Irish equivalent of a quarter of a million. Keegan deliberately left the boxers at home when he travelled to London. 'I knew the UK had a disciplinary problem and there was a bit of a drink culture in both teams. When I say drink culture, I mean that when they finished boxing and were beaten it was out to the pub and nightclub and this was something we wanted to change.'

The British performance director couldn't have been more helpful. 'He opened his office to me and put about four files in front of me and said, "Have a look through them and if you find anything interesting there is a photocopier out in the hall."'

Theoretically, the British model was top of the range. 'UK Sport had just brought in consultants in everything from psychology to strength and conditioning and told the boxing guys what they needed to do. They had written up a series of programmes and I just photocopied them. It was great. Learning was such a huge part of the journey we were on.' Keegan spent another three days on the floor of the gym, watching the coaches and boxers in action. 'They had a great team, a great bunch of well-educated coaches. They had a much better system in the UK in terms of educating coaches. They had better facilities than us and they had some phenomenal talent.

'But they didn't see any need to change. What I had read about upstairs in terms of the process wasn't being activated on the floor by the coaches. They had brought in the consultants because UK Sport said to do it as opposed to them feeling they had to do it themselves. So they didn't take responsibility themselves for making the changes.'

Ultimately, the changes were implemented. In an ironic twist of fate Keegan was subsequently interviewed and offered the post as head of Great Britain's High Performance Boxing Programme in 2006 and again in 2008, but turned it down.

So instead of linking up with Great Britain, Keegan targeted France, then the most successful Western European nation in boxing. At the 2003 World

Championships in Bangkok, France finished fifth in the medal table, headed by Russia, Cuba, Kazakhstan and the host nation Thailand. So Keegan emailed his French counterpart, Dominique Nato, seeking permission to bring an Irish squad to a French training camp.

No response. Undeterred, Keegan dispatched a second, third, fourth email. He lost count of the number of emails he sent. He contacted the French Boxing Federation so often that he befriended Nato's PA who spoke excellent English. 'She was a lovely woman. I kept emailing him through her. I sent so many emails that I must have peed them off. But I managed to develop a working relationship with his PA and she probably started feeling sorry for me. Eventually, she said, "Our director is going to allow you permission to attend a training camp in Paris prior to the European Union Championships."' France was hosting the event in Strasbourg in June 2003.

Created in the nineteenth century by the Emperor Louis Napoléon III, Bois de Vincennes is the largest public park in Paris. Located on the eastern edge of the city, it houses France's National Institute of Sport and Physical Education (INSEP). It was here that the French Federation hosted their Irish visitors in May 2003. Deep down, Keegan suspected he knew exactly why his French counterpart was so reluctant to host the Irish. He kept his counsel, however, but warned the boxers to be on their best behaviour.

'I called the guys together and told them the story. It has taken us three months to get into this camp. There must be a reason for this. Why would he not want them to train alongside his boxers? He must have an impression of us that's not good. So when we go, we have to stand tall, stand proud, spar hard and when we use the gym leave it as we found it. Let's make a good impression and in fairness to the guys they were up for it.'

An Italian by birth, Dominique Nato, the national technical director of the French Boxing Federation and their Olympic coach, was an ex-French professional heavyweight champion. He was a large man in every sense. He spoke reasonably good English and Keegan invited him out for coffee one night after everybody had settled into the training camp. After the usual small talk, the Irishman broached the thorny issue. 'I said I was puzzled as to why he waited so long to give us the nod to get into the camp.'

Nato didn't mince his words. He told Keegan that the Irish boxers had a reputation for excessive drinking and poor behaviour. He had personal experience of seeing two Irish boxers drunk at an airport while wearing their Irish gear. He didn't want that culture near his boxers. Keegan assured his French counterparts that those days were over.

Mindful of the warning he had issued before they left Dublin, the boxers didn't let Keegan down. 'We behaved. There was no gargle, or anything, but we took a pasting in the ring,' remembers Egan, who had just moved into the light heavyweight division. John Dovi, the French champion in the 81 kg category, was one of the country's pin-up boxers at the time. He won a silver medal at the World Championships in Houston in 1999 and a bronze in Belfast two years later when he stopped Ireland's Alan Reynolds in the quarter-finals. 'I took a bit of a beating from him and went home with my tail between my legs,' recalls Egan.

Seeing how other boxers trained proved an invaluable learning experience for the Irish. 'Their boxers were terribly fit. They set a pace in round one and maintained it until the end of the fight. In those days fights were over four two-minute rounds. I was thinking, "How can they last that pace?" Back then, we would get the score after each round. I was like a hybrid-car: I didn't go any faster than I had too. My attitude was I don't have to win by twenty-nine points; I just have to win. Being a counter-puncher, I was on the back foot anyway. I wasn't lazy; it was just the way I boxed.'

Egan knew he was improving, but it wasn't until the European Union

Championships in Strasbourg that he realised the tactical shrewdness of Zaur Antia. In the semi-finals he came face to face again with his French adversary John Dovi. 'He was nine years older than me and had one of the best jabs in the game. It was up high so you could never see it. Being the genius that he is, Zaur told me it was all about getting the timing right. I wasn't to get too close to him. This tactic would force him to throw his left jab when he was slightly over-extended. Then I'd throw my left jab as I'm a southpaw.

'So I decided to try this approach when we met in the EU Championships. Dovi was very confident; he's clever and he's waiting, waiting, waiting. But then I take that step back, and so he has to overreach with his left. I nail him with my left and I do it repeatedly. I see Dovi looking at me and I know he was thinking, 'What the hell is going on here?''

The contest finished 19-19, and Egan won it on a countback to guarantee himself a silver medal. Even though he eventually lost in the final, Egan knew he could implicitly trust Antia. 'I realised then that Zaur knew what he was talking about. This was the proof of the pudding. A minor adjustment made by a coach can change the course of a boxer's career.'

Ireland ended up winning five medals at the EU tournament. McCloskey secured silver, while Murray and Reynolds took home bronze medals, as did Brian Gillen, a member of Belfast's Holy Trinity Club. The eighteen-year-old made a spectacular debut in the senior ranks earlier that spring, winning the Ulster and Irish Elite bantamweight titles. What made these achievements all the more remarkable was that Gillen suffers from Cystic Fibrosis, the debilitating lung condition.

Ultimately, he had a short-lived career in Ireland; he was beaten in the 2004 Elite bantamweight final by Eric Donovan. Later he moved to Wales. After being refused entry to the 2005 Ulster Senior Championships following a dispute over where he could do his weigh-in, he won a Welsh featherweight title in 2007 and represented his adopted country at the Commonwealth Championships in the lightweight category in Liverpool later that year.

The World Championships in Bangkok in July 2003 represented an altogether more exacting challenge. Antia was unable to travel due to visa issues. While no medals were secured, the eight-man team performed credibly. Egan was the stand-out Irish boxer, reaching the light heavyweight quarter-finals, before losing 27-13 to the eventual gold medallist, Evgeny Makarenko from Russia.

Light flyweight Conor Ahern was only a rookie. Trained by former Irish champion Ned Hendricks in Baldoyle Boxing Club on Dublin's northside, he had yet to win an Irish Elite title. He lost his first bout, as did Gillen, Murray and Reynolds. But Moore and Lee won theirs. The latter lost his next fight to eventual middleweight gold medallist Gennady Golovkin from Kazakhstan, now rated as one of the outstanding pound-for-pound professional champions of his generation. Moore was beaten by a Russian, Andrey Mishin, who exited in the quarter-finals.

All the time Keegan was pumping everybody he met on these international trips for more information. Antia recognised that he had linked up with what he describes as 'a very special person'. 'He had huge energy; he was a very smart man, very intelligent. He asked me questions about the Soviet system. But he wasn't just looking at the Soviet system; he was looking at all the systems to try to make ours better.'

Through his contact with the French coach, Dominique Nato, Keegan secured an introduction to the German coaching staff and soon afterwards the Irish squad were invited to a camp in Germany. They used a more scientific approach compared to their French counterparts, which fascinated Keegan. 'The Germans had a background in science back to the GDR days. Okay, some of the science wasn't too pretty, in terms of blood and doping and all the rest.

But there was a lot of science behind their performance and we had access to it. This guy who collected me from the airport would give me test results for German boxers. I would get them translated and study them to see how they compared with what we were doing in Ireland.'

Less than a year after the foundation of the HPU, Keegan achieved one of his major goals. Six Irish boxers, Murray, McCloskey, Moore, Lee, Egan and Reynolds, along with Keegan, Walsh, Antia and John Cleary, left Dublin Airport in November 2003, en route to Chekhov, a small town one hundred kilometres south of Moscow.

Their final destination was a large grey building situated in a pine-scented forest. From the outside it looked like just another drab relic from the Soviet era. Inside though was a dream factory. It was the epicentre of Russian boxing, where the nation's finest pugilists were aiming to restore their country's reputation as the world's foremost power in amateur boxing. Antia's impeccable contacts within the Russian system allied to his ability to speak the language had facilitated this historic breakthrough. 'We couldn't have survived there otherwise,' says Walsh. 'Zaur was respected by his Russian peers. I have been around a lot of coaches and he's top class. For me he is the best technical coach in the world. What he has brought to the team is unbelievable.'

It was minus thirty degrees centigrade when the Irish party – rigged out in new all-black tracksuits – ventured outside the terminal building in Domodedovo International airport in Moscow. The change of strip was Keegan's idea, as Egan explained in his autobiography. 'He felt our poor results and our behaviour after continued failure was living proof that we had lost respect for the crest.'

At first, the boxers thought it an act of sacrilege to dispense with the traditional green-coloured gear. 'We were saying, what is he [Keegan] doing with these black tracksuits? Normally we would be wearing green with a bit of orange. But it was his way of stripping everything down and starting afresh,' said Egan. Over time, the boxers grew to respect their new gear which featured a sprig of shamrock as the new crest, while the words 'Member of the High Performance Team' were embroidered on the shoulder of their tracksuit tops.

The Russian camp was a mind-blowing experience. The ground was covered in snow; it was freezing cold, and for ten days the visitors had to row in with established practice in the camp which housed seventy Russian boxers. Everybody lined up at six-thirty in the morning in front of their coaches for the playing of the Russian national anthem followed by a speech delivered in Russian.

The shivering Irish boxers then went for a short walk in the knee-deep snow before heading for breakfast, where another nasty shock awaited them. 'The food was not what we would normally eat,' according to Walsh. Egan described what they were presented with for breakfast on day one as 'black cow's tongue'. The Irish learned that doctors managed the boxers' diets. They were expected to eat everything on the plate and if they didn't something else was put on the plate next time. Keegan suffered more than anybody else in the Irish party. 'I struggled with the food because I am a fussy eater and I lost about 5 kg during the trip.'

The Irish trained on their own in the mornings before linking up with their hosts in the afternoon. The first thing that Egan noticed when he stepped inside the gym was the three-inch thick soft canvas which covered the floor. 'When I stood on it, the first thing that came into my mind was "fuck, I can't move." It was a very hard surface to move on.'

The Russians showed no mercy. 'We were doing tic-tac stuff with them; two minutes over twelve rounds. But these lads were hitting us hard. They weren't holding back. It was a long ten days,' admits Egan.

'The whole experience was an eye-opener,' says Walsh. Basically, when we came home we had to tear up the script and start all over again. Technically, physically and mentally we were destroyed in every training session. The only one that kinda held his own was Andy Lee. We tailored our training once we came home. From then on, it was all explosive stuff. It took us the best part of a year to change the boxers' engines.'

'It was a culture shock, for sure,' recalls Lee. 'But it was a good indication of where we were at. It was designed to be that way. It toughens you up. At times though, I said to myself, "What the fuck am I doing here?" But I stuck at it because it was make or break.'

Fundamental changes were needed in the fledging High Performance Programme. 'We used to train for two and a half hours. The Russians were training for an hour and fifteen minutes, but at a high level of intensity. Boxing had changed. Now rounds lasted two rather than three minutes, so the boxing had to be quicker and more intense,' said Walsh. Video analysis of the Russian sparring sessions demonstrated why the Irish boxers were failing against the top guys. 'Our problem was that we weren't attacking enough,' says Egan. 'Through the video analysis, we noticed they were attacking every three or four seconds, whereas we could spend eight or nine seconds doing nothing. It was way too long, particularly in a two-minute round. It was there in black and white. We weren't working hard enough; we were not throwing enough punches so we had to up the pace.'

For their next visit to Chekhov, in preparation for the 2005 World Championships, the Irish visitors were a lot more streetwise; so much so that they engaged in a spot of espionage. The Irish boxers wore heart monitors during sparring. The Russian coaches became increasingly intrigued as they watched the HPU's conditioning coach John Cleary strap the monitors around the boxers' torsos.

Billy Walsh recalls the story: 'We actually monitored Kenny in a contest against one of the Russians and his heart rate measured between ninety-three and one hundred percent max during the eight-minute contest. They didn't have any monitors, but they were watching how we used them. We said to them, "Tomorrow your guys can wear the monitors and we will give you the information on a disc."

The Irish suggested that Aleksei Tishchenko, the then reigning Olympic and world featherweight champion and future double European and 2007 world featherweight title holder Albert Selimov wear the monitors. The Irish kept their side of the deal and supplied the hosts with the boxers' heart-rate data on a disc. Before handing it over, however, the Irish downloaded all the information on to their own laptop.

'It was just a bit of espionage. We discovered that they operated near their maximum heart rate for the duration of the training sessions. We knew then this was the kind of conditioning our boxers needed in order to compete at the highest level.' says Walsh.

'On the first visit we were going out there as amateurs. It was just a question of learning as much as we could. On the second trip we went with a plan. We were looking at heart-rate data, plyometric power out of the lower body and lactic toleration,' explains Keegan. When the HPU staff compared the data produced by the Russian boxers on the second visit it wasn't much different from the Irish figures. 'We weren't just doing this to improve the science. We wanted to impact on the belief of the team and wipe out any reason why our boxers would feel they couldn't compete against the best. They had to believe in their own potential.'

Back in Ireland, the influence of the HPU manifested itself when the IABA agreed to stage the 2004 Elite Championships in December 2003 to facilitate the boxers' preparations for the European Championships in Croatia in February 2004, which was the first of three Olympic qualifiers. Compared to the Sydney Olympics the bar for boxers seeking to qualify for Athens 2004 had been raised even higher. The number of weight divisions was reduced by one – light middleweight was dropped and other weight limits were changed. Only 284 boxers would be allocated places at the Athens Games, twenty-eight fewer than in Sydney.

At the December Elite finals, Moore suffered a shock defeat in the welterweight final to Henry Coyle, but the other five who had been to Russia won their titles. Ireland, though, endured a serious wake-up at the European Championships in Pula. Lee was the only Irish boxer to make an impact; his seven colleagues all failed to win a bout. The nineteen-year-old Limerick middleweight won a bronze medal and qualified for the Athens Olympics. Finally, Ireland's slide into the abyss at international level had been halted. Lee's first round 31-17 win over David Tsiklauri from Georgia was the first time an Irish boxer had won a bout at the European Championships since 1998.

But the achievement came at a high cost. 'I still have the scar from the damage I did to my right hand in the first fight. I fought Darren Barker from the UK with a broken hand in the next round. Then I had it injected for the medal fight against a Serbian, Nikola Sjekloća. The doctor wouldn't inject it for the semi-final and I lost.' The German Lukas Wilaschek, who beat Lee 28-17, was stopped in the final by Gaydarbek Gaydarbekov from Russia.

Even though there were three more qualifying tournaments in Plovdiv (Bulgaria), Warsaw (Poland), and Baku (Azerbaijan), none of the other Irish boxers made it through. 'Kenny (Egan) should have qualified. He was our best performer throughout the year. He went to the first qualifier and bombed it. He went to the second one in Plovdiv and did the same and lost again in the last one in Baku,' recalls Walsh.

Egan believes he wasn't mentally ready for the challenge. 'Back then I was thinking, "Jesus am I good enough for the Olympics?" I bottled it mentally. I admit that now. Then I used to say it was bad luck. It was a combination of not being good enough and a lack of confidence. I hadn't learned enough. I had only been with Zaur for about eighteen months at the time.' Egan roomed with Lee at his final training camp in France before he departed to Athens. Egan headed to Crete for a holiday.

Even though Gary Keegan headed the HP Programme, he wasn't part of the official IABA Olympic delegation in Athens. The ISC brought him to the Games, but he wasn't allowed to stay in the athletes' village. The IABA appointed Sean Canavan – a long serving member of the IABA's Central Council and the then secretary of the Antrim Boxing Board – as team manager. According to OCI President Pat Hickey, representations were made to the OCI to thwart his appointment. 'Some people moved heaven and earth to try and block it. The IABA stood by their man and as it turned out Sean Canavan was one of the best managers we've ever had. The situation is that we leave it up to the sports bodies to nominate their team manager.'

Keegan has no issues with Sean Canavan. 'He was the team manager for the Athens Games and a better official or a nicer man you wouldn't meet. He was hugely supportive of the High Performance Programme and he knew it was a new thing and it was trying to find its feet. That was the way the system was in terms of how team managers were selected. We got on with it. But you would think that the person leading the programme would be the person who would lead the team into the Games. I went out to Athens effectively as a spectator,' says Keegan.

In the event, due to his damaged hand, the Games proved an anti-climax for Lee. 'The whole training camp prior to the Olympics was all about managing my hand,' says Lee, who had further underlined his potential at the European Union Championships in Madrid two months earlier when he had won a silver medal.

Lee comfortably beat Mexican Alfredo Angulo 38-23 in his first bout in Athens. But he damaged his hand again and had to have it injected for his next fight against twenty-year-old Hassan N'Dam N'Jikam from Cameroon. The latter had won the African middleweight title the previous year and has since proved his pedigree in the professional ranks winning interim WBA and WBO world titles. 'My hand was numb but I have no excuses,' acknowledges Lee.

Walsh, though, still has nightmares about the contest which finished 27-27 with the Cameroonian getting the nod on a countback of punches. 'I can still clearly remember what happened. Andy had a routine. He liked to come into the changing area through the back entrance but he always went out before a fight to look around the arena. But this being the second round of the Olympics we weren't allowed near the arena before his fight. So his normal routine was disrupted.

'So when we got to the curtain to come out we could hear the crowd chanting "Andy Lee, Andy Lee." The hairs were standing on the back of his neck. When the curtains opened, there were six Irish guys dressed as leprechauns, jumping up and down in front of us. Andy just lost his concentration. He went into the ring but his head wasn't in there. I didn't get him focused until he was back in the corner after the first round. Had he seen the Irish fans in the arena before the fight, he might have been okay, though he was restricted by his hand injury as well.'

As it transpired, even if he had got the decision, Lee would have been ruled out of the quarter-final due to an eye injury. According to the official report presented to the IABA by Sean Canavan, Lee was examined by Irish team doctor Sean Gaines and a Greek neurosurgeon after the fight and taken to hospital for treatment for a dilated left eye. He was detained for forty hours, partially because there was no ophthalmic surgeon on duty over the weekend.

He was released after being examined but not passed fit to box. The quarter-final had taken place twelve hours earlier.

Outside the ring, Lee did experience one life-changing event as a result of his Olympic experience. At a reception in Áras an Uachtaráin for the Irish Olympic team following their return, Lee met his future wife, Maud.

Overall the new HPU remained on target to win a medal in in four years' time in Beijing. After all, it had taken the French a quarter of a century to make the breakthrough. But within months of the Athens Olympics the IPU had to re-think their strategy after Lee accepted an offer to turn professional.

CHAPTER 10

WOBBLE ON THE
WAY TO BEIJING

*'Emanuel Steward talked about bringing me to America and how he would make
me into a world champion. It was like a young soccer player being
phoned up by Alex Ferguson.'*

Andy Lee

F our boxers from the HPU, Andy Murray, Paul McCloskey, James
Moore and Andy Lee turned professional after the Athens Olympics. But the
loss of the latter was by far the most damaging blow to the still fledgling programme. Losing boxers to the professional ranks has always been a feature of
Irish boxing but Lee was a special case. He was going to be the HPU's pin-up
boxer ahead of the Beijing Olympics.

'Initially he said he was turning professional and then he decided to stay.
We had it all set up. He was getting a grant of €32,000 from the Sports Coun-
cil. We got it increased to €40,000 and we got him a sponsored car,' recalls
Billy Walsh. Then he rang me later and said, "Billy, I can't sleep. If I don't do

this, I will regret it for the rest of my life." All I could say to him was "If that's how you feel there is no point in me trying to persuade you otherwise.'"

Lee was signed by the famous American trainer-manager Emanuel Steward, who discovered Thomas 'Hitman' Hearns, one of the iconic figures in professional boxing during the 1980s, and trained a cohort of other world champions. Steward's courtship of Lee began on Christmas Day 2002.

'I thought it was a wind-up given the day it was,' Lee recalls. 'He talked about bringing me to America and how he would make me into a world champion. It was like a young soccer player being phoned up by Alex Ferguson.'

It transpired that Lee had been on Steward's radar since the previous September when the Irishman beat a hotshot, American Jesús Gonzáles, en route to winning a silver medal at the World Junior Championships. Steward had been tracking Gonzáles' career.

Coincidentally, a friend of Lee's, Belfast-based Damian McCann, was trying to persuade Steward to allow him to brand his gym with the famous 'Kronk' trademark. McCann sent him tapes of Lee's performances.

Steward and Lee stayed in contact during the next three years and ultimately the latter opted to link up with him in the original Kronk Gym in Detroit. 'I thought about the decision long and hard,' says Lee. 'At the end of the day it was Emanuel Steward. I had to take it, though it was very difficult. I was very close to Billy [Walsh] having gone to the Olympics together. It would have been an easier decision to stay. I had the run of the place and I would have been the big dog.' Walsh believes that had he stayed he would have won a gold medal in Beijing. Lee, though, has no regrets. 'I never regret any decision I've made. Even if I hadn't won a world title, I still wouldn't have regretted leaving. I had an amazing experience in the US.'

Interestingly, he has stayed in touch with Zaur Antia. 'We talk quite regularly and any chance I get to promote him I do. I don't think he gets enough credit. He's a very smart guy and he has this ability to hone in on the talented boxers. He is one of the main reasons why there has been such a change-around in Irish boxing.'

The Limerick southpaw stayed around long enough to retain his Irish middleweight title in March 2005. At the same championships future IBF super bantamweight world professional champion Carl Frampton won the flyweight title. Later that month, Lee won the Home Nations' middleweight title in Liverpool. Frampton bowed out in the flyweight semi-final, a prelude to what was an unfulfilling amateur career.

From the staunchly loyalist enclave of Tiger's Bay in north Belfast, he won two Irish Elite titles in different weight categories (fly and feather) in 2005 and 2009 but acknowledged that he ought to have achieved more. 'I didn't always do what I was told. I'm far more dedicated now. Zaur [Antia] was one of the best coaches I ever worked with and Billy [Walsh] is a real nice guy. It was just better for me personally to be training by myself. I can be easily influenced and do the wrong thing. One of the things that I'm kinda annoyed with is that I turned professional without telling Billy or Zaur. They wouldn't have changed my mind but I should have told them what I was doing.'

Lee, meanwhile, marked his exit from the amateur ranks with a memorable win. In April 2005 the Home Nation winners took on a visiting Cuban team in Liverpool. Lee lost 16-12 to double world bronze medallist Yordanis Despaigne as the visitors romped to a 7-1 win. A week later, the Cubans visited the National Stadium. A six-man Irish team, augmented by two British boxers, hammered them 6-2, with Lee avenging the loss to Despaigne, who later defected to the US where he turned professional.

Ireland's preparations for the 2005 World Championships in the Chinese city of Mianyang were thoroughly professional. There was another trip to Chekov, this time during the summer, and the final training camp took place in the mountains outside Manila, capital of the Philippines.

Newcomer Darren Sutherland was the star performer in Mianyang, reaching the quarter-finals in the middleweight category. But his progress was halted by the eventual gold medallist Matvey Korobov from Russia. Nine years later, in Las Vegas, the Russian was sensationally stopped by Andy Lee in their WBO world middleweight title fight.

Welterweight Roy Sheahan was unlucky in Mianyang. He drew 21-21 with eventual silver medallist Magomed Nurutdinov from Belarus but lost on a countback. Kenny Egan lost 26-35 to Sweden's Babacar Kamara, while Conor Ahern (flyweight) and Eric Donovan (featherweight) also bowed out in the early stages. Ahern was beaten 31-17 by Georgian native Nikoloz Izoria, who had been coached in his native Poti by Zaur Antia until he left to take up a coaching position with the IABA two years earlier. 'I left my heart behind with those boxers whom I had trained for eight years,' says Antia. Meanwhile, Donovan proved no match for Romanian Viorel Simion who romped to a 40-25 win.

Prior to the 2006 European Championships in Bulgaria, the Irish returned again to Russia, though to a different location: the training camp was in Dagestan, a politically unstable region in the North Caucasus. Only four boxers travelled: Donovan, Sheahan, Egan and newcomer Darren O'Neill who replaced an injured Sutherland in the middleweight category.

Egan was the stand-out performer at the Europeans in Plovdiv. Despite injuring his thumb in his first round win over Germany's Robert Woge, he progressed in the competition. He knocked out a French opponent Mamadou Diambang in the quarter-finals before being stopped by the eventual gold medallist Artur Beterbiyev from Russia in the semi-final.

Egan knew what to expect having sparred against him at the training camp in Dagestan. But the defeat didn't gnaw at him like previous setbacks had. 'I finally got a place on the podium at a major championship. It wasn't that hard. I was thinking, "Why couldn't I have beaten those guys previously?" It was all part of the growing-up experience for me.' Meanwhile, O'Neill and Sheahan reached the quarter-finals, while Donovan bowed out in the second round.

Now the focus shifted to the World Championships in October 2007. They were switched to Chicago after the original hosts Mexico failed to meet certain criteria. Cuba declined an invitation, citing security concerns. The real reason was a fear that some of the team would defect once they reached US soil. The event was the first qualifier for the now looming Beijing Olympics, so the absence of the traditional market leaders was welcome news.

The target set for the HPU by their pay masters, the Irish Sports Council, was to get three boxers qualified for the 2008 Olympics and win a medal. The pressure was building, but so too was their talent base. Of particular significance was the pioneering work of IABA President Dominic O'Rourke in enticing members of the Travelling community to train in his own club, St Michael's, Athy. Two of his recruits, the Joyce cousins, John Joe (Johnny) and David Oliver quickly graduated to the HPU. Indeed, in an ironic twist, David Oliver Joyce beat his clubmate and the defending featherweight title holder, Eric Donovan, in the Elite final in February 2007. John Joe Joyce won the Elite lightweight crown, while other newcomers to emerge included Belfast teenager Ryan Lindberg (bantamweight), who beat Carl Frampton in the semi-final, and Letterkenny native Cathal McMonagle, who was crowned super heavyweight champion. The 2007 Elite also featured a triumphant return to the ring for Darren Sutherland and a first title for another Gerry Storey prodigy, light flyweight Paddy Barnes.

Ireland hosted the fifth edition of the European Union Amateur Boxing Championships in the National Stadium in June, 2007. The host country topped the medal table. Egan, Sutherland and Sheahan won gold medals in light heavyweight, middleweight and welterweight categories respectively, while Carl Frampton – now boxing in the featherweight division – and super heavyweight Cathal McMonagle claimed silver medals.

Meanwhile, flyweight Conor Ahern and lightweight Eric Donovan together with John Joe Joyce (light welterweight) all reached the quarter-finals but were beaten in their 'medal' fights. Donovan lost to future light world champion Domenico Valentino from Italy who surprisingly had to be content with a bronze medal in Dublin. Newly-crowned light flyweight champion Paddy Barnes suffered an eye injury during his quarter-final bout against Frenchman Nordine Oubaali which resulted in the referee stopping the contest in the second round.

Outside the boxing community, the decision of the IABA to overlook Keegan for the position of boxing team manager for the Athens Olympics in 2004 went unnoticed. So the first public indication of friction between the Central Council of the IABA – which runs the organisation on a day-to-day basis – and the HPU came prior to the World Championships in Chicago.

'We set criteria: for a boxer to be selected he had to have won a gold or silver medal at two tournaments,' recalls Billy Walsh. Based on this criteria, five boxers; the St Michael's, Athy, trio of David Oliver Joyce (featherweight), Eric Donovan (lightweight), and John Joe Joyce (light welterweight) together with Darren Sutherland (middleweight) and Kenny Egan (light heavyweight) were chosen by the HPU. 'But the Central Council decided to send a full team,' recalls Walsh.

According to Gary Keegan, the HPU wanted to develop a selection process which was transparent. 'We wanted to move in a direction where everything was transparent and clear for everyone to see. The boxers would have been aware of it before we entered the competition space.

'Selection criterion is not always perfect. The one we had was probably slightly imperfect. But it was transparent; everybody knew what they had to do. Everybody had signed up to it. It wasn't as if we pulled it out of a hat at the last minute. Remember we had selected many, many teams to compete in tournaments. But it is only when it comes to the European and World Championships and the Olympic Games that people really get exercised.'

The row between the HPU and the Central Council had simmered for several years. 'The High Performance Unit and the Sports Council wanted the High Performance director to have full control over the selections of teams. I, as president of the association, felt this wasn't right,' recalls Dominic O'Rourke.

The issue came to a head before the World Championships. Against O'Rourke's wishes, the team selected by the HPU became publicly known. 'I left my mobile phone in my car one evening after work. When I went back to get it, I had thirty missed calls. I knew something was up. Boxers were on to me wondering why we weren't sending a full team to the world championships. I was very annoyed and I called a Central Council meeting for the following Saturday and they agreed to send a full team.'

The Central Council added six boxers to the travelling party: Cathal McMonagle (super heavyweight), John Sweeney (heavyweight), Roy Sheahan (welterweight), Conor Ahern (flyweight), Ryan Lindberg (bantamweight), and Paddy Barnes (light fly). All, bar Sweeney (who was beaten by Ian Tims in the 2007 Elite heavyweight final) were reigning Elite champions. With the exception of McMonagle and Sweeney they were also all training full time with the HPU.

The selection of Paddy Barnes proved inspired. His love of boxing was nurtured on weekend trips to Ardglass, a coastal village in county Down – an hour's drive from his home in north Belfast. His uncle Jimmy Linden lived there. 'I used to go down there to visit my three cousins every weekend.' Linden ran the

East Coast Boxing Club in nearby Ballyhornan. 'I joined the club when I was eleven. It seemed the natural thing to do,' he recalls, though he actually made his boxing debut in the Kronk Club in Belfast. 'I joined on a Wednesday and had my first fight the following Sunday which I lost.'

Barnes was no overnight success. But he was persistent. He reckons he lost around his first twelve fights before breaking his duck, and he struggled to make an impact in his early teenage years. 'I never qualified for the All-Ireland Boys' Championship Finals. I was always beaten in the Antrim Championships. But one year I got a bye. So I got down to Dublin and won the final.'

He felt being crowned U-16 boys champion of Ireland would be the pinnacle of his career. 'I thought I was a legend.' By then he had switched to the Holy Family Club in Belfast, where he came under the influence of legendary coach Gerry Storey. Even before he officially joined the club, he trained in their famous headquarters, the Reccy, situated on the second floor of a modest building in the New Lodge Estate. It was five minutes' walk from his home. 'Gerry would bring me down every night. I was taking it seriously. I had stopped drinking with my mates,' chuckles Barnes, breaking into his trademark impish grin before he adds, 'I think I had my first drink when I was eleven.'

Barnes had little interest in formal schooling and left when he was seventeen. 'I stayed on an extra year, I don't know why because I wasn't good enough to do A levels.' In 2006 Barnes secured a temporary job with the Royal Mail. Although he worked the graveyard shift, 6pm to 6am, the money was good. 'I was getting four hundred pound a week; it was brilliant.'

He faced the classic sportsperson's dilemma when offered a full-time post. At the same time, he was selected to box for Northern Ireland at the 2006 Commonwealth Games in Melbourne. 'I left [the Royal Mail] two days early, without telling them, because the Commonwealth Games was coming up and

I wanted to get back training.'

He was a month short of his eighteenth birthday when he journeyed to the far side of the world. Barnes has come to detest travelling, but this was his first adventure abroad and he loved Australia. He has less-fond memories, though, of his time in the ring. He was beaten in the first round in the light flyweight category by the eventual bronze medallist Simanga Shiba from Swaziland. 'I was leading by something like nine points going into the last round. I don't know what happened. I felt I blacked out or something. I was devastated. Even then I was very competitive. But I kept my head down and I won my first Irish senior title in 2007.'

By then the HPU had expanded and Arklow native Jim Moore – who coached his son James to win a bronze medal at the 2001 World Championships in Belfast – was supervising training for a cohort of younger boxers. Barnes recalls his training. 'I was still a junior and trained on a Saturday with them. I wasn't on funding so I wasn't in Dublin on a full-time basis.'

At this stage the HPU was not concerned over their decision not to select Barnes for the World Championships, according to Billy Walsh. 'He didn't look anything special. As we didn't have many boxers in his weight category, he was sparring against youth and juvenile boxers and they were able to handle him.

'Later on, we found out that having him spar against these guys wasn't stimulating him. He needed better opposition to bring out the best in him. We brought him to a training camp in France where he was absolutely fantastic when he got in against Jérôme Thomas, a flyweight who won a silver medal for France at the Athens Olympics. On the basis of that performance, we would have added him to the team for Chicago, but the IABA selected him anyway,' notes Walsh. Gary Keegan also agreed with that outcome. 'We were happy to be overturned on that one.'

Barnes was ascending the ladder at a rapid pace, but he wasn't entirely happy. 'After France we went to another training camp in Germany. I was never away from home for so long before and I hated it. Training full time was a shock. But it brought me on. I was a different fighter afterwards. I was a nobody when I went to Chicago. I just wanted to go out and see how I measured up against the world's best.' And in a classic understatement, Barnes adds with a smile: 'I didn't do too badly.'

On 31 October 2007, at the World Championships in Chicago, he became the first Irish boxer to qualify for the Beijing Olympics – then ten months away. It was a surprise. But what was far more surprising was how his ten colleagues struggled in the UIC Pavilion in the Windy City. Barnes was completely oblivious to the gathering storm clouds. After all, he was just twenty.

'I hadn't qualified for the Olympics in my head at all. I beat a North Korean [Jon Kuk-chol 33-19] then stopped an Iranian [Sadegh Farajzadeh] in the second round before beating a Japanese [Kenji Ohkubo 24-6] to reach the quarter-finals. After I qualified, I remember Billy saying to me, "You're on twenty grand a year now." I had no funding up until then. So I went from zero to €20,000 a year.

Barnes's breakthrough couldn't disguise the reality that the 2007 World Championships were an unmitigated disaster for the HPU. The crisis gathered momentum slowly in Chicago. Early on there were no real concerns, though Conor Ahern, Ryan Lindberg, John Joe Joyce, Roy Sheahan, and Cathal McMonagle made early exits in the UIC Pavilion.

Kenny Egan, Eric Donovan and Darren Sutherland were progressing through the rounds in the UIC Pavilion together with heavyweight John Sweeney, who was ultimately beaten 28-5 in the last sixteen by the eventual silver medallist Rakhim Chakhiev from Russia. Sutherland and Donovan also came unstuck in the last sixteen. Sutherland lost his middleweight bout

20-13 to Alfonso Blanco from Venezuela, who later captured the silver medal. Donovan's conqueror, Italian lightweight Italian Domenico Valentino, also won a silver medal.

Egan, who captained the World Championship team in Chicago, started the tournament well. He stopped Julius Jackson from the Virgin Islands in the second round. The Neilstown boxer then beat Julio Castillo from Ecuador 16-10. Now he was in the last 16; eight minutes and one win away from realising his boyhood dream of wearing the tracksuit with the five Olympic rings on it. At face value he had nothing to fear from his Croatian opponent Marijo Šivolija who had given him a walkover at the EU Championships in Dublin a few months previously. However, in a surprise defeat, Egan lost 17-9.

Egan was shocked by his performance. 'All I had to do was to reach the last eight. It was the most straightforward way to qualify for the Olympics. I was confident, having reached the last eight of the World Championships in Belfast in 2001 when I was nineteen and again in Bangkok two years later.'

Even Barnes was unhappy, despite qualifying for his maiden Olympics. 'I was thinking, "Shit, I'm going to have to go to China on my own." I was disgusted that nobody else qualified. Thank God John Joe Nevin, then Kenny [Egan], Darren [Sutherland], and John Joe Joyce qualified [the following spring]. I probably wouldn't have gone otherwise,' he suggests.

Performances aside, Dominic O'Rourke has no regrets about the IABA's insistence on sending eleven boxers to the event. 'What happened in Chicago proved that the Central Council was right to send a full team. Apart from Paddy Barnes, John Sweeney, who we also added to the team, reached the last sixteen where he was beaten by an excellent Russian. He did as well as any of the high-profile boxers in the High Performance. My theory has always been that if a boxer wins an Irish title he is entitled to wear the jersey and represent Ireland. We will never know whether they're good enough until they get a chance.

'One of my best memories from my time as president comes from the World Championships in Belfast in 2001. I argued that we should send a full team which we did. Super heavyweight Eanna Falvey was probably not expecting to go but he was selected. Even though he was beaten by a Russian, he gave a tremendous performance. When I went into the Irish dressing room afterwards he shook my hand and thanked me for giving him the chance to box for Ireland in the World Championships. I will always remember that.'

On reflection Ireland's performance in Chicago wasn't quite as bleak as it first appeared. McJoe Arroyo from Puerto Rico, who had eliminated bantamweight Ryan Lindberg, qualified for Beijing as did Russian super heavyweight Islam Timurziev who stopped McMonagle. So, six of those who denied Irish boxers a place at the Olympics, qualified themselves and five of them ended up on the podium.

China's Zou Shiming, who beat Paddy Barnes 22-8 in the quarter-final, won his second successive world title in Chicago at light fly. The clash marked the beginning of one of the classic rivalries in modern amateur boxing and arguably the best ever in the light flyweight class. Barnes was blissfully ignorant of Shiming's pedigree before stepping into the ring to face him. 'I was new on to the scene so I didn't have a clue who he was. It wasn't until after the fight that Billy told me he was a two-time world champion and an Olympic bronze medallist.'

These caveats, however, were of minor concern to the Irish boxing fraternity. It seemed there wouldn't be sufficient room on the proverbial bandwagon for all those clamouring for Keegan's head and the disbandment of the entire HP programme.

The back-stabbing started before the squad left Chicago, recalls Egan. 'People who should have known better were saying that the HPU was a waste of money and should be scrapped. The boxers stuck together. Paddy [Barnes] getting through put the tin hat on it.'

The critics were sniffing around, looking for information as to what transpired at the official post-mortem meeting which was held in the team hotel. 'I remember one guy, in particular, was mad for news. He wanted the whole HPU disbanded. Nobody said much. We just got back to Ireland with our tails between our legs.'

For Egan, in particular, there was a sense of déjà vu about the experience. 'I had fucked up on three occasions before the Athens Olympics. Now I had done it again. There were two more qualifiers to come. Was I going to get six chances to make the Olympics and still fail?' Given the fragility of his self-confidence what happened in Chicago was a shattering blow.

John Treacy was acutely aware of the possible fall-out. The ISC couldn't tell the IABA how to proceed but they dropped enough hints to let them know the lie of the land. 'Let's put it this way. The Sports Council would have been staunch backers of the High Performance Unit in 2007. Behind the scenes we would have been very supportive.'

The President of the IABA Dominic O'Rourke held his nerve at the next Central Council meeting when there were calls for Keegan to be replaced. 'There was a big uproar after Chicago, but I supported the High Performance. I could see from a coaching point of view that the boxers were improving and the system was good. We still had two more qualifying tournaments to come. So why cut off the head at that stage? Wait and see how the boxers did in those qualifiers. As it transpired four more boxers qualified,' he says.

The HPU staff were devastated with the performances, so much so that they brought in an independent facilitator to assist with a review. 'We were disgusted that we didn't achieve more in Chicago and we did feel under a lot of pressure. Some guys didn't perform at all and we were trying to figure out why that had happened. We had a little problem with the tapering phase; we had spent too much time away,' says Billy Walsh. 'We should have spent less time in our final training camp in Germany and more in the US prior to the start of the championships. But we learned from our mistakes. We have got the tapering right since and adapted to being away for longer periods.'

The HPU's own review and the facilitator's report threw up another issue. 'We had been over coaching the boxers. It ended up where Kenny [Egan] was expecting me to tell him what punch to throw next and everybody was in a comfort zone,' says Walsh.

So when the boxers returned to training in December they discovered the schedule had been ripped up. Two weeks before Christmas everybody headed for the hills of Donegal, where a local man Eunan Devenney had prepared a set of challenges for the boxers around the twin towns of Ballybofey and Stranorlar. 'We got up at 6am and brought them to the hills around Barnesmore Gap where they ran through hail, rain and snow. It was tough but enjoyable and stimulating,' recalls Walsh.

Unwittingly, the trip resulted in an unanticipated bonus. John Joe Nevin, a settled Traveller from Mullingar, who was coached by Brian McKeown in Cavan Boxing Club, was earning rave reviews for his performance in the under-age categories. A stylish counter-puncher, only a controversial public warning prevented him from achieving a clean-sweep of all the underage All-Ireland titles. In 2006 Nevin, boxing in the light flyweight category, reached the quarter-finals at the World Junior Championships in Morocco, before bowing out to an American, Luis Yáñez.

His interest in boxing came via his cousins. 'When I was a kid they were all running off doing boxing. I kept wrecking my father's head about getting me gloves. Eventually he had to give in. He sent me down to the boxing club in Mullingar when I was seven.' John Joe honed his footwork watching his idol, Prince Naseem Hamed, then the glamour professional performer in the lighter weight divisions. Nevin sported a pair of Prince Naz's replica shorts in his first fight, and being a cocky eight-year-old he couldn't resist showing off the 'Prince Shuffle'. His twelve-year-old opponent didn't take kindly to his showboating and promptly sent him sprawling out through the ropes. 'I still have a video of the fight at home and I got the worst hiding for doing the shuffle.'

The turning point in his early career came when he opted to join his older cousin David Nevin in Cavan Boxing Club. 'David had been boxing with Brosna Boxing Club, but I think there was a bit of a row in the camp and he came over to me when he was boxing at youth level,' recalls Brian McKeown. 'Several more cousins, including John Joe, arrived shortly afterwards. He was only twelve, but I could see straight away that he had ability. He had that bit of arrogance and confidence that flows from having talent.'

There was one problem though, according to his new coach. 'He had no left hand. But he could thump anybody with his right. Everybody thinks he's just a 'fancy Dan' but he can thump an opponent as well. Unfortunately he was very light. So I sat down with him and we agreed that he wasn't going in like a 'kamikaze pilot' against older and bigger opponents just to get a trophy. We worked on developing his skills and the only contests he competed in were championship events or representative bouts,' said McKeown. Nevin's father, Martin, became his chauffeur, often making the round 120 km trip from Mullingar to Cavan five nights a week.

The HPU's junior boxing coach Jim Moore had alerted his boss, Gary Keegan, to Nevin's potential. 'Jim came into my office one day and informed me that John Joe would win a senior title in 2008 and would go on to qualify for the Olympic. He was certainly on the money.

'Jim Moore is an unsung hero in my mind. He developed a truly world-class talent pipeline in the space of three years, which is nothing short of amazing.

Anybody in sport will tell you how difficult that is to do. But Jim, one of our Irish coaches, did it, and by doing so he ensured a rich vein of talent, including the likes of Joe Ward came through to the senior squad in subsequent years.'

In December 2007 the Irish junior squad were participating in a four-nation round-robin tournament against England, France and Germany in Ballybofey at the same time as the senior squad were undergoing their post-Chicago debriefing sessions on nearby Barnesmore Gap. Before one of the shows Walsh spoke briefly to the boxers.

Nevin retains vivid memories of the speech. 'He said, "Some of you will be aiming to make the Olympics in 2012 but some of you can make it in 2008." I could see he was looking at me when he said it. I spoke with Billy afterwards and he suggested I give the nationals a go,' recalls Nevin, who was the captain and star Irish performer in the four nations' tournament, comfortably winning his three bouts.

Just seven months after winning the Irish U-19 flyweight championship, Nevin entered the 2008 Elite championship in the bantamweight division. The key contest came in the semi-final when he faced the defending title holder, Ryan Lindberg who had boxed at the World Championships in Chicago. 'He was a tremendous boxer and I was surprised when I beat him,' said Nevin, who then defeated TJ Doheny 8-3 in the final.

The victory earned the eighteen-year-old the right to challenge for a place at the Beijing Olympics. The next European Olympic qualifying tournament which was scheduled for Pescara in Italy, was just six weeks away. 'I'll never forget what I said to a reporter after the fight. He told me I had three chances to make the Olympics. I was young and cocky, and I replied, "All I'll need is one", and that's all I needed.'

Nevin breezed through the tournament in Pescara. He needed only to reach the semi-final but won the gold medal by outpointing Veaceslav Gojan from

Moldova 17-10. Just forty-nine days earlier he had won his first Irish Elite title. Now he was going to the 2008 Olympics. Nobody was more surprised than Nevin. 'Getting to Beijing was never part of the plan really,' he remarked later. 'I mean I remember watching Andy Lee in 2004 and thinking how I'd be only be nineteen by the time of the next Olympics. There wasn't a hope in hell of getting there. So the target had been London 2012.'

'But I had no fear in Pescara. I was just a young lad and I went out to enjoy myself. The older lads were putting pressure on themselves,' suggests Nevin.

McKeown was struck by how quickly his prodigy matured once he joined the senior ranks. 'As soon he got into the seniors he started to blossom, helped by the High Performance Unit. They had a training regime Monday to Friday and the boxers were on a balanced diet. They had a back-up team of physio-therapists and nutritionists on hand. These are the extras that an ordinary club boxer doesn't have. He could be coming to me training four nights a week but then eating a kebab or a bag of chips on the way home or nothing if trying to make a weight.'

But if Nevin was justifiably ecstatic it was another tale of woe for Kenny Egan and, in particular, Darren Sutherland. He lost by a point (23-22) to Great Britain's James DeGale. They would cross paths again in Beijing. Sunderland believed he had done enough to nick the verdict, as he outlined in the *Irish Independent* a few months later. 'I put on a great performance at the tournament but was robbed in the quarter-finals. For about ten minutes afterwards, I lay on the floor. I'm not embarrassed to say I might have been crying.'

John Joe Joyce also narrowly missed out in Italy. He finished with a bronze medal. But a 17-13 semi-final loss to Romanian light welterweight Ramazan Magomedov put paid to his Olympic ambitions for the time being. Egan also secured a bronze medal, but it was the most worthless piece of metal he ever won. As in Chicago, he was one win away from securing his place when he blew it. It wasn't even particularly close. Ramazan Magomedov from Belarus beat him 17-13.

Keegan later told Egan that when he saw him leaving the dressing room he knew he was doomed. Egan remembers, 'My eyes were glazed over and my head wasn't in the stadium.' Just to rub salt into Egan's wounds, Magomedov, having secured his place in the Olympics, pulled out of the final. The Irishman decided it was time to think of a career outside boxing.

'My brother Willie and I went into town and I think we paid one hundred quid to do the theory test to apply for a taxi plate. I said, "Right, I will get a taxi plate under my arse now and that will do me." I was disgusted with myself. Thank God, I never went through with my plan. I have been lucky with decisions like that. I was going to buy property on my return from Beijing at the height of the property boom but thankfully didn't go ahead with that either.'

Egan and the other Irish boxers had one last chance to qualify for Beijing at the final qualifier in Athens. Again the HPU were under the spotlight as none of the HPU's high profile boxers had qualified for Beijing. Walsh's priority in the lead-up to the Athens qualifier was to make sure Egan's head was in the right place. 'We knew from the sports psychologist that he was constantly looking to the future. So we got him to focus on the present. We got him to think about one punch at the time, one round at a time, one fight at a time.'

RTÉ's boxing commentator Jimmy Magee suggested that Egan have a chat with golfer Pádraig Harrington who had won the British Open the previous year. Coincidentally, Harrington won his second major, the US PGA, during the Beijing Olympics.

'The media subsequently made a lot more out of it than it actually was. It was just a chit-chat over a cup of tea,' said Egan. 'My confidence was high. I genuinely thought I deserved to be at the Olympics, whereas four years previously I didn't think so. I had to reach the final [of the European Olympic qualifier in Athens] to qualify but I was fairly confident given who I was up against. There was a Greek light heavyweight Anastasios Berdesis, who was fairly handy, but he was in the other half of the draw and got beaten in the semi-final.'

After a box-off in mid-March in the National Stadium, a nine-man Irish team was chosen for the final European Olympic qualifier in Athens in April. There were no surprises. Newcomers Willie McLaughlin (welterweight), Ross Hickey (lightweight), Tommy Sheehan (heavyweight) and Cathal McMonagle (super heavyweight) bowed out early. Flyweight Conor Ahern and featherweight David Oliver Joyce exited at the quarter-final stage, leaving Egan, Sutherland and John Joe Joyce standing at the business end of the tournament.

The latter did have a slice of good luck in the quarter-final of his light welterweight bout against local hero Gevorg Galstian. The contest ended 18-18, but the Irishman got the verdict on the countback. In the semi-final he comfortably beat a German opponent Harum Sipahi 27-12, to become the second member of the travelling community to secure a place at the Beijing Games.

'There was a lot of pressure going to Athens. After Pescara, I just wanted to disappear. I was four points away from the Olympics and I'm thinking: "That was my chance." Back in the spring, my mother booked a holiday for us in Lourdes. She was looking to choose a date. I said pick a date during the Olympics. My feeling was that, if I didn't qualify, at least I could go there and clear the head. So, now, all the family are going to Lourdes, while I'm in Beijing," Joyce revealed later in an interview with Vincent Hogan in the *Irish Independent*.

Darren Sutherland underlined his potential in Athens. He was in a different class to the rest of the middleweights as he beat Finnish, Norwegian and Serbian opponents by a combined tally of thirty-six points. Neither did he have to go the distance in his medal bouts as Victor Cotiujanschi from Moldova retired in the third round of the semi-final while France's Jean-Mickaël Raymond did likewise in the gold medal bout.

Egan breezed through as well. He beat Italian Alessandro Sinacore 23-14 in the first round before accounting for Holland's Daniel Kooij 13-4 in the second. With all the coaches' words 'Take your time, one punch at a time' ringing in his ears, Egan stepped into the ring for the most important eight minutes of his career against a German opponent, Gottlieb Weiss. It was all square after the first round. Then something strange happened as Egan felt all the pressure seep away and suddenly he was energised. 'I'm not a religious man so I can't say I got a flash or anything. It was just a question of going back to what I knew best and collecting the points. It was plain sailing after that. Long before the end I knew I was going to the Olympics.'

Just for good measure, Egan beat Kennedy Katende from Sweden 15-10 in the final to join Sutherland and Joyce as gold medallists at the tournament. For once though, the colour of the medals didn't matter. But what did matter was that Ireland now had five boxers destined for the Beijing Olympics in five months' time. It would be Ireland's biggest team since the Barcelona Games fourteen years previously.

CHAPTER 11

NIGHTMARE
IN VLADIVOSTOK

'It was the worst place I ever stayed in my life. But I was the only one who said,
"Get me out." My new hotel was brilliant. I think the other lads were jealous
because they were afraid to speak up when they had the chance.'
Paddy Barnes

ladivostok, situated on the eastern tip of the Russian sub-continent, was once the base for the Soviet Union's formidable Pacific naval fleet. It has an established reputation of being an unwelcoming port of call for foreign visitors. In the wake of the October Revolution in 1917 it was occupied by troops from countries as diverse as Czechoslovakia and Canada as well as the world superpowers at the time: the United States, the United Kingdom, Japan and China. However, the taking of the city by the Red Army on 25 October 1922 marked the end of the Russian Civil War and the expulsion of the visitors. The city, which has a population of just over half a million, was closed to foreigners for the remainder of the twentieth century.

This was the improbable venue for Ireland's final training camp ahead of the Beijing Olympics in August 2008. The five-man team, captained by Kenny Egan, and their support staff were in Vladivostok at the invitation of the Boxing Federation of Russia. Their eleven Beijing-bound boxers were there as well. No other country was invited to the ten-day camp. While the Irish were there the Venezuelan Olympian squad turned up but weren't allowed in.

The HPU still had its critics in Ireland. Eyebrows were raised at the decision to send the team to a Russian training camp on the eve of their biggest-ever challenge. What if they were demoralised by their opponents during sparring? What if Egan, Sutherland, Joyce, Nevin and Barnes were drawn against Russian opponents in the early rounds?

The coaching staff had no such qualms, according to Billy Walsh. 'For us it was the best preparation possible. The top five Russians guys in each of the weight divisions were in the camp. So our lads would be tested in every skill imaginable. It was just a two-hour flight from Beijing so in terms of acclimatising it was ideal.

'We hadn't too many options to be honest. The Olympic Council were trying to put us in a club in Beijing. Our answer to that was, "We're a national team going to the Olympics. We don't train in a club." We had the option of France or Germany but felt it was too far from Beijing. Russia was our best bet.'

Zaur Antia's impeccable contacts did the rest, and the Irish party, which included physiotherapist Scott Murphy, strength-and-conditioning coach John Cleary and sports psychologist Gerry Hussey packed their bags for a six-week sojourn in the Far East. One journalist saw off the Irish squad as they departed from Dublin Airport on a soft July morning on the thirteen-and-a-half hour flight to Beijing, via Frankfurt.

Formwise, the boxers were on top of their game. At the European Union Championships the previous June in Poland, Nevin, Sutherland and Egan all won gold, while Barnes won a silver. Just for good measure, David Oliver Joyce (featherweight) and Con Sheehan (heavyweight) – neither of whom had qualified for Beijing – had won gold medals as well. The only disappointment was John Joe Joyce's defeat in the quarter-finals to the eventual silver medallist, Gyula Káté from Hungary.

The itinerary, meticulously drawn up by Gary Keegan, was a master stroke in planning. The Irish boxers were among the first competitors to arrive in Beijing. They got an opportunity to look around and familiarise themselves with the place before it became overcrowded. But most of all they rested. 'Everybody was shattered after the flight,' remembers Walsh. During the three-day stop they dropped off their luggage, including their John Rocha-designed suits, which they wore during the opening ceremony. They also obtained their official accreditation, which can prove a tiring and time-consuming process if left to the eve of the Games.

A feature of the Beijing Olympics was the sheer number of 'volunteers' the organisers laid on. They lavished attention on the Irish party during their familiarisation trip. Soon though, it was time to take a rickety flight south to Vladivostok where a shock awaited the boxers. The Irish found Vladivostok almost as inhospitable as the foreign troops did during the Russian Civil War.

Billy Walsh still has a picture on his iPhone of the bathroom facilities. 'Let's put it like this: if anybody offers you a free trip to Vladivostok, say no quickly. It's a kip to put it mildly,' says Walsh. 'We were in a hotel; but you couldn't call it a hotel. Every time you went through the front door it was as if you were taking your life in your hands.' Security men armed with AK47 rifles were positioned on every floor of the building.

To try and make the place feel like home, containers from Ireland filled with food items, including cornflakes, pasta and Jaffa cakes, had been transported to Vladivostok. However, there was a danger the boxers would become preoccupied with the filth, the heat and the gun-toting security guards and lose their focus.

'We called a meeting straight away to spell out our message: "You can throw the toys out of the pram and sulk and moan. But we are getting ready for the Olympic Games and we won't get better preparation anywhere else. We have to put up with this in order to get what we want,"' Walsh informed the boxers in no uncertain terms.

The squad doctor, Jim Ryan, was billeted in a more upmarket hotel five minutes' walk away. Paddy Barnes ended up staying with him. 'We had to move him [Barnes] there because he was cracking up,' reveals Walsh.

Barnes has a slightly different take on the story. 'It was the worst place I ever stayed in my life. I remember Gary Keegan coming in to us and saying, "I know boys it is a bad hotel; if you want, we can move." He asked each of us the same question. But I was the only one who said, "Get me out. There is no way I'm staying here." My new hotel was brilliant and I was there on my own in the end because the team doctor had to leave early. I think the other lads were jealous because they were afraid to speak up when they had the chance.'

Barnes's decision to move out allowed Egan to swap rooms. He was originally billeted with Sutherland and Nevin in a tiny room, where a sizeable amount of the floor space was occupied by a huge noisy fridge. For the remainder of the trip he shared with Joyce. Having rested up for a couple of days and passed the time doing quizzes, playing cards or watching films on portable DVD players, they got down to work.

Once inside the gym, the Irish boxers discovered that Russian training camps are location indifferent. All are run in an identical manner. The surface of the sparring areas was fitted out with the same sponge-like material that the Irish found so intimidating on their first visit to a Russian camp five years previously. 'There is no running around on that surface. You had to stand your ground,' according to Egan.

'There were sixty or seventy Russians there, and there was no question of them taking it easy against us because we were going to the Olympics at the end of the month. They were doing their best to take our heads off. But it was a great camp,' says Egan.

Paddy Barnes concurs. 'I had never fought a Russian before. In fact, I still haven't boxed a Russian. So getting to spar with them every day was brilliant. I felt I was matching or coming out on top of them each time and my confidence grew from there.'

In the run-up to the Games there had been much debate among the Irish coaching staff as to how best to taper the training workload of the boxers in order to ensure that when they stepped into the ring in Beijing they were at their peak physically, mentally and psychologically. Arguably, they had got it wrong in Chicago; they couldn't afford to make the same mistakes again.

'Zaur was adamant that your last spar before going into competition had to be a good one. Then you go into the competition on a high and you're chomping at the bit. On the other hand, if you take a beating in your last spar it affects your confidence going into your first fight. They listened to Zaur in 2008,' suggests Egan.

So, ten days before the boxing commenced in Beijing, the Irish boxers were involved in a test match against the Russian number ones. Egan found himself face-to-face with his nemesis, Artur Beterbiyev, the 2009 world champion and double European title holder. On his way to winning the gold medal at the latter championships two years earlier, the Russian stopped Egan under the twenty-point rule.

'Beterbiyev was an animal,' remembers Egan. 'I wanted to finish on a high before heading to Beijing. I said to myself, "F... it, I'm in good shape. I will stand my ground here." I boxed him for four two-minute rounds, and I felt I got the better of him. I said afterwards, "That's me now, I'm ready.'"

Not alone did Egan excel, but so too did his four colleagues, particularly Sutherland who got the better of the then Russian superstar and world champion Matvey Korobov. There was one unintended consequence; the Irish performed so well in Vladivostok but more particularly in Beijing that they were only invited back to train with the Russian squad on one occasion subsequently.

'Our lads boxed out of their skins that day, beating their number ones. Obviously there were no official results declared, but everybody knew who had done well. That night we had a meeting with the team. It was still ten days out from the Games, but we felt we were ready. Two days later, the Russians came to us, looking for another sparring session, but we declined. They put their Olympic team through another spar before leaving for Beijing. We felt we overcooked them. Korobov, for example, flopped at the Olympics," says Walsh.

For Keegan, the epiphany moment came one afternoon while he was watching the two squads doing their warm-up together. 'I said to Billy, "What do you see that's different?" He didn't know what I was on about. For me, what was different was that other than the fact they were wearing GAA jerseys one couldn't separate our lads from the Russians. On our first visit to Russia they stood out as being awkward and not having the same confidence levels as the Russians.'

Two days before the opening ceremony of the Games of the XXIX Olympiad, the Irish boxers arrived back in Beijing Capital International Airport. Complete with their Olympic accreditation, they breezed through security and were whisked off to their accommodation in the athletes' village.

This was a newly-constructed complex, containing nine thousand rooms in forty-two buildings, spread over a sixty-six hectare site that was a twenty-minute walk from two of the iconic landmarks of the Beijing Games: the Bird's

Nest Stadium and the Water Cube Aquatics Centre. Sutherland and Nevin roomed together, as did Barnes and Joyce. Egan was due to share with canoeist Eoin Rheinisch but as his slalom event was taking place in the district of Shunji outside the city he didn't use the accommodation in the Olympic village.

The global nature of boxing was underlined by the fact that the two hundred and eighty-three boxers officially accredited at the 2008 Olympics came from seventy-seven countries across all five continents. Only Russia had a representative in each of the eleven categories, though China, Cuba, Kazakhstan and Morocco had ten each. Ireland's five representatives left them in mid-table.

In the weeks leading up to the Games, one of the medal contenders in Egan's light heavyweight category, Ismayl Sillakh from Ukraine was banned for two years after failing a dope test. Incredibly, his replacement, Greece's Anastasios Berdesis – whom Egan avoided in the final qualifier in Athens – suffered a similar fate. So, Turkey's Bahram Muzaffer received a late call-up. For the boxers though, the overriding concern was the all-important draw, scheduled for the Grand Ballroom of the Asia Hotel on the morning of the official opening ceremony.

There was drama before the actual draw, which was overseen by the president of the International Boxing Association (AIBA) Dr Wu Ching-kuo. Three boxers, including Great Britain's Frankie Gavin, the 2007 lightweight world champion, failed to make the weight, resulting in automatic exclusion.

John Joe Joyce drew the short straw – a first round clash against Gyula Káté from Hungary, a former world and European championship bronze medallist. He had beaten Joyce in the quarter-finals of the European Union Championships just eight weeks previously, having earlier eliminated the Limerick-born light welterweight from the World and EU Championships respectively in 2007.

In contrast, Barnes and Sutherland received byes in the first round, leaving them two wins away from a medal, though the latter wasn't entirely happy as Walsh revealed at the time. 'Darren is just desperate to get into the ring. He's not happy about getting a bye.'

At eight minutes past eight on 8 August 1988 the Chinese president, Hu Jintao, declared the 29th summer Olympic Games open. Less than twenty-four hours later the boxing was under way.

CHAPTER 12

BONANZA IN BEIJING

'Naturally, I counted the scores, and I won it by two or three points. But, look, I hold no grudges against Zhang. If I was offered any medal at the start of the game, I would have taken it with both hands.'

Kenny Egan

The Beijing Workers' Gymnasium, originally built in 1961 for the World Table Tennis Championships, hosted the boxing programme at the 2008 Olympics. Kenny Egan was in action in the first session. Although it is slightly more than 8,000 kilometres from his native Neilstown to downtown Beijing, Egan wasn't short of support. Chants of 'Kenny! Kenny! Kenny!' resonated around the arena that Saturday afternoon as he pummelled his opponent from the Virgin Islands, Julius Jackson, 22-2: the same boxer he had stopped at the World Championships in Chicago. High up in the bleachers, Gary Keegan watched in stoic silence.

Egan was exuberant; he bounced into the mixed-zone afterwards where the boxers and coaches meet the media. And, in what turned out to be a prophetic comment, he told RTÉ's Marty Morrissey that he was the first Irishman in action and would be the last one out.

But it wasn't until twenty-year-old John Joe Joyce stepped into the ring the following morning that ringside observers got the first indication that this was a very special Irish team. Egan's fight was as straightforward as one can reasonably expect at Olympic level. Joyce's battle against his 'bogeyman', the Hungarian boxer Gyula Káté, was the exact opposite.

The portrait of St Jude, the patron saint of lost causes, tattooed on Joyce's right forearm seemed an appropriate portent for what might transpire. After all, the Hungarian had accumulated seventy-nine points against the St Michael's Athy boxer in their last three contests.

'Sixty-four boxers in the Worlds and I drew him in the first round. This time when I drew him again, I was thinking, "There's something meant to be,"' remarked Joyce to journalists in the mixed zone, after prevailing 9-5 against his nemesis in a tactical contest. 'I've drawn him so many times that I knew God was going to be on my side this time.'

Having celebrated his nineteenth birthday just nine weeks previously, John Joe Nevin was Ireland's youngest male competitor in Beijing. 'It was hard on me because I was so young,' he recalled four years later in an interview in the *Irish Independent* on the eve of his first fight at the London Olympics.

Arguably, this uncertainty impacted on his performance because he never quite reached the heights he scaled at the qualifying tournament in Pescara. Nonetheless, he won his opening bout – beating African champion Abdelhalim Ouradi from Algeria 9-4, despite being docked two points in the first round of a scrappy contest.

The Irish were now on a roll. Egan underlined this growing confidence when he outclassed Bahram Muzaffer, the Turkish boxer who had received the late call-up, to win 10-2 and nail down a place in the last eight – one win away from a coveted medal. Just as the decision in the Egan fight was announced, the favourite in the light heavyweight category, Russian world champion Artur Beterbiyev was entering the arena alongside his Chinese opponent Zhang Xiaoping. Like Egan, the Chinese boxer had bombed at the World Championships in Chicago. But it was Beterbiyev who failed on this occasion, suffering a shock 10-2 reversal, after leading 2-0 at the end of the first round.

As Egan emerged from the shower afterwards, Beterbiyev, who had previously ignored him outside the ring even though they sparred each other at the training camps in Russia, finally acknowledged the Irish champion. 'In broken English he said, "Ken, good luck." It was a nice touch,' recalls Egan.

While the Irish captain was now through to the quarter-finals and the other four Irish boxers were in the last sixteen, John Treacy couldn't relax. 'Living through those fights my heart was in my mouth, to be honest. There is only one way to measure high performance and that's to win medals.'

Treacy's caution appeared justified as in the next forty-eight hours two of the team made their exits. As it transpired, Joyce and Nevin were both beaten by the eventual gold medallists in their respective categories. It mattered little to Joyce, who was desperately unlucky to lose to Felix Diaz from the Dominican Republic after a bruising encounter.

Joyce's fate was sealed fourteen seconds from the end of the final round when Diaz landed what was ostensibly the winning punch. The contest actually ended 11-11 but Diaz got the verdict on a countback. Joyce's cause wasn't helped by the fact that he was penalised two points in the first round for holding, which gave his opponent a seemingly unassailable 5-1 advantage. The rest of the fight was every bit as eventful. Fearful that Joyce would pick up another public warning for holding, Billy Walsh was particularly vociferous in the corner. He ignored a series of warnings from South Korean referee Kim Jae-bong, who eventually lost patience and ordered the coach from the auditorium.

Joyce battled back bravely and was two points ahead with sixty seconds remaining but he couldn't hold out. Prophetically, he sensed afterwards that he might have missed his best ever chance of capturing an Olympic medal. With his voice breaking, a tearful Joyce told the assembled Irish media: 'I have to live for years with what I did today. The hardest part is that this is the Olympics. Hopefully, I'll come back. But … it's hard. I'm young, but four years is a long way away.'

Walsh, too, warned that Joyce might not get a second chance. 'There's no second chance here and you might not be here in four years. Johnny [John Joe] could find it very difficult to qualify in four years' time. That's the name of the game. It's sport, it's cruel and we all suffer.'

While Joyce did win a bronze medal at the European Championships in Liverpool six weeks later, he didn't make it to the London Olympics in 2012.

Nevin's Beijing adventure also ended in the last sixteen but he could have no complaints as he went down 9-2 to a Mongolian opponent Enkhbatyn Badar-Uugan. The 2008 Olympics were always going to be a learning experience for the youngster. 'I remember back in 2007 people were telling me I was too young to enter the Elite championships. But Billy (Walsh) said to go for it. He said I could win the title and go on to qualify for the Beijing Olympics. But he said, "If you qualify, they're not your Olympics – your Olympics will be in 2012."'

Attention then switched to Barnes and Sutherland, who had byes into the last sixteen. First into the fray was Sutherland, who had already announced that he planned to turn professional immediately after the Games. He was three points down within a minute against Algerian Nabil Kassel, who had also received a bye into the last sixteen. But once the twenty-six-year-old Irishman found his range with his left hook, his opponent was on the defensive. He took the first of four standing counts, just before the end of the first round.

The Algerian fought back in the second stanza to lead 10-9 at the end of six minutes. It was also tight in the third round until just before the end when Kassel took a second standing count, though incredibly the Sutherland punch that sent his opponent reeling was not registered by the judges. With the scores tied at 14-14 early in the final round, the contest was still wide open until the Algerian finally gave up the ghost in the closing two minutes. Sutherland scored with a succession of shots. At 21-14 the fight came to a premature end when a left jab, right hook combination sent the North African stumbling through the ropes.

Sutherland's post-fight interview was as entertaining as the fight itself. 'I've never been in a dull fight in my career and there was never a period in that fight when I was going to protect a lead. I'm here to fight. But I'm not like a dancer trying to move out of the way. I can box but I like to fight.'

Barnes's Olympic debut was less dramatic but equally rewarding. The twenty-one-year-old was 3-2 down at the end of the first round. He restricted his Ecuadorian opponent, José Luiz Meza, to one point in the second round while he scored four. The third round was marked level (3-3), but Barnes comfortably outpointed his opponent 5-2 in the final round on his way to a 14-8 win. 'Having waited for a week, I was very, very nervous. I couldn't sleep all week. I wanted to go home. I had been preparing for this all year.'

Despite a brave ninth place finish from Robert Heffernan in the 20 kilometres, Roisin McGettigan reaching the final of the steeplechase and Paul Hession's exploits in the 200 metres, by the end of the first week of the 2008 Games, the focus of the Irish nation had switched to the boxers. Barnes, Sutherland and Egan were now one victory away from a place on the medal podium. Keegan's original forecast of one podium place in Beijing seemed outrageously conservative, but Walsh was preaching caution. 'We have won nothing yet.'

The only fly in the ointment in the Irish camp was the appointment by the

IABA of Jim Walsh, the secretary of the association's Munster Council, as the boxing team manager for the Beijing Olympics in preference to Gary Keegan, the director of HPU.

Team managers at the Olympic Games have a different role compared to their counterparts in Gaelic football and soccer. In boxing, the team manager is responsible for everything that happens outside the stadium, while the coaches take over once the boxers enter the competition arena. Essentially, team managers co-ordinate all the logistics surrounding the boxers' participation in the tournament. While they have overall responsibility for the welfare of the boxers, they are not specifically involved in coaching them.

Within the IABA this issue had festered for nearly a decade. The crux of the problem is that the Central Council of the association has a tradition of appointing one of their own long-serving members as team manager for international tournaments, including the Olympic Games, which angers the coaches and the boxers and is frowned upon by the Irish Sports Council.

'I remember talking to Gary [Keegan] about this the first week the High Performance Unit was set up. I told him, "Make sure you are the team manager for the next Olympics." But he didn't push it' recalls Billy Walsh.

The IABA had overlooked Keegan for the position of team manager for the Athens Olympic Games in 2004. Nobody had paid much heed then, but in Beijing it snowballed into a major controversy. While the then minister for arts, sports and tourism Martin Cullen sat in the plush VIP seats at ringside, the man who had led the HPU had to watch his protégés from a bucket seat high up in the bleachers. Ironically, the VIPs had better access to the boxers than Keegan who had to meet them near a side entrance to the stadium.

Seven years after the controversy, Dominic O'Rourke, who was the IABA president at the time, has finally broken his silence on the issue. According to his version of events, Keegan attended a meeting with the Olympic Council of Ireland together with the officer board of the IABA. 'I said to Gary: name your team [of boxing officials]. Gary Keegan named his own team of officials but didn't name himself. He could have named himself.' Keegan's reaction to this was simply to say, 'It was never my position to appoint myself. That's all I'll say about it.'

Keegan knew more than twelve months in advance of the Games that he wouldn't be team manager in Beijing but opted not to tell the boxers until much later. 'For Billy and me the focus at the time was not doing anything that deflected from the preparation of the team. It wasn't new to us. We only raised it in the boxers' psyche closer to the Games because they needed to know how things were going to be organised so it wasn't a shock to them when it happened.'

The fact that it was announced five months before the Olympics that Keegan had been appointed as director of technical services at the Irish Institute of Sport (a position he was to take up after Beijing) appears to have been a source of irritation within the IABA.

'The Board of Directors of the IABA decided that we would keep him on [as director of the HPU] because if anything happened to the boxers at the Olympic Games it would have fallen back on the association that we got rid of Gary Keegan. That's the truth of it,' says O'Rourke.

The Olympic Council of Ireland (OCI) is perennially caught in the crossfire of this ongoing saga. 'We leave it up to the sports bodies themselves to nominate the manager and we accept their decision unless there is something really horrendous like they are sending their granny or auntie. We had this issue in Athens and I believe it may arise again in Rio. In my opinion, Gary Keegan had no role whatsoever in Beijing. He was involved in High Performance and could go where he wanted. As far as we are concerned, the coaches are the important people. This is an internal dispute in boxing and we try not to get involved in it,' says OCI President Pat Hickey.

However, the ISC takes a different view. John Treacy described what happened in Beijing as not ideal. 'Fortunately it had no impact on the boxers' performance. Sports are beginning to move on from the stage of giving the job of team manager to somebody who has given twenty years' service to the sport. There is merit in that if you don't have professional people in place. But sport has kicked on and the governing bodies need to make sure that they have high performance people travelling to these major games with their teams. End of story,' says Treacy.

The strained relationship between the ISC and the OCI on this issue was underlined by a report in the *Irish Examiner* during the height of the controversy. In it, Hickey said the OCI were 'never asked before they left Ireland or over there for any accreditation for Gary Keegan. Dominic O'Rourke gave us a list of who he wanted accreditations for and that was approved and we followed the rules rigidly.'

However, Paul McDermott, a spokesman for the ISC, said they had made a direct request to the OCI at the Olympic Performance Committee to have Keegan accredited. 'We felt that Gary, who had been head of High Performance for the previous five years, had a role and a very useful role to play at the Olympic Games, and it was because we felt so strongly about it that a formal request was made through the channels.'

Official accreditation at the Olympic Games is the passport which opens all doors. Keegan didn't have that laminated pass in Beijing, which made life very difficult for him both on a personal and professional level. For the duration of the Games he stayed in a fourth-floor apartment in the Chaoyang district of Beijing. The boxers visited him every day.

He had to be persuaded to go and see them in action. 'He was so heartbroken he wasn't even going to come to watch us boxing; he was going to watch it in the hotel. I went down and had a chat with him. He said he would be there for the sake of the team. So he came. I popped in regularly to see him but it was terrible that he wasn't with us in the Olympic village,' says Egan.

Coaches as well as athletes dream about making it to the Olympics. 'My dream was to go to the Olympics too. In 1996, I'd been involved in the final camp for Atlanta and I remember Gussie Farrell [who was one of the Irish boxing coaches at the Atlanta Olympics in 1996] saying to me, "It won't be long before you get your turn." So even before the programme, I felt I had a chance of going to an Olympics,' said Keegan in an *Irish Independent* interview.

Reflecting on it all now, he is at pains to stress that the accreditation issue is history. 'It's gone; it doesn't matter. At the time it was difficult; very difficult. You're in the blood, the sweat, the tears, the emotion, the planning and the strategy. I was there for every step and then to be pulled out at that point when you are so personally connected. I never wanted to be a spectator. I hadn't been a spectator from the concept of the programme. I had always been in it. It was difficult but you get over that.'

So there was no John Rocha-designed suit for Keegan, not even an official kit bag, but he did bring home four precious mementoes from Beijing: four vests signed by the boxers. A fifth signed by Nevin was pilfered from his bag. Another memento – an autographed picture of the three medallists, Egan, Sutherland and Barnes – now hangs in the living room of his home. Delivered exactly a year after the Olympics, it was a present from team doctor Jim Ryan who wrote a message on the back of it.

On the eve of Egan's Olympic final bout Keegan couldn't sleep. Alone in his apartment, he composed two long messages of thanks on his mobile phone. He forwarded one to the boxers who had missed out on the Olympics and the other to those who had worked with or helped out with the HPU during the previous five years. Dr Ryan transcribed the exact message on to the back of the picture. Timed and dated: August 23, 2008, 2.14am it read:

'On the eve of the Olympic final in the city of Beijing I find sleeping a little difficult. My thoughts are of the journey and not the destination and the people I have had the privilege of sharing this five-year experience with. I want you all to know that although you are not here to witness our arrival at the Olympic Dream in person; you were all very much in this apartment room with me this morning. I can't find words (because I left my dictionary at home!) to describe what all your contributions have made to me personally and our boxers, contributions equal to and as valuable as the rest of our support team who are here right now. Thank you all for staying the distance on what has sometimes been a difficult journey for all of us. I am honoured to say I was part of your team.' Gary Keegan.

'When I got the picture I was happily upset, but when I turned it over and saw the text message you can imagine how I felt. It was a big moment for me. It is the most precious gift I received out of the Games,' says Keegan.

Inside the Irish camp, coach Zaur Antia was experiencing every father's worst nightmare, but only Walsh knew about the turmoil he was enduring. While Antia was on route from Vladivostok to Beijing with the rest of the squad on 6 August, his wife Nona and their youngest son George were flying to Georgia to visit Zaur's eldest daughter and her husband in their home in Poti. Twenty-four hours later the country was at war with its giant neighbour, Russia.

After the break-up of the Soviet Union, a war between ethnic Georgians and Ossetians had left part of South Ossetia under the de facto control of a Russian-backed government. Tensions began to escalate again in April 2008, culminating in Georgia launching a large-scale military operation against South Ossetia on the night of 7 August. The Russian response was swift and brutal. They airlifted troops into South Ossetia and launched air strikes against targets in Georgia, including the Black Sea port of Poti ,which they eventually occupied, albeit temporarily. The Antia family found themselves trapped in a war zone. One bomb landed five hundred metres from Zaur's parents' home and shook the entire port area, killing sixteen people.

There was virtually a communication black-out in the besieged city, and Zaur spent three fruitless days trying to make contact with family members in Poti. 'It was terrible, I was flipping,' he remembers. 'I couldn't contact them or find them anywhere.' Eventually he got through to a friend in the Georgian capital of Tbilisi who was able to trace the whereabouts of his family. 'My wife and children were hiding in the mountains in her sister's house and I was able to make contact with them.'

Everybody wasn't so fortunate: 244 Georgian civilians, including boxing acquaintances of Antia's, and 169 members of their armed forces were killed in the conflict. Had his eldest son, David – who was born in Georgia – gone back with his mother, he could have been conscripted into the Georgian army. The war ended on 12 August, though the last of the Russian troops didn't leave Georgia until October. 'It was a very difficult time, but I had to put my professional relationship with the boxers first.'

Barnes had good reason to fret before his bronze medal fight against Poland's Łukasz Maszczyk. The Holy Family boxer made his senior international debut on 15 October 2006 in an international against Poland in Loughrea, County Galway. Maszczyk toyed with him, winning by 16 points (25-9). 'I wasn't confident at all. He had hammered me.' Twenty-three months later, though, the Belfast light fly was a different proposition.

Barnes's fight was scheduled first for the session on Tuesday, 19 August. It was to prove a historic evening for Irish boxing. By now, the Irish fans were more plentiful and boisterous than ever before. The fight was level 2-2 after round one. Then Barnes went to work in his trademark frenetic fashion. Maszczyk must have wondered where the timid youngster he had previously demolished was. Barnes won the second 5-3 and the two subsequent rounds 2-0. Long before the finish, he knew he was in medal territory. His six-point winning margin (11-5) underlined his dominance. 'It demonstrated how much I had improved. I'm sure he was confident going into the fight,' he recalls.

Just over two hours later, Kenny Egan stepped into the ring for his medal bout against Washington Silva from Brazil, whom he had sparred with at the training camp in the Philippines prior to the 2005 World Championships. In truth, there was never a doubt about the outcome, Egan oozed class. His opponent couldn't cope with the Irishman's southpaw style as reflected in the fact that he failed to register a single score against Egan. The Irishman clocked up eight points to secure a place in the semi-final. Ireland had just enjoyed their most productive session at an Olympic Games since that famous Saturday morning in Barcelona in 1992. John Treacy could finally relax. Meanwhile, Irish boxing aficionados garnered extra satisfaction from the fact that these two medals came in two weight divisions in which Ireland had never medalled previously. Ireland had now won a total of twenty-two Olympic medals, exactly half of them in boxing.

Twenty-four hours later, it was the turn of Darren Sutherland to attempt to make it a round dozen. His opponent Alfonso Blanco Parra from Venezuela had beaten him 20-13 at the World Championships in Chicago on his way to winning the silver medal. The Irishman exacted revenge in the most decisive manner imaginable. In arguably his greatest-ever performance in the ring, Sutherland totally outclassed his opponent as the scoring confirmed. He won the first round 3-0; the second 3-1, the third 3-0 and the last 2-0, for an overall 11-1 triumph. For the Irish team it was a momentous breakthrough. For the first time since the 1956 Olympics in Melbourne, Ireland would have three boxers competing in the Olympic semi-finals.

Even before the official opening of the Beijing Olympics, Zou Shiming was one of the host country's top tips for a gold medal. When the country's top athlete, defending Olympic champion, Liu Xiang hobbled out of the track before the heats of the 110-metre hurdles, resulting in nearly ninety thousand disappointed fans exiting the Bird's Nest Stadium in record time, the nation's focus switched to the Workers' Gymnasium.

A bronze medallist at the Athens Olympics, Shiming was a double world champion and had beaten Barnes en route to winning his second title in 2007. For the first time in the tournament the Irish fans were not the most vocal in the stadium. Instead, thousands of Chinese jammed the arena to support Shiming. From an Irish perspective the fight was an anti-climax. Seven years later Barnes acknowledges that he lost to the better boxer, but he still bristles about the score. He has valid reasons for being annoyed. Frankly, the 15-0 verdict was absurd.

'I knew I lost the fight, but the scoring was a disgrace. I remember hitting him in the first round and his head flew back, but he got a point for it. He was very muscular and was a bit too fast for me. I've never watched the fight, but boxing judges I know slowed it down and they said the score should have been 12-4 which I would have accepted.'

But the five judges: Wayne Rose (Australia), Enrico Apa (Italy), Pierre Chiasson (Canada), Kim Jae-bong (South Korea) and Armando Carbonell (Columbia) thought differently. As is his wont, though, Paddy had the last word. Selected for a random drug test after the fight, Barnes memorably declared in a TV interview that it was the judges who should be drug tested after handing down such a decision. 'It was funny,' acknowledges Walsh. 'Paddy is a great guy; very passionate. Sometimes he lets it all flow. That's who he is.' The authorities could have thrown the rule book at the boxer, but Barnes has no regrets. 'I still say the judges should have been sacked. There is no place for such people in sport.'

Winning the bronze medal changed his life, though it wasn't until he returned to Ireland that he realised the impact of the Olympic Games. 'I never watched the Olympics or any other sport on TV when I was growing up. I didn't appreciate how big it was until I got home. People wanted to have their picture taken with me. I was thinking, "Why do they want a picture with me?" They looked on me as a hero.'

In contrast to Barnes, Egan and Sutherland were hotly tipped to win their semi-final bouts. Based on form, the latter ought to have had the measure of his British opponent James DeGale. Sutherland had won four of their previous five clashes – the most recent being a 22-16 success in the final of the EU Championships in Poland, eight weeks previously, when as Walsh recalls, 'He put DeGale on his ass.' Winning the bronze medal seemed to satisfy Sutherland's ambitions, though the fact that, according to Egan, Sutherland did a two-hour warm-up may have contributed to his lethargic performance. Whatever the reason, it was obvious that Sutherland was a shadow of his former self, even though the fight was level 1-1 at the end of the first round.

Billy Walsh has clear memories of how the fight went down. 'Zaur and I looked at each other at the end of the first round; we couldn't believe what was happening. Then we began to realise he had settled for the bronze medal, which was disappointing because for me he could have been the gold medallist. He obviously wanted to go pro after the Games. Getting into the shop window as an Olympic medallist was going to help him. But if he had got the gold medal how much more value would it have been to him. Zaur and I were gutted.'

Technically, Sutherland was still in the fight after two rounds when he trailed 3-1, but sensing his opportunity, the British middleweight pressed home his advantage to win the third 5-1 and ultimately take the bout 10-3. Forty-eight hours later, the Londoner captured the gold medal with a surprise win over the Cuban Emilio Correa Bayeux, whose cause wasn't helped when he was deducted two points for allegedly biting his opponent's shoulder in the first round. DeGale's winning margin was two points.

Kenny Egan was literally the last man standing for Ireland. He ought to have felt the pressure; in fact, he was arguably the most relaxed Irishman in the stadium as he revealed in his autobiography, 'It was just a happy time in my life, where everything was good.' Like Sutherland, he faced a British opponent, Tony Jeffries, who he had beaten in the gold medal bout at the EU Championships in Poland the previous June. Egan simply had too much class and speed for his opponent and won probably more convincingly than the 10-3 verdict suggests.

Just as he was doing a post-fight interview with RTÉ, the other semi-final between the surprise local pin-up hero Zhang Xiaoping and Yerkebulan Shynaliyev from Kazakhstan, who had beaten both Zhang and Jeffries on his way to winning a bronze medal at the 2007 World Championships, was getting underway. It was a grim low-scoring affair that ended 4-4. A hush descended on the crowd as they awaited the result of the countback. The arena erupted into a crescendo of noise when Xiaoping surprisingly got the decision.

The possible consequences of the result for Egan never occurred to him. 'I remember I wanted the Chinese fighter to win because Shynaliyev is very small and harder to hit. Afterwards, I said to myself, "Lovely, now I have a chance of winning the gold medal." It never dawned on me that I was going to get a raw deal in the final,' he recalls.

At the time, Egan didn't share those views with the media. Instead, he entertained us with a humorous account of his woes when he was a lesser-known figure in Irish sport. We never checked the veracity of the tales he regaled us with. Perhaps the stories were apocryphal but they were entirely in keeping with the giddy mood that prevailed in the mixed zone late that Friday night.

Egan claimed he had once served US golf superstar Tiger Woods and his then wife Elin their dinner at Dublin's City West Hotel, when the US team were in Ireland for the Ryder Cup in 2006. At the time, Egan was doing a 'nixer' as a waiter to earn a few extra bob, but the job had unusual downsides, he insisted. 'It got to the stage where I was walking by tables and women were slapping me on the arse and all sorts. I'm a quiet lad. I'm not into that kind of stuff. I was sweating going around the place. It's not right, but it was a bit of crack up there.'

Prior to travelling to Beijing, he had sold his car. 'If there is anybody out there who wants to sponsor me a car, they are more than welcome. As I said, I'm still living at home, so if somebody wants to sponsor me an apartment for a year, they can give me that too. I'm on the bones of me arse.'

Listening nearby, Zaur Antia might not have fully grasped the nuances of Egan's Dublin accent but he thought the country's newest sporting hero was much too happy. And he wasn't slow in telling him either. 'I said to him, "This is nothing [the silver medal]. Now, go and rest and think about the final." I'm afraid some boxers are just satisfied to win a medal and the fire is gone. That is what happened with Darren [Sutherland] because once the fire is gone it is very difficult to bring it back.'

While the mood back in Ireland was positively radiant that Sunday morning as thousands tuned in to RTÉ to watch the build-up to the final, inside the Workers' Gymnasium the Irish fans were much more sombre. The arena had been virtually taken over by Chinese fans, who were creating an unbelievable din having seen Zou Shiming win the country's first-ever gold medal in boxing a couple of hours earlier. For once, the 'Olé, Olé, Olé' chorus from the Irish was drowned out.

'We just had to deal with it,' says Walsh. 'Look, the Chinese fighter had massive support but we had our own plan.' The unspoken fear though among the Irish observers was that unless Egan could knock out his opponent his chances of getting the verdict was at best debatable.

His fate hung with the five judges sitting around the ring: Kassymkanov Berikbol (Kazakstan), Peter Dorko (Hungary), Artit Somchai (Thailand), Enrico Apa (Italy) and Juan Ponce (Cuba). The light heavyweight final was the penultimate contest on the 2008 Olympic boxing programme. Egan got off to the worst possible start. He was tentative in the opening three minutes and was two points down at the end of it. Walsh knew he now faced an uphill battle. 'We've done the stats over the years. Eighty percent of boxers who win the first round win the contest. If you win the first round, it is very hard for judges to change tack because they want to be on the winning side as well.'

Egan was less perturbed. 'I had a terrible start so when I heard I was two points down at the end of round one I said, "Fair enough." But I had a good second, a great third and a good fourth. I also knew that once they (the judges) kept him ahead I was never going to win the fight.'

The second and third rounds were drawn 3-3 and 2-2 respectively, although any objective view of what actually happened in the ring – as opposed to the reaction of the partisan crowd – would argue that Egan won both of them. Still Egan was only two points behind going into the last two minutes, but Xiaoping nicked it 4-2 according to the judges to win the contest 11-7. From an Irish perspective, there was no fairytale ending to a remarkable success story.

Six weeks after he returned to Ireland, when the first wave of celebrations had subsided, Egan sat down and watched the contest again. 'Naturally I counted the scores and I won it by two or three points. But, look, I hold no grudges against Zhang. He was doing what he had to do. If I was offered any medal at the start of the game, I would have taken it with both hands.'

The staff in the HPU did a detailed analysis. 'He should have won it by five points,' according to Walsh. 'Of course, it was a tough one to take. But what a journey for this guy! He failed to qualify for the Athens Games; he only made it to Beijing in the final qualifier. Then he goes and reaches the final and performs with all that charisma,' says Billy Walsh.

Egan earned a bonus of €15,000 from the ISC for his efforts in Beijing, bringing his total funding under the carding system for the year to €55,000, making him the highest paid athlete in the carding scheme. Katie Taylor was the second biggest recipient with €50,000. The other medallists in Beijing, Sutherland and Barnes received €15,000 and €10,000 respectively in bonuses; officially they were called performance incentive payments, bringing their annual grants to €35,000 and €38,333 respectively. Nevin and Joyce both received a €5,000 bonus bringing their 2008 grants to €25,000 each. Uniquely the five Irish boxers were all eliminated by the eventual gold medallists: Zou Shiming (light fly), Enkhbatyn Badar-Uugan (bantam), Felix Diaz (light welter), James DeGale (middle) and Zhang Xiaoping (light heavy).

Of the thirteen Olympic sports funded by the ISC only five (boxing, badminton, sailing, swimming and fencing) achieved their targets in 2008. Yet in terms of funding, boxing still lagged behind. The IABA received a grant of €255,462 from the ISC in 2008, less than other sports organisations such as the Athletic Association of Ireland (€1.3 million), Horse Sport Ireland (€1.03 million), Badminton Ireland (€401,150), and Irish Sailing (€334,019).

Admittedly, the IABA's High Performance programme fared better with a grant of €540,000, though this figure was less than the equivalent programmes in equestrian (€736,635), athletics (€681,000), rowing (€635,000) and hockey (€550,000) received.

Twenty-four hours after the final, Egan, Barnes, and team psychologist Gerry Hussey finally got a chance to visit the Great Wall of China. It was to prove the last moment of true peace that Egan had for a long, long time. He wasn't to know it, but the biggest battle of his life was about to begin.

CHAPTER 13

THE IN-BETWEEN YEARS

'Boxing is a crazy sport; putting two guys in a ring and allowing them to beat the head off each other for nine minutes. It's absolute madness. On the other hand, it's nature at its best. It is the survival of the fittest and there is no escape. On a hurling field if you have a bad day, there are fourteen other guys to cover for you. If you have a bad day in the ring, you are alone.'

Darren O'Neill

Just six weeks after the closing ceremony of the Beijing Olympics, Europe's Elite boxers assembled again for the 2008 European Championships in Liverpool's Echo Arena. Ireland's Beijing medallists Kenny Egan, Darren Sutherland and Paddy Barnes stayed at home, while John Joe Nevin's non-selection resulted in a public spat between his club coach Brian McKeown and the president of the IABA Dominic O'Rourke.

However, John Joe Joyce – who was unlucky to lose on a countback to the eventual gold medallist Felix Diaz in Beijing – got some measure of compensation when he picked up a bronze in the light welterweight category. Joyce was beaten in the Euro semi-final by the silver medallist Hungarian Gyula

Káté, who he had beaten in the first round in Beijing. Ross Hickey (light) and Eamon O'Kane (middle) also secured bronze medals as Ireland finished eleventh in the medal table.

Ryan Lindberg (bantam), David Oliver Joyce (feather) and Con Sheehan (heavy) were beaten in their medal fights while Conor Ahern (fly), Willie McLaughlin (welter) and Darren O'Neill (light heavy) exited the championship at an earlier stage.

It was a particularly frustrating time for Darren O'Neill, a one-time talented underage Kilkenny hurler who opted to pursue a boxing career after being selected to represent Ireland at the 2006 European Championships. Two years down the line, though, his career had effectively run into the sand. Sometimes he wondered whether he was simply born at the wrong time.

O'Neill had watched from a hotel bedroom in Galway as his friend Kenny Egan received his Olympic silver medal. He had never beaten Egan – but had fashioned wins over the Olympic champion Zhang Xiaoping and the bronze medallists Yerkebulan Shynaliyev and Tony Jeffries. 'I was delighted for both the lads [Egan and Sutherland] because I knew them so well, but I was also completely demoralised. I had beaten the Olympic gold and bronze medallists, along with world and European medallists, yet I still hadn't won a national Elite title. So I decided to give it one more go.'

As a junior, O'Neill competed in the light heavyweight division, though he usually weighed in at least three kilograms shy of the 81 kg limit. A Russian, Igor Mikhalkin – now enjoying a career in the professional ranks – ended his chances of a medal at the European juniors in Warsaw in 2003.

Still, seventeen-year-old O'Neill looked an identikit candidate for the new HPU. Fifteen months later O'Neill stepped into the ring at the National Stadium to face Egan in the Irish Elite light heavyweight final. Egan was three years older and aiming for his fifth Elite title and third in a row in the category.

After just one round the challenger was telling his coach and father, Ollie, to cut off his gloves because he was leaving.

'I thought the scoring was scandalous to be honest. I was 6-1 down after the first round. I was probably a bit naïve but I came back to the corner expecting to be ahead or level. So I said to my dad, "I'm getting out of here." Predictably, Ollie O'Neill persuaded his son to change his mind, but the deflated rookie lost 27-7.

The two boxers clashed again in 2006. 'I remember throwing a left hand early in the second round. I knew straight away I had left myself completely exposed. Kenny ducked to the left. I was off balance and before I could tense up he cracked me with a body shot. I went "arrgh" and spent the remainder of the round trying to recover. He went five points up which basically ended the fight which was a pity.'

By now, O'Neill was studying to become a primary school teacher in St Patrick's College in Drumcondra. He used to hitch a lift to training from Sutherland, who was studying nearby in Dublin City University (DCU), for the journey across town to the National Stadium. O'Neill was immersed in his studies for his summer exams in 2006 when he received a call from Billy Walsh. Sutherland had sustained a serious eye injury in an international match against Russia which ruled him out of the European Championships in Bulgaria at the end of the summer. Walsh believed that O'Neill was the ideal candidate to replace the middleweight even though he boxed in the light heavyweight category.

O'Neill got another shock a couple of days later when he stood on the scales. The arrow stopped when it reached 84.9 kgs – nine kilograms over the 75 kg middleweight limit. 'I remember thinking, "My God, what's happened to me?" I'd never been so fat in my life. With the exams coming up, I was stuck in my room studying all day. It was easier to throw a pizza in the oven than do any cooking.'

He had a sporting decision to make before he accepted Walsh's invitation. He was a member of the Kilkenny U-21 hurling squad at the time. In his last appearance in a challenge match against Tipperary he scored three points from play and held the future Tipperary midfielder star James Woodlock scoreless. It looked like he would make the team for the forthcoming championship.

'A lot of people would have stayed and hurled with Kilkenny because it is such a big thing in the county. In boxing you do a lot of things by yourself – from the suffering to the success – but it was also a family thing for me.' Darren's family is steeped in boxing lore. His father, Ollie, his godfather Tom and his uncle Joe founded Paulstown Boxing Club; his mother Carmel is club secretary, and his two brothers Aidan and Daniel box with the club.

O'Neill accepted Walsh's invitation and spent the summer of 2006 shedding the weight in preparation for the Europeans. Together with Egan, Roy Sheahan and Eric Donovan he travelled to a Russian training camp in Chekhov. The latter pair, both members of St Michael's Boxing Club in Athy, were coached by IABA President Dominic O'Rourke, and had competed at the World Championships in Chicago in 2007 but had missed out on Olympic selection.

Unlike the majority of his colleagues, O'Neill didn't baulk at the food. 'Maybe it's the country boy in me but I'd eat anything. I used to say to the boys, "Just eat it. Don't ask what it is." I can tell you there were no Michelin stars in any of the Russian or Ukrainian training camps we attended over the years. I didn't care. Some of the boys struggled and used to go out shopping for pot noodles and stuff like that.'

The judging at the 2006 European Championships frustrated O'Neill to the point of distraction. 'The scoring back then was crazy with a massive number of points being awarded. In one of the finals the score was 43-30.' Donovan bowed out in the preliminaries but O'Neill, Sheahan and Egan all reached the quarterfinals but only the latter won a medal.

O'Neill is unlikely to ever forget the name of the Scottish boxer who beat him. Fundo Mhura was born in Malawi and represented his native country in the welterweight division at the Commonwealth Games in Melbourne the previous March. However, he had moved to Scotland when he was five weeks old and boxed for his adopted country at the Europeans and moved up to the middleweight category.

'Basically all he did for the entire fight was run around the ring. He'd come in with a shot to the body or a one-two. I remember in the second round he stepped in and threw this body shot. I stepped back and he missed me. In those days the crowd could see the scoring live on a TV monitor and everybody started to boo. I realised later he had got a point for that shot even though it hadn't gone next or near me.

'With twenty seconds to go in the third, I hit him with a body shot which put him down. When he got up he let off two shots neither of which hit me. Then the bell went. I assumed it was the end of the round. Instead, it signalled the end of the fight which was stopped under the twenty points rule. It was such a pity because I would probably have stopped him in the fourth round.'

O'Neill was back in Ireland for the latter stages of the All-Ireland U-21 Hurling Championship. Kilkenny beat Tipperary by a goal in a replayed final. Future Kilkenny All-Ireland winning senior captains, James 'Cha' Fitzpatrick, Michael Fennelly and TJ Reid all featured, as did future senior medallists Kieran Joyce, John Tennyson, Richie Hogan and Richie Power. These players became household names, not just in Kilkenny but nationwide, due to their exploits on the hurling field in subsequent years which underlines what O'Neill potentially missed out on by opting for boxing.

Meanwhile, O'Neill injured his left hand in the semi-final of the 2007 Tammer Tournament in Tampere, Finland. His Estonian opponent Alexander Rudjuk lasted less than a round but the damage was done. O'Neill had to concede a walkover in the final, but that was the least of his worries. Now committed to the middleweight division, the chances were he would have to beat the defending Irish title holder, Darren Sutherland – fit again following surgery on his eye injury – in order to win an Elite title and boost his chances of being selected on the Irish team for the 2007 World Championships.

Due to Darren's injury he had no choice but to train for the championships using his right hand only. But he recalls how positive he was feeling despite this setback, 'I was still boxing out of my skin. I sparred Kenny [Egan] and was thinking, "Nobody is going to beat me." Disaster struck, however, when in his final spar O'Neill broke his right thumb. In his absence Sutherland comfortably retained his middleweight title, beating European bronze medallist Eamon O'Kane in the final. This put him in pole position to secure a place on the team for the World Championships in Chicago the following November and put him ahead of O'Neill in the pecking order for Beijing.

O'Neill had a chance to reverse that at a tournament in the Ukraine later that year. Mindful of the intense rivalry between the pair, the HPU unit brought O'Neill and Sutherland to the training camp and organised for them to be on the opposite sides of the draw in the subsequent tournament. O'Neill boxed a Ukrainian in the semi-final. Again, disaster struck, as he recalls: 'I broke my right thumb again, in a different place. I actually boxed on and caught him with a lot of body shots. He got the decision 13-9 but his coach apologised to me afterwards and said I should have won.

'Darren [Sutherland] was the body shot specialist and having seen me hurt this lad badly with body shots there was a feeling he could put him away. Instead, he lost by a big margin. If I hadn't broken my thumb out there, I could have been selected for the World Championships.'

Like the other members of the HPU, Sutherland underperformed at the

Worlds, but he beat O'Neill 21-15 in the Elite final in 2008 which essentially ended O'Neill's Olympic ambitions. However, Sutherland's decision to turn professional after winning a bronze medal in Beijing left a vacancy in the middleweight division which O'Neill slotted into.

By the time 2009 rolled around, much had changed in the HPU. Though it was widely anticipated that Walsh would succeed Gary Keegan as its new head, neither the Sports Council nor the IABA seemed in any particular hurry to fill the post. Walsh effectively ended up with two jobs: he was acting head of the HPU and head coach.

Meanwhile, Ireland's star performer at the Beijing Olympics, Kenny Egan, was on a slow but seemingly inevitable path towards self-destruction as a result of his drinking. But as far as the outside world was concerned it was business as usual in the HPU.

In fact, performances were actually getting better. At the 2009 European Union Men's Elite Championships in the Danish city of Odense, Irish boxing reached another milestone when they topped the medal table with an unprecedented haul of nine: gold for David Oliver Joyce (feather), Darren O'Neill (middle), and Con Sheehan (heavy). Declan Geraghty (fly), John Joe Nevin (bantam), and Willie McLaughlin (welter) all won silver while Eric Donovan (light), Philip Sutcliffe (light welter) and Egan (light heavy) captured bronze. Every team member won a medal as Ireland didn't compete in the light flyweight or super heavyweight categories.

But Ireland's ambitions extended way beyond the EU Elite Championships at this stage. They had set their sights on the World Championships which were taking place in September in Milan's Mediolanum Forum. For Paddy Barnes, however, the World Championships turned into a nightmare. Inevitably, it was a controversial judging decision which caused the rumpus. Though Barnes's opponent Peter Mungai was forced to take two standing counts, it mattered little to the judges who gave the Kenyan the verdict by a farcical eleven points (15-4). The Irishman did not even earn a point for forcing his opponent into the second count late in the fight.

'I went ballistic,' acknowledges Barnes. 'I had done loads of hard training, spending months away from home and then to be treated like that. I just couldn't believe it, particularly after the two standing counts. So I took off my gloves and kicked them out of the ring. They were probably the same judges that I had in the Olympics in Beijing. Had the fight been judged on the scoring system which is used now I would have won 30-25 because of the two counts. Those judges should have been drug tested as well,' he suggests, with a grin. After his defeat in the Olympic semi-final in Beijing he made similar comments about the judges.

Barnes was sent home the next day and his grant was suspended. 'I didn't realise until the day after the fight that I was being sent home. I wanted to go home anyway. My grant [from the Sports Council] was withheld for a few months, but eventually I got it all back.'

His emotional reaction to dodgy decisions stems in part from his ultra-competitive instincts. 'I don't know where I got it from. But I just love to win and I hate when anybody gets the better of me. I'm not the fastest runner but when I go training on the track, for example, I'm never last. I always want to beat somebody. Sometimes it's heartbreaking when you don't get a decision. You can do all the training in the world and do well in the fight and there is still no guarantee that you will actually win. The judges have to like you,' he laments.

Kenny Egan fared only marginally better inside the ring – and infinitely worse outside of it – in Milan. He made a tame exit in the quarter-finals, losing to a French opponent, Abdelkader Bouhenia, (17-9), whom he had beaten before. At his best, he believes he could have won a gold medal in Milan, or at least ended on the podium, but he hadn't done enough conditioning work in the run-up due to his binge drinking. Worse still, he went on another bender in Milan after his exit and got so drunk that he had to be helped into the team hotel by a referee and a Brazilian doctor. Billy Walsh had to sit up with him all night in case he got sick or choked. The escapade earned him a five thousand euro fine from the IABA.

In boxing it is arguably more difficult to win a medal at the World Championships than at the Olympic Games. Up until this year there was no pre-qualifying so all the top boxers who are fit compete in the worlds. Just fourteen countries medalled in Milan in 2009. Ireland was one of those countries – thanks to the exploits of bantamweight John Joe Nevin. Still only twenty, he came of age at the event. By the time he faced Chinese opponent Gu Yu in his medal fight he had accumulated forty-three points and conceded just eleven in his previous three contests. He edged his Chinese opponent 7-5 before going down by the narrowest of margins (5-4) to Russia's Eduard Abzalimov in the semi-final. The latter lost to Bulgaria's Detelin Dalakliev in the final.

While Ireland had won twelve Olympics medals in the previous fifty-seven years, Nevin's bronze was only the sixth world championship medal garnered by an Irish boxer since the launch of the event in 1974. And it was the first since James Moore won bronze in Belfast in 2001.

The build-up to the next significant event on the international boxing calendar, the 2010 European Championships in Moscow were fraught with difficulties as well. The previous March, the *Irish Independent* revealed that IABA President Dominic O'Rourke had been chosen instead of Billy Walsh to head up the HPU.

'I applied for the job, did two interviews, during which I laid out what I had done as a coach and various other things and I got the job,' says O'Rourke.

Billy Walsh says, 'I didn't get the job. End of story really. It was a difficult time and I did come close to packing it all in. Then I would be letting other people win. I'm not a quitter.'

The ISC reacted by withholding funding for the position. A stand-off developed between the two organisations which effectively left both Walsh and O'Rourke in 'limbo'. 'This was a matter between the trustees [of the IABA] and the Sports Council and I wasn't involved,' says O'Rourke. While coy about what went on behind the scenes, John Treacy, the then chief executive of the ISC, said: 'Let's put it like this. We would have been huge supporters of Billy Walsh and we didn't want anything to disrupt that pipeline or investment.' He rejects the notion that the Council ought to have been more forceful on the issue by becoming directly involved. 'We cannot tell national government bodies what to do,' he argues. Of course, by withholding funding the ISC were effectively forcing the IABA's hand on the issue.

Remarkably the controversy had no impact on the performance of the Irish team at the European Championships in Moscow; in fact, it appeared to galvanise them. Of the nine boxers selected all but flyweight Declan Geraghty had won Elite titles in their respective weight divisions at the 2010 Irish Championships.

Kenny Egan (light heavy), Paddy Barnes (light fly), John Joe Nevin (bantam) and John Joe Joyce – who had moved up to the welterweight category – had competed at the Beijing Olympics, while Eric Donovan (light) and Darren O'Neill (middle) had boxed at the 2006 European Championships.

Apart from Dublin-born Geraghty, the only other international rookies on the team were Derry native Tyrone McCullagh, who boxed out of the Donegal-based Illies Golden Gloves Boxing Club, and Mayo teenager Ray Moylette, who had won a gold medal at the World Youth Championships in Guadalajara, Mexico in 2008.

After his travails in Milan at the 2009 World Championships, Paddy Barnes was on a mission of redemption in the Russian capital, though he wondered how the judges would score the fights involving the host country. 'Russia is one of the hardest countries to go to and try to win something.' On this occasion his luck held; he avoided the Russian champion David Ayrapetyan, who was beaten 5-3 by Elvin Mamishzade from Armenia. The latter proved his pedigree by going all the way to the final.

On the other side of the draw, Barnes breezed through, beating his three opponents – from Hungary, England and Spain respectively – by a combined tally of eighteen points to qualify for the final. And he delivered in the decider, restricting his opponent to a single point while he scored four. Barnes was Ireland's sixth gold medallist at European level; the first ever in the light flyweight category and the first since featherweight Paul Griffin won in 1991.

'Winning that European gold medal in Moscow was probably one of the biggest achievements of my career. It's up there with my Olympic medals and I would rate it better than the Beijing bronze. I remember when the Irish national anthem was being played I was looking around at the other boys on the team and I thought it was a great moment.'

It was a stunning European Championships for the Irish. Billy Walsh and Zaur Antia were the two busiest coaches in the Ice Stadium on the penultimate day of the event. Five of the Irish squad made it through to the last four; only the host country had more boxers in the semi-finals. In the event Tyrone McCullagh (feather), Eric Donovan (light) and Egan (who lost again to Frenchman Abdelkader Bouhenia at light heavyweight) had to be content with bronze medals. Arguably, though, it was the performance of Darren O'Neill which was the pick of the lot.

Unlike his colleagues, O'Neill held down a full-time job outside boxing; he was a primary school teacher in Donaghmede on Dublin's northside. While he was allowed to take official leave for the championships, which were held in June, he had to pay for a replacement teacher while he was away in a training camp in the Ukraine. 'I wasn't entitled to get leave to go to the camp, which was a bit ridiculous.'

Even though O'Neill had opted to concentrate on boxing rather than hurling, his love affair with the game was far from extinguished. He brought a couple of hurleys and half a dozen sliotars on all his boxing trips abroad. Conor McCarthy, the squad's physio, who was from Waterford, would be his hurling partner, while later his room-mate John Joe Nevin joined him for a puck around.

While O'Neill loves boxing, he doesn't have a blind loyalty to it. 'It's a crazy sport; putting two guys in a ring and allowing them to beat the head off each other for nine minutes. It's absolute madness. On the other hand, it's nature at its best. It is the survival of the fittest and there is no escape. On a hurling field if you have a bad day, there are fourteen other guys to cover for you. If you have a bad day in the ring, you are alone.'

The 'sweet science', as boxing is sometimes euphemistically labelled, was rated 'the toughest sport in the world' by the TV sports network ESPN in 2014. An eight-member panel, made up of sports scientists from the US Olympic Committee, academics who study the science of muscles and movement, and sports journalists, classified sixty sports under ten different headings, ranging from analytic aptitude to endurance. Boxing came out on top. Ireland's indigenous games of Gaelic football and hurling were not included in the study.

O'Neill played competitive hurling at a reasonably high level. He discovered to his cost that there was no comparison between the fitness requirements of the two sports. 'I was often very fit for a hurling game. Then I'd step into a boxing ring and be beat after one round. Boxers require a different kind of fitness. Our heart rate is up to ninety-five percent of its maximum for the nine minutes of a fight.'

Tiredness sets in rapidly as the boxers' glycogen stores – in layman's terms, the fuel for their muscles – rapidly depletes. Being hit accelerates the rate of fatigue, while inappropriate dieting to make a weight will leave boxers drained of energy in a multi-fight tournament. O'Neill personally experienced what it's like to box when his glycogen stores were running low. 'This happened to me when I was boxing in the 75 kg category and had to lose weight quickly to make the limit. I was cutting out too many carbohydrates and, as a result, the glycogen stores in my muscles were burning rapidly.'

The psychological demands of the sport are equally complex. Taking hits plays tricks with the boxers' minds, according to O'Neill. 'Boxers try and not think about being hit. Occasionally after being hit you would go "Oh God" and once that creeps into your head you're beaten. Instead of thinking about scoring, you're thinking about curling into a ball and protecting yourself. Sometimes ego can take over and an opponent will try to disguise the fact he's hurt by rushing in and leaving themselves open.'

O'Neill's coming of age as a top-class international boxer accelerated at the training camp in Ukraine prior to the Europeans in 2010. None of the boxers showed any inclination to spar against the Ukrainian middleweight Sergey Derevyanchenko, as O'Neill recalls: 'All the boys were avoiding him. But I was in his weight division and I volunteered to spar him as I figured I would probably meet him at some stage in competition.

'I was down close under my arms thinking I could relax for a second. But from about two inches [range] he nearly upended me with a shot into my ribs. It was like falling off a bike and not being able to catch your breath. I didn't want to show him I was in trouble, but my legs were stuck to the ground. I was thinking, "Shit, I'm going to be drawn against this fella one day."'

Every subsequent day during the camp O'Neill braced himself for three minutes of torture from the Ukrainian. Gradually his confidence levels soared. Still, his heart sank when he checked the draw sheet in Moscow. He would have to beat Derevyanchenko to secure a medal. By the time the quarter-final came around O'Neill's mental resolve was resolute despite his physical appearance.

O'Neill cut his nose in a tense 4-2 first round win over Ronald Gavril from Romania. He comfortably beat England's Anthony Ogogo 10-1 in the next round but sustained a cut over his eye. 'I was black and blue even before I got into the ring with Derevyanchenko. I decided I was going to make it as hard as possible for him to beat me. I started exceptionally well and was two points up after the first round. I slipped a bit in the second, probably trying to defend the lead, and it was all square after six minutes. There was a break with twenty seconds remaining. I glanced over at the corner and Billy pointed one figure down so I assumed I was one point down.'

The direction of his entire career probably hinged on what happened in those twenty seconds. 'I managed to level it up. Then, right on the bell I circled around to my own corner and threw a jab and a left hook. The jab knocked his head back and the hook struck him on the shoulder. Even though his head popped back, I think it was the other punch that the judges counted. Anyway, they gave me the score and I won 7-6. It was crazy and while winning my first Elite title and qualifying for the Olympics were the highlights, winning that fight was the most satisfying victory of my career.'

O'Neill comfortably beat Bulgarian Mladen Manev 6-0 in the semi-final before succumbing 16-7 in the final to the Russian Artem Chebotarev. 'Fighting a Russian in Russia in a final was never going to be easy. I was 5-4 down after the first round and then at the start of the second I did a double jab and knocked his head right down. I said "lovely", and though he came back with a flurry, most of his shots hit my arm, though one got through my guard.' The judges saw it differently. Chebotarev went 8-5 after this exchange of blows, effectively sealing the result.

Still, O'Neill became only the fifth Irishman and the first since 1998 to win a silver medal at the European Championships. Coincidentally, it was another middleweight, Belfast's Brian Magee, who had won that silver medal twelve years previously in Minsk.

The only disappointing result at the 2010 European Championships was John Joe Nevin's below-par performance in the quarter-final of the bantamweight category, where he bowed out tamely (7-1) to nineteen-year-old Gamal Yafai from Birmingham. 'I went into those championships too confident. I was eyeing up the gold medal. I thought I had nothing to do but turn up. I took my eye off the ball and paid the price. These things happen,' says Nevin who avenged the defeat at the Feliks Stamm Memorial tournament in Warsaw the following April.

Overall, though, the championships were a resounding success for the HPU. At the 1939 European Championships in Dublin Ireland finished second in the medal table behind Italy with a total of three medals – two gold and one bronze. Russia did not compete internationally in those days. As anticipated by Paddy Barnes, the Russians dominated the 2010 event, winning seven of the eleven gold medals on offer and one bronze. Ireland's haul consisted of one gold, one silver and three bronze medals.

So just seven years after the establishment of the HPU Ireland was the second most successful country in the signature championship on the most competitive boxing continent on the planet. Among those waiting to greet the team on their arrival back in Dublin airport was Dr John Lynch, then chairman of the IABA's Board of Trustees. He asked to see Walsh privately, where he informed him that he had brokered a deal between the association and the ISC. Dominic O'Rourke was to be appointed director of boxing development, while Walsh would be in charge of the High Performance Programme with the title head coach. 'Happy days, but it hasn't really transpired like that,' says Walsh.

O'Rourke rejects the notion that there was ever any malice between them. 'We got on ok, we're boxing people. The two of us had the same goal. It wasn't as if we fell out.' O'Rourke's contract with the IABA which finished on 31 August 2014 wasn't renewed. 'I was disappointed. But I had no say in it. The association is bigger than any one individual.'

CHAPTER 14

A HIGH PRICE

'Darren was a very special young man. He was a character, flamboyant yet insecure. He used that flamboyance to make himself believe. He was the only guy on the team that I texted every day. I deliberately did that because he needed reassurance. Once he had a little bit of attention, everything was okay.'

Billy Walsh

I t was a Monday afternoon, 14 September 2009. Kenny Egan was drinking in the Oliver St John Gogarty pub in Dublin's Temple Bar when his mobile rang. He's not certain now who made the call. He thinks it was Hazel O'Sullivan, the ex-girlfriend of his fellow Olympian Darren Sutherland. He will bring her brief message to the grave. Darren was dead. He was discovered hanging in his Bromley apartment in Kent earlier that day by boxing promoter Frank Maloney. All Egan could say was 'Jesus Christ'.

That evening, throughout the country, similar phone calls were made. Gary Keegan was driving along the M1 after work when he took a call from a friend who was close to Darren. 'I nearly crashed the car. The shock was incredible.' He rang Billy Walsh who was on his way home to Wexford. Walsh can still recall how Keegan broke the tragic news. 'Gary just said, "I have bad news. Darren has been found dead." I had to pull in to the side of the road. I couldn't believe it.'

Darren O'Neill was celebrating his twenty-fourth birthday with his two housemates in the Porterhouse North bar in Glasnevin when the call came. 'The number came up as Jimmy Haplin's, who was Darren's old coach in St Saviours Olympic Boxing Academy.' O'Neill sensed straight away that something was awry. 'I had returned the previous day from the World Championships in Milan. Jimmy was with us on the trip working as a coach so I was wondering why he was ringing me so soon afterwards. I went outside to answer his call. When I walked back in, my friends knew straight away that something was up. The colour had drained from my face. It was horrifying. It was such a shame because I think he would have been one of the greats,' says O'Neill.

Darren was a unique individual. Even though he was only twenty-seven when he died, he packed more life experiences into those years than many will manage over a full-term life span. His parents, Anthony Sutherland and Linda O'Brien, met in a blues club in London. They were both emigrants. Anthony was from the Caribbean island of Saint Vincent, while Linda hailed from a large family in Glasnevin on Dublin's northside. They fell in love and Linda was determined that the couple's first child would be born in her native city. Darren arrived in the Rotunda Hospital on 18 April 1982, but lived most of the first ten years of his life on Tottenham Court Road in north London.

Even though Anthony Sutherland never boxed he had an abiding interest in the sport. Father and son spent Friday nights together on the couch, watching 'Fight Night' on ITV, which featured household names like Nigel Benn, Chris Eubank, Michael Watson and Steve Collins. Darren loved boxing, so much so that he sneaked around to the local community centre, where he took part in a mini-boxing tournament, won a trophy and got a bloody nose! When his mother saw him, she banned him from boxing. He didn't step into the ring again until he was fourteen.

When his father secured a job with his brother, who was a building contractor on Saint Vincent Island, the family headed to the Caribbean. The island is about a third the size of Ireland's smallest county, Louth, and has a population of approximately 100,000. In an extended interview with the author in 2008, Darren recalled his life on the island. 'It was a real change in lifestyle. I went from being forbidden to leave my road to being able to go on all these adventures. I imagined I was heading off into the jungle, though really it was only a forest.' The biggest shock came, however, when he enrolled in the local primary school. Much to his horror, he discovered that corporal punishment was still legal. 'I was very chatty and tended to answer back a lot. So I got my share of slaps on the hand from the leather strap.'

According to Darren, his mother found it hard to settle being so far away from her family, so in the mid-nineties the family uprooted again and moved to Ireland, settling in a housing estate in Mulhuddart in west Dublin. The family budget was stretched to breaking point due to Darren's penchant for enrolling in every sports club in the parish. Having already bought him a new pair of football boots and a karate outfit, his mother baulked at the notion of purchasing him a pair of boxing gloves when he joined St Brigid's Boxing Club in nearby Blanchardstown.

Gary Keegan was still running the club. 'Anybody who met Darren Sutherland will never forget their first meeting. When he walked through the door of the gym, the first comment he made was that he was going to be the first Irish black world champion in professional boxing. He was fourteen years old at the time,' recalls Keegan.

'From the moment he stepped into the ring it was obvious that he had huge potential. The most impressive thing was his long rangy jab which was very powerful. He was in the Boy 4 Division and got to the latter stages of the All-Ireland in his first season at a time when there was a particularly talented bunch of boxers coming through.'

His life took an unexpected turn while studying for his Junior Certificate in 1998. Comedian Brendan O'Carroll was making a boxing-themed film in west Dublin, which was to have been called *Sparrow's Trap*. It proved an ill-fated project; the financial backers pulled out two days before filming was due to begin, leaving O'Carroll with reported debts of £2 million. The film was never released.

Unwittingly, Keegan helped Darren secure a walk-on role in the film. 'I got a call from the County Board saying this film was being shot and they were looking for a black boxer and I think we were the only club who had one at the time. So I sent him along. He was getting one hundred pounds for the day, which was great because he liked to have a few quid in his back pocket.'

Darren was looking forward to meeting future European super bantam-weight champion Esham Pickering, who also had a role in the production. When he went to Pickering's dressing room – a double decker bus – he bumped into the boxer's trainer, Sheffield-based Dubliner Brendan Ingle. He was then one of the most influential coaches in British professional boxing having mentored Prince Naseem Hamed for eighteen years.

'The story goes that immediately he [Darren] saw Brendan Ingle, he rec-ognised who he was. So he dropped his bag and started throwing punches and telling him he was going to be the next big thing in terms of professional boxing and Ingle was pretty taken by his personality,' says Keegan.

Half an hour later, Darren had secured an invitation to train in Ingle's famous gym in Wincobank in Sheffield. 'He loved the whole idea of me being a black Irishman,' recalled Darren, who couldn't wait to tell Keegan the excit-ing news. He was taken aback by his coach's vehement opposition to the idea.

'I had a bit of a falling out with him over the issue,' confessed Darren.

'I was against it I guess really at the beginning,' says Keegan. 'We had done our research and the evidence was there to suggest that professional boxing is a man's world, not a boy's world. Even at adult level the percentage of guys who make it to the top is so small it is just a tiny factor.

'My view at the time was, let Darren have a really good amateur career. He had started well and we wanted to see where it would go. But he saw the offer as an opportunity for him and he just wanted to go and there was no holding him back.' After that, Keegan only had contact with Darren when they had the occasional cup of coffee if they bumped into each other in Blanchardstown Shopping Centre when Darren was back visiting his family.

Darren had completed his Junior Certificate before he headed off to England at the tender age of sixteen. He trained twice a day, cooked and washed for himself, had a part-time job as a sales assistant in a sports shop and studied for three A levels. He secured an A grade in sports science, though he had to drop his other two subjects due to time constraints.

Such was his commitment to boxing that on occasions he didn't come home for Christmas. When I interviewed him in December 2008, Darren acknowledged that he had made mistakes. 'I specialised too soon. I had no life outside boxing.' And he realised just how fickle the sport was.

Ryan Rhodes was the rising middleweight star in the Ingle stable. In 1999, however, he was sensationally knocked out by another English middleweight, Jason Matthews. Darren remembered seeing Rhodes get knocked out. He thought at the time, 'What makes me any different?', and he ended up hating boxing. 'I was due to turn pro and got cold feet. I would have come back earlier, but I didn't want to come back a failure. I was embarrassed.' In due course, he packed his bags and left Sheffield. He knew that the key to his future lay in education. Returning to school at the age of twenty was a challenging experience, however. Eamon Gaffney, the principal of St Peter's College in Dunboyne – where Darren's younger sister Nicole was a student – accepted him into the school's Leaving Certificate cycle.

Darren thrived; he became the school's DJ, was named Student of the Year and obtained 475 points in his Leaving Certificate which helped him secure a sports' scholarship in Dublin City University, where he studied for a degree in sports science.

Gradually he fell in love with boxing again. He didn't return to St Brigid's Boxing Club. Instead, he joined St Saviours Olympic Boxing Academy based in Dublin's Dorset Street, where he trained under the watchful eye of John McCormack. Success at Elite level was not instantaneous. In the 2002 Elite Championships a nineteen-year-old Sutherland lost to eventual champion John Duddy. The following year he bowed out to the future WBO world champion Andy Lee, whose decision to turn professional in early 2005 was just the break Sutherland needed.

Outright victory in a multi-nation tournament in Liverpool in 2005 under-lined his potential; he beat his Beijing nemesis James DeGale 27-13 in the final. But he needed convincing before signing up to the HPU project. 'He came in to see what we were doing,' recalls Walsh. 'He was unsure of getting involved. He never wanted the Olympic Games; he wanted to be a world pro-fessional champion. Then he got caught up in our ethos and the Games and thrived in it.'

According to Gary Keegan, Sutherland knew what he wanted from the HPU. 'He was checking us out as much as we were checking him out at the start. He was a challenging individual to work with. He challenged us to be better and challenged us to consider him as an individual and we had to do that and learn that one size doesn't fit all. Above anybody else Darren taught us that.'

The stray thumb of a Russian boxer, Danil Shved, nearly ended Sutherland's career in May 2006 in the National Stadium. The accidental blow damaged the muscle in his left eye. 'The muscle that moves the eye upwards was damaged. It was an awful time. The doctors weren't sure if the injury would ever clear up. I couldn't leave the house because of the double vision and I was embarrassed as it looked as if I was cross-eyed,' he recalled. In his absence, Darren O'Neill boxed at the middleweight division at the 2006 European Championships and looked set to challenge for a place on the Irish team in the 75 kg category for the 2007 World Championships.

Following surgery, Darren got the all-clear to resume boxing, though he was again contemplating giving it up at the end of 2006. 'The turning point came when I went for a run on Christmas Eve with all those demons in my head. I just thought: "Screw this. Let's have it! I owe nobody anything. I'll do this for myself." I had no doubts from then on. I knew I'd beat him [O'Neill] and go to Beijing,' Sutherland revealed in an *Irish Independent* interview on the eve of the Beijing Olympics in 2008. In the event, O'Neill missed the 2007 Elite Championships due to injury. Darren retained the middleweight crown – a victory which ultimately set him on the road to Beijing.

It was no surprise when he signed professional forms with British promoter Frank Maloney after his triumphant return from China. Born in Peckham, south-east London, Maloney – whose late father, Tommy, was a native of Tipperary and whose mother, Maureen, is from Kimmage in Dublin – made his name in boxing in the nineties. Against considerable odds, he signed British-born boxer Lennox Lewis shortly after he won the gold medal in the heavyweight category for Canada at the 1988 Olympics. Lewis later became the third boxer in history to win the world heavyweight title on three occasions. A flamboyant figure, Maloney ran for the office of Mayor of London in 2004, finishing fourth. Last year he was on the front pages of the tabloids when he revealed he was undergoing a sex change and now wanted to be called 'Kellie' Maloney.

On 17 November 2008, Darren moved to London; initially he stayed with Maloney and his second wife, Tracy, in their semi-detached home in the leafy dormitory town of Chislehurst in Kent. At the inquest into Darren's death there was evidence given that Maloney had re-mortgaged his home to secure the finance to sign the Olympic bronze medallist.

Darren returned to his alma mater, DCU, to make his professional debut on 18 December 2008 against Georgi Iliev. The Bulgarian journeyman lasted just two minutes and forty-four seconds before the referee intervened to save him from further punishment. Now branded 'The Dazzler', Darren had three more professional fights during the first half of 2009, winning them all within the distance. Indeed, his four professional fights only lasted a total of thirty-eight minutes and forty-eight seconds.

However, his final fight in the York Hall in Bethnal Green, London, on 30 June was the toughest. Against a Ukrainian opponent, Gennadiy Rasalev, who was three inches taller, he shipped a lot of punishment. By the end of the first round his right cheekbone was beginning to swell and a nasty cut opened up under his right eye at the start of the fourth round. Ironically, the referee stopped the fight after seventy-six seconds of the fourth round on the instructions of the ringside doctor who had examined a cut over Rasalev's left eye. Billy Walsh actually saw the fight. 'I was on holiday in Bulgaria and I just happened to walk into a bar and it was on the television. I noticed he [Darren] got a bad cut under his eye.'

To the outside world, Darren's dream of becoming a world professional champion looked on target. But sometimes everything is not as it appears, as Darren's Beijing colleague Kenny Egan knew only too well. In the months after the 2008 Olympics, Egan was one of the most fêted and photographed males in Ireland. Ahead of the Beijing Games, the HPU had prepared the boxers for virtually every possibility. What they hadn't counted on was one of them becoming a celebrity. Darren Sutherland didn't drink and he was focused on signing a professional contract, while Paddy Barnes lived in north Belfast. So inevitably the media spotlight fell on Egan. For somebody who was already developing a dependence on alcohol it proved a near fatal cocktail. Walsh sensed the worst even before Egan started to miss training. 'You had only to look at the papers; he was in every nightclub in Dublin, pictured with every model in the place.'

The issue became public in March 2009, when Egan and a friend Stephen O'Reilly headed off to party in New York without telling anybody. However, the latter wrote an oblique message on a Twitter account he had opened for Egan stating: 'This could be my last Tweet for a while. Cannot say any more!!!! Kenny Egan has left the building. Take care y'all!!'

Predictably, his unexplained absence – he was due to box for Ireland in an international against the US that weekend – and the message on Twitter sparked a media frenzy. Journalists camped at Dublin Airport and outside Egan's parents' home in Clondalkin. By the time the pair arrived back after their seven-day sojourn in the Big Apple the reporters had left the airport. However, as a precaution, Keegan and Walsh arranged with a friend who worked in the airport for Egan to be ushered out a side entrance.

The boxer spent the next few days in Keegan's home, where he sweated the alcohol out of his system by running on the nearby strand in Bettystown. 'I got off the plane in an awful state. I had fallen in a lift in New York and my face was cut. Fair play to Gary [Keegan] he looked after me. The media wanted to get a picture and they were offering a couple of thousand for it.'

Nineteen days later, Egan was due to box Olympic gold medallist Zhang Xiaoping in a re-match of their Olympic final on the undercard of the Bernard

Dunne-Ricardo Cordoba world title fight in the O2 Arena in Dublin. Not surprisingly, Egan was in no fit shape to box anybody – never mind the Olympic champion. 'I'm not joking; the first morning I had run about two hundred metres on the beach when I had to stop. Half of me was saying: "I will be ready" [for the fight]. The other half was saying: "There is no way I will be ready." I was offered good money (€20,000), but I had to pull the plug on it. It's a big regret of mine that I didn't fight the Chinese guy.'

He travelled to Belfast to link up with the Irish squad who were training in the University of Jordanstown. The media finally got their 'Egan picture' in comical circumstances. The team's transit van wouldn't start one morning and the boxers got out too push it. An eagle-eyed photographer noticed the commotion and snapped the picture. Next day the caption in the papers read: 'Kenny EgAAn'.

Egan continued to drink. Such was his state of mind when he heard the tragic news of Darren's death he assumed that the training scheduled for the rest of the week would be called off. 'So I just kept on drinking right through the funeral and for a few days afterwards.

'That was me being a selfish bastard. I thought that with the funeral I would be able to drink away under the radar and nobody would be looking for me to go training. When I turned up at the funeral I was shaking like a leaf. I remember giving his father a hug and I'll never forget his comment, "Don't ever go professional."'

At times, when his demons threatened to overwhelm him, Egan also thought about ending his life. 'Being honest, in my drinking days I thought I would be the first of our group to die. I thought about suicide. There is a big bridge over the West Link beside my house and I thought of jumping off it a few times when I was sick of everything. 'Darren was the perfect athlete – the way he trained, his diet, getting up at 4am to eat his porridge. I remember waking up in the middle of the night once when we roomed together on a trip, and he was skipping. I don't know what happened to him, no one knows for sure. Was it the pressure? Was he lonely? It was just terribly sad.'

Gary Keegan believes that Sutherland had the potential inside the ring to make an impact in the pro game. 'In fact, what happens in the pro game between the four corners really suited his style, ability and skill. But the environment outside the ring wasn't conducive to what he needed. He needed a support network around him. He needed reassurance; he had phenomenal potential and capabilities, but he needed people that he could trust,' says Keegan, who knew that Darren was struggling at the time to adjust to his new life as a professional boxer. 'His death was a major shock to us and one which I haven't gotten over. It is still devastating.'

Billy Walsh remembers he got an inkling of Darren's state of mind when he visited the HPU shortly before the boxer's death. 'He wanted to see the physiotherapist because he was having some problems with his knee and asked if the psychologist was around.' During the visit Walsh discovered that an infection had developed in the cut that Darren had sustained in his previous fight. He had been unable to spar and his next fight was due on 16 October. 'He would never get into the ring unless he was one hundred percent fit,' says Walsh.

'What happened was awful. One can only imagine what it was like for his parents. He was a very special young man. He was a character, flamboyant yet insecure. He used that flamboyance to make himself believe. He was the only guy on the team that I texted every day. Just little messages like, "How are you today?" "How are things?" I deliberately did that because he needed reassurance. Once he had a little bit of attention, everything was okay.' Walsh goes on to recall a poignant comment Darren made to the other boxers from the HPU on that final visit. 'He said to them: "Do you know how lucky you are? I have to pay for this treatment and everything else.'"

Meanwhile, Egan's drinking continued to spiral out of control; so much so that in early 2010 Walsh sent him home. 'He was shocked when I did that. I told him to come back when he wanted to be a High Performer again.' Egan admitted in his autobiography that he was also addicted to porn. 'I was completed addicted to porn too. I'd wake up and be watching the stuff for hours. I was in a terrible way,' he admitted.

Eventually Egan joined Alcoholics Anonymous in April 2010. He went back training and secured a bronze medal at the European Championships in Moscow the following June. However, he fell off the wagon during a trip to Uganda with the A-Z children's charity later that summer. In his autobiography he gave a candid account of how he lapsed at a farewell party thrown for him before he left Uganda.

'I was looking at this Smirnoff bottle of vodka on the table and I swear it was looking back at me,' recalled Egan who admitted that he should have left the party at that point. Instead, he succumbed to temptation. 'I could feel the gorgeous warmth of the vodka going down my neck. I felt it in my veins and it was so, so nice.' Ninety minutes later, he had to be carried out of the house. 'Shortly afterwards, I was down for the count,' he said.

His mother noticed that he had lapsed when he returned home. One morning she took him to the graveyard where two of her sons – both of whom had died when they were infants – were buried. Egan recalled in his autobiography how his tearful mother berated him for his behaviour as she pulled weeds off their graves. Later that day, a shaken Egan phoned Walsh.

Walsh remembers the call. 'I was in the office in the gym. He was sitting outside in his car but he didn't want to come in. We drove up to the track in Sundrive. Even though it was pissing rain, we got out and walked around for maybe an hour. He told me about the incident with his mother. He was crying and shaking when he recalled how his mother had said, "I couldn't save them but I'm going to save you." I cried with him,' recalls Walsh.

Dominic O'Rourke arranged for Egan to book into a rehab treatment centre in Enfield and he hasn't touched alcohol since 12 August 2010. Egan confesses, 'I don't have a relationship with alcohol now, none whatsoever. Whenever I think about having a drink I fast forward ten days and visualise where I would be and it's not a nice place. I think I would have had this problem with alcohol irrespective of my boxing career. But it probably wouldn't have surfaced until later in life. It was a blessing in disguise that I hit rock bottom so quickly, otherwise I could have been drinking away until I was forty or fifty and end up with nothing.'

Even though his boxing career petered out, Egan succeeded in rebuilding his life outside of the ring. He joined Fine Gael and was elected to South Dublin County Council in the 2014 local elections. Last Christmas he announced his engagement to his fiancée Karen Sullivan.

For the Sutherland family the torment continues. Less than a year after their son's death they were given permission to exhume his body, which is interred at St Finian's Cemetery in Navan, in order for a second post mortem to be carried out. The official inquest into Darren's death was held in the Coroner's Court in Croydon in March 2012. During the four-day hearing a clearer picture emerged of the boxer's state of mind immediately prior to his death. One of the medical witnesses, as well as Ismay Bourke, a friend of the boxer, revealed that Darren had spoken to them about committing suicide.

Evidence was given that the eye injury which Darren had sustained in his last fight, and which had become infected, was a major source of worry for the boxer, who had become increasing concerned over the possible financial implications of breaking his contract with Frank Maloney.

Darren had been treated by his GP, Dr Natasha Haugh, for the injury. She had seen the boxer three times: twice for his infected eye cut and once for sleeping problems. She said he had been suffering from low mood and complained he did not have much of a support network where he lived. He was prescribed sleeping tablets to help restore his sleeping pattern and had begun seeing a counsellor.

Detective Sergeant Lee Dunmore of the Metropolitan Police headed the investigation into the boxer's death. In his evidence, Dunmore said he believed the boxer had killed himself because of depression, loneliness from living in London, concerns about leaving the sport and repaying Mr Maloney, problems with his training, and an unhealed eye wound.

The family did not give direct evidence to the inquest. However, in a statement read to the inquest Anthony Sutherland said that the day before his death, his son revealed he was having doubts about his professional future. 'He said he wished he had given up boxing when he came back from the Olympics. He said if he gave up, he would have to pay Frank Maloney £75,000.'

He didn't want to fight on 16 October but had added, 'I'm damned if I do and damned if I don't, because if I do I'm going to get beaten, but if I don't Frank is going to pull me out and I'll have to pay him his money.' In her statement, his mother, Linda, said her son was 'anxious' but she did not believe he was depressed. She added, 'Although Darren had concerns and worries, I do not believe he was suicidal at the time of his death.'

In his direct evidence, Frank Maloney said he received a phone call while he was on holiday in Portugal from Darren's psychologist Joe Dunbar who said he was concerned about the boxer. Maloney later received a call from Sutherland's trainer Brian Lawrence who told him the boxer had been at the gym and told him he did not want to box anymore. Maloney acknowledged that he had told Darren he would not let him walk away with the £75,000 contract he had signed but that he could keep the purses for the fights which had already taken place.

The coroner, Dr Palmer, recorded an open verdict. Explaining his rationale not to record a verdict of suicide, Dr Palmer declared, 'A coroner in contemplating such a verdict has to be satisfied beyond reasonable doubt, not only that the individual did an act unaided, but also must be sure that he fully intended that it should end his life. Here I am persuaded that there is sufficient doubt to make me hesitate to return a verdict of suicide.

'The words I've heard over the last four days are words like: happy, always smiling, a gentleman, nice guy, charming, personable, determined, diligent, panicky, a worrier, a closed individual. He was anxious. He always tried to do the best and be the best he could. He lit up the room. He didn't want to let anybody down. Perhaps he was too sensitive and intelligent to be a boxer. And we heard he sustained this cut. Many boxers get cuts and they heal up. This clearly distressed him. There were clearly lots of reasons why he felt distressed.' Dr Palmer added that he would write to the British Board of Boxing Control to explore whether changes could be made to ease the transition from amateur to professional boxing.

In a statement read out by solicitor James Evans, the Sutherland family called for such changes to be made. They said: 'If anything is to be learned from the tragedy of Darren's death, it should be that the support mechanisms that exist for amateur boxers should also be there for them when they begin their lonely path on the journey to professional life. My clients hope that in this Olympic year and especially being this year held in London, that all young sports men and women who make the transition from amateur to professional status ensure that they surround themselves with those who they can trust and rely on.

'The Sutherland family will do all they can to come to terms with the way and circumstances surrounding Darren's tragic and untimely death. They will hold dear to them the memory of Darren, their beloved son, brother, friend and confidant.' The family also paid tribute to their lost loved-one, who they described as an 'ambassador of goodwill for Ireland'.

A statement issued to the author by the coroner's office in Croydon summarises the life and tragic death of the boxer:

'Darren Sutherland won a medal at the Beijing Olympics and became a professional boxer in October 2008. He sustained a cut to his face in June 2009 that was slow to heal and caused him much distress as he was unable to spar or fight. He became disillusioned with boxing but appears to have been unable to see a way out of what he perceived as contractual, moral, family and other obligations. He sought professional help for mental health issues in September 2009. He is last known to have been alive on the afternoon of 13 September 2009. He was found hanging from a radiator in his flat on 14 September 2009 and was pronounced dead at 15:11h. His intention cannot be determined beyond reasonable doubt. Conclusion of the inquest: open.'

CHAPTER 15

NEW KIDS ON THE BLOCK

'I come from a boxing family. Boxing was something I wanted to do from the age of six. I wanted to get in there and slap somebody's head off.'

Joe Ward

Not since the halcyon days in the fifties, when the duels between Fred Tiedt and Harry Perry had the crowds hanging out of the rafters, did the National Stadium witness the scenes that unfolded on the night of the Elite finals on 25 February 2011. The place was heaving long before the finalists in the men's and women's categories climbed into the ring for the traditional pre-fight preamble from Master of Ceremonies Al Morris.

Olympic silver medallist and double European bronze medallist Kenny Egan headed up arguably the most medal-laden group of Irish boxers ever assembled under one roof on Irish soil. Paddy Barnes, fresh from winning the Commonwealth title the previous October in India to add to his European gold and Olympic bronze, was there seeking his fifth consecutive light fly-weight title.

European silver medallist Darren O'Neill was due to fight a young Donegal middleweight, Jason Quigley, who had an impeccable pedigree at underage level. John Joe Nevin was a world bronze medallist, while Ross Hickey and Tyrone McCullagh had won bronze medals at European championship level. Indeed, the competitive nature of Irish boxing at the time was underlined by the fact that Tommy McCarthy and Steven Ward who had both won silver medals at the 2010 Commonwealth Games didn't make it through to the Elite finals; both were beaten by the eventual heavyweight champion Con Sheehan.

The most decorated boxer in the stadium that night was Katie Taylor, who by then had won three world, four European and three European Union titles. But, as had become the norm, there was no female lightweight in Ireland prepared to get into the ring with her so she was awarded a walkover.

There was no mistaking who looked the most confident male boxer before a punch was thrown. It wasn't Egan, who was bidding for a record eleventh successive senior crown, or Barnes, or Nevin, or O'Neill. I commented on this in the *Sunday World*: 'As the fighters were introduced to a packed National Stadium, seventeen-year-old Joe Ward displayed no nerves. He strutted into the ring, a mixture of self-assurance and arrogance. It was obvious that the youngster wasn't in the least intimidated at the prospect of sharing a ring with Egan for the first time.'

He had only become eligible to compete at Elite level the previous October when he celebrated his seventeenth birthday; the age limit has since been raised to nineteen. A settled traveller from Moate, County Westmeath, Ward's maternal grandfather Joe Joyce is the self-styled King of the Travellers and a renowned bare-knuckle pugilist. Long before he stepped into the ring to face Egan, Ward had built his reputation. 'I come from a boxing family,' says Ward. 'Boxing was something I wanted to do from the age of six. I wanted to get in there and slap somebody's head off. The club in Moate is about a mile and a half from my house and I used to jog there. As I got older the boxing became more like a business'

An only child, Ward came under the influence of his grandfather from an early age. 'Grandad: he does the real fighting. It is probably due to his career that I am in boxing. He was possibly the most influential person of all in the family because we all looked up to him because of what he's done.'

Ward played Gaelic football at underage level with Moate but a desire to express his individuality prompted him to focus solely on boxing once he reached his mid-teens. 'I wanted to be involved in a sport where I only had to depend on myself. I didn't like it when I had to depend on fourteen others.'

Watching the Irish boxers – including his cousin John Joe Joyce – compete at the Beijing Olympics fuelled his interest further. Even though he has never lacked self-confidence, Joe Ward was surprised when he won the light middle-weight AIBA World Junior title at the age of fifteen – just ten months after the 2008 Olympics. 'Young lads always think they're the best. Being realistic about it, though, I never thought I would be a world champion at that age. But I boxed very well out there and ended up with the gold medal.'

Ward won the title in June 2009, following a third round stoppage of local favourite Hayk Khachatryan in Yerevan, the capital city of Armenia. His per-formances during the event were simply stunning; he won three of his four fights – including the final within the distance – scored a total of forty points and conceded just six. By then he was a regular weekend visitor to the National Stadium for weekend squad sessions. Usually his mother drove him but occa-sionally he took a bus to Heuston Station and a taxi to complete the trip to the South Circular Road.

In 2010 he boxed at the renamed World Youth Championships in Baku. (This competition is better known by its former name the Junior Champi-onships.) Now competing in the middleweight category he was, once again, a class apart, beating both Russian and Cuban fighters before comfortably accounting for Australian Damien Hooper 6-2 in the gold medal fight. Five months shy of his seventeenth birthday, he became the first Irish boxer to win two world titles.

'Actually, my main goal in Baku was to finish in the top two to qualify for the inaugural Youth Olympics in Singapore later that year. Beating the Cuban and the Russian on the way took the pressure off so I could perform in the final,' he remembers.

His luck ran out in Singapore. He broke his hand in the first round of his first fight against Hooper who went on to win the title. Ireland's other boxer at the tournament, eighteen-year-old Ryan Burnett – who has since turned professional – won a gold medal in the light flyweight category in Singapore. The Belfast native beat Salman Alizade of Azerbaijan – who had beaten him in the World Youth Championships final three months earlier – to become the first Irish boxer to annex an Olympic youth title.

Despite the fact that he was still a teenager, Ward was adamant that he was entering the 2011 Elite Championships in the 81 kg category, which set him on course for a showdown against Olympic silver medallist Kenny Egan. 'I'm that sort of person; I always want to be the number one guy. Being only seventeen, I probably had no fear. I know a lot of people thought I was too young and rightly so. I enjoyed going up against one of the greatest amateur boxers of all time.'

Understandably, the bookies made him the 9/4 outsider. Not only was he competing at senior level for the first time; he had moved into the heavier light heavyweight category which Egan had dominated for more than half a decade. Having gone off the rails in the wake of his silver medal success in Beijing, Egan was slowly rebuilding his career and had been abstinent from alcohol since the previous August. But for once the bookies were wrong, as I reported in the *Sunday World* twenty-four hours later.

'Ultimately what we witnessed may have been the beginning of the end of one era and the launch of, arguably, an even more exciting one. Even though the referee Sadie Duffy took centre stage by issuing two public warnings to Egan for dropping his head, which cost him four points, there was no doubting Ward's ultimate superiority as reflected in the 11-6 final score.'

'I'll be back,' declared a defiant Egan afterwards. 'I'm not finished yet. This was just a blip. As I said to his face in the ring, he hasn't the flight to London [for the Olympics] booked yet. He's a strong lad for his age. The referee gave me two public warnings. I deserved one of them. It is very hard to come back after giving away four points in an Elite final.' As it transpired, the defeat did signal the beginning of the end of Egan's career. After enduring two more defeats against Ward, by margins of 19 and 20 points respectively in the 2012 and 2013 Elite deciders, Egan announced his retirement from competitive boxing. Ward's grandfather Joe Joyce made a triumphant by-pass through the ring after the decision was announced before he was ushered away by stewards.

Ward promised afterwards he would go one better than his opponent and win an Olympic title. 'I remember watching him in the Olympics. Kenny is a wonderful boxer; ten Irish titles and an Olympic silver medal, but I will go one better. I'm a mature seventeen-year-old. I'm one hell of a tough man as well,' said Ward when quizzed by journalists immediately after his victory. He also paid tribute to his first coach, Seamus Donnington. 'He's crying down there in the audience. He made me the man I am.'

Reflecting now on that famous night, the win remains one of the defining moments of his career. 'The feeling was indescribable when the final bell sounded. That bell always sounds good when you know you have won the fight. But to become one of the youngest ever boxers to win an Elite title and to beat Kenny in the final made it very sweet.'

Ward's win grabbed all the headlines the next day. But it was an equally momentous night for nineteen-year-old Michael Conlan from Belfast, who won his first Elite title in the flyweight category, beating Chris Phelan 11-7. To understand the significance of the win, it is necessary to explore his back story. His father, John, is a Dubliner and boxed for Drimnagh Boxing Club during his teenage years before moving to Belfast where he married a local girl and reared three sons: James (Jamie), who is now a professional boxer, Brendan and Michael.

The family watched big fights on television. As a twelve-year-old Michael was transfixed by the boxing action at the Athens Olympics in 2004. 'I was only a pup but I remember watching Andy Lee and Amir Khan. He was only seventeen but he did so well [he won a silver medal]. I said to my parents, "I'll be there one day."'

John Conlan – now the IABA High Performance coach in Ulster – brought his three sons, whom he later coached, to the St John Bosco boxing club on the Falls Road, where the careers of Olympians Freddie Gilroy, Sean McCaffrey and Martin Quinn had been forged.

Conlan had an outstanding underage career, culminating in his selection to box for Northern Ireland at the Commonwealth Youth Games in Pune, India, in 2008 when he was sixteen. He was beaten by a Kenyan in his medal fight. He made an apparently seamless transition into the senior ranks, winning his first Ulster senior title in 2009 when he beat Ruairi Dalton 3-2 – who had previously beaten Conlan's brother Jamie – in the final.

Losing to seasoned international Conor Ahern in the semi-final of the 2010 Elite Championships left Conlan devastated though. 'I was leading by five points going into the third round. But I kinda panicked. I didn't know what to do and I started to move instead of continuing what I had been doing up until then. He started to pull back the points and eventually won by three.'

Afterwards, the boxer had an unexpected visitor to his dressing room; Zaur

Antia. He invited Conlan to train with the HPU. 'He obviously saw something in me. It was great but I was raging at the time because I thought I was going to win the fight.' In the event, Conlan didn't accept Antia's invitation. Instead, he headed to the US to box with an Ulster team, winning his three fights.

Nonetheless, he got a call-up to wear the green vest in a prestigious two-leg international against Italy in March 2010. At the World Championships in Milan the previous September, Italy finished second to Russia with two gold medals which elevated them to the number one boxing nation in Western Europe. This didn't sit well with the ambitious Irish squad. But nobody could have foreseen what transpired in the second leg of the duel in the Donegal Celtic Sports and Social Club in west Belfast. Ireland won the first bout 7-5 in the National Stadium. The visitors were a bit miffed with some of the refereeing decisions, particularly Eric Donovan's 11-8 victory in his lightweight contest against world champion Domenico Valentino, the 2009 AIBA World Boxer of the Year.

The visitors' fortunes didn't improve in Belfast. Conlan made a dream debut in front of his own fans, dropping the highly-rated Italian flyweight Vincenzo Picardi, who had won bronze medals at Olympic, world and European level. The Irish got a fortunate decision in the featherweight category when James Fryers prevailed 5-4. Then when their pin-up hero Valentino lost for the second time in forty-eight hours – this time to David Oliver Joyce – the Italians had enough. They refused to continue and the remaining seven bouts were abandoned. The premature end to the event spoiled the occasion for Conlan. 'I was on a high after winning my fight but I couldn't enjoy the occasion as much as I could when they cleared off.'

Conlan's luck ran out at the 2010 Commonwealth Games, the following October in Delhi, when he lost on a countback in the first round to an unheralded Australian, Jason Moloney. 'My headgear came over my eyes in the first round; I tried to push it up. But I kept getting caught and I ended up eight points down. I pulled it back to 10-10 but lost 21-20 on the countback.'

Worse was to follow, however, when Conlan endured a shock 6-3 loss to Declan Milligan in the Ulster final in February 2011. 'I battered him; I don't think I've ever boxed as well since. But he got the verdict. All the papers were saying the result was a disgrace. I told every reporter that night that I was going down to Dublin the following week to win the Elite title.'

Conlan kept his promise, though it was by no means straightforward. His first-round opponent, Ryan Burnett, was the Olympic youth champion. Conlan won 4-3 before accounting for the defending title holder, Gary Molloy (10-5) in the semi-final. But his final opponent Chris Phelan appeared to hold all the aces when he led 5-0 but Conlan turned the contest on its head in the last two rounds, outscoring his opponent 11-2. This time he did accept the invitation to join the HP programme, though he didn't secure funding until he won the gold medal at the prestigious Gee Bee Tournament in Helsinki two months later. Even though he had been training virtually full time for the previous couple of years, moving to the HPU proved an intimidating experience initially.

'The likes of Kenny Egan were absolute heroes in my eyes and I didn't want to look stupid. I just clicked with them straight away, though at times life was very boring. Basically, all we did was eat, sleep and train. The older lads went to the bookies during the down time but they couldn't inveigle me to join them. I didn't have a clue about betting,' recalls Conlan.

Apart from Egan, one of the most disappointed boxers in the wake of the 2011 Elite finals was nineteen-year-old Ray Moylette. A seemingly innocuous incident the previous Christmas had a profound negative impact on his career. He was fooling around outside the family home with one of his dogs, a full-bred Staffordshire bull terrier called Mitzi, when he slipped on ice and broke his left hand. The Elite Championships were just eight weeks away. He made a valiant effort to defend his title but the odds were stacked against him. 'My preparations weren't ideal. I was only able to spar with one hand. I wasn't good enough against James McDonagh who beat me (5-3) in the quarter-finals of the light welterweight category. I thought afterwards that my boxing year was over, though it was only February.'

However, as he was receiving funding from the Irish Sports Council, Moylette was contractually obliged to continue to train with the HPU. In 2008, he overshadowed the growing fame of his Islandeady neighbour, future Taoiseach Enda Kenny when he became the first Irish boxer to win a gold medal at the World Youth Championships in Guadalajara, Mexico.

One of a family of seven, his brother Richard, who was eight years older, was the inspiration for his career. 'He won a Boy 2 All-Ireland title and my goal in life was to win two All-Ireland titles, and box once for Ireland in order to surpass his achievements.' They brought their rivalry into the ring once Ray got older. During one infamous spar Richard ended up with a broken nose courtesy of a vicious right hook delivered by his kid brother, who sported two black eyes afterwards. 'There was blood everywhere and my mother banned us from ever sparring against each other again.'

Ross Hickey ended up not only winning the light welterweight title at the 2011 Elite Championships but being named Boxer of the Tournament. He looked certain to be selected on the team for the European championships in June. However, he decided to join the Defence Forces later in the spring. His introductory phase of training clashed with Ireland's preparations ahead of the Europeans in Ankara and he couldn't make the final camp in Germany.

The beaten finalist Philip Sutcliffe – son of double European bronze medallist Philip Sutcliffe – was troubled by a hand injury, so Billy Walsh took a punt on Ray Moylette for the Europeans, which were brought forward twelve months to avoid a clash with the Olympic Games in London. 'I went out there without a bother in the world. All I wanted to do was to win one fight,' says Moylette.

The designated team captain, Paddy Barnes, was ruled out with a wrist injury as was newly-crowned welterweight champion, Wexford native Adam Nolan. It was a bitter blow for Barnes as he was the defending title holder in the 49 kg category. 'I was absolutely gutted that I wasn't there to defend my title, but it was simply not worth the risk,' he recalled. So a nine-man team – seven of whom were national champions – journeyed to Ankara and prayed that they wouldn't draw a Turkish boxer in the early scraps.

Ireland trained alongside the Great Britain squad at their final training camp which gave Michael Conlan an opportunity to test his skill against their flyweight champion, Khalid Yafai, a hot-shot prospect and favourite to win the gold medal. 'He even had his own blog,' recalls Conlan. 'He was writing about Ireland having a new kid Michael Conlan in his category. He said, "He's nothing that I haven't seen before."

'I began to doubt myself, even though I actually felt I had done all right against him in sparring. So guess who I'm drawn against in the first round? Khalid Yafai! The first round was tense; I was one up after the second and I won 19-10. So I stuffed him. It was a massive boost to my self-confidence. I couldn't believe it. He was the favourite and I had beaten him so easily.'

Another familiar flyweight awaited Conlan in the quarter-final: Italy's Vincenzo Picardi, whom Conlan had sensationally beaten in his full international debut in Belfast the previous year. 'Having dropped him twice in Belfast I was too confident. Instead of doing what I normally do, I went in and tried to knock him out. He beat me comfortably enough (26-20).'

Two of Ireland's other leading medal hopefuls, John Joe Nevin and Darren O'Neill, also bowed out in the bronze medal fights. The latter went down 17-10 to Dmitro Mitrofanov from the Ukraine, who was beaten in his semi-final bout, while Nevin lost by a point (13-12) in the bantamweight category to the eventual silver medallist Dmitriy Polyanskiy from Russia. The Irish camp was furious with the decision and lodged a protest.

'Normally when there is only a point in it the decision could go either way. But in this case it was ridiculous. I thought I had won by about eight points. I have the DVD of the fight at home and you can hear boxers from other countries booing the decision. The Russian coach shook my hand afterwards and gave a gesture which suggested he thought I should have got the decision,' says Nevin.

Four others, Michael McDonagh (lightweight); Willie McLaughlin (welterweight), Con Sheehan (heavyweight) and Cathal McMonagle (super heavyweight) also left Ankara empty-handed, but Ward and Moylette were on a roll. The latter had the more difficult path to glory. After stopping an Israeli in the first round, he had a single point to spare (17-16) over a Serb in the next round before edging out a Russian, Maxim Ignatiev, again by a single point (14-13) in the quarter-final. He had two points to spare over Gaybatulla Hajialiyev from Azerbaijan to guarantee himself a silver medal and become the first Connacht boxer to reach a European championship final. He was in a dream world. So much so that he did a Bruce Lee impression with a spectacular flip off the ground after edging out Hajialiyev in the closing thirty seconds of their contest. 'Once I got the bronze medal my funding was secured for the next two years so I felt no pressure during the rest of the tournament.'

Meanwhile, Ward – still four months away from his eighteenth birthday – was marauding through the light heavyweight division. He launched his international championship career at senior level with a 10-7 win over an Estonian boxer before beating an Italian by two points in the quarter-final. He then hammered a Hungarian Imre Szellő 18-8 in the semi-final. So for the second

European Championships in a row Ireland had two boxers in the finals.

Moylette faced a familiar foe, England's Tom Stalker, in the light welter-weight final – the latter had won a bronze medal at the Europeans in Moscow two years earlier and was the defending Commonwealth champion. The pair were level 5-5 after round one. Moylette won the second round 7-3 to take a 12-8 advantage into the last three minutes and went on to claim a comprehensive 18-8 success. As the bell sounded to end the contest Moylette celebrated with an impromptu hand-walk around the ring. 'When I was a child my father would have me walking around the house on my hands. It became a bit of a party trick. I hated doing it, but it was great for my strength and core stability. Everything went so well for me that week that I decided to do it.'

His brother Richard arrived back in Ireland from Australia on the same day that Ray came home with a European gold medal. Their mother relented and let them into the ring for spar. 'It was just exhibition stuff.' But the victory in Turkey was achieved at a considerable cost. After breaking his left hand, he had overused his right which became increasingly painful. 'Progressively it just got worse and worse; it was very painful during the championships because the fights were so intense. But adrenalin is the best pain killer of all.' Moylette underwent surgery in December 2011 to correct the ligament damage in his right hand but never recaptured his previous form.

The 'Eye of the Tiger' blared around the arena as Ward and his opponent Nikita Ivanov – who was seven years older – made their way from the dressing room. The Moate youngster might have been the underdog but he had the Russian on the run from the start. He led 7-3 after three minutes. Ivanov was full of venom at the beginning of the second round, but there was little method to his fury and he was deducted two points after he was twice penalised for low blows. Ward won the round 8-3, to take a virtually unassailable 15-6 lead into the final stanza. Only a knock-out could stop the Moate marauder now. He shaded the round 3-2 for a comprehensive 18-10 victory. Still just seventeen years old, he was the European light heavyweight champion.

'I didn't have high hopes before the tournament. I was going to one of the biggest tournaments in the world where I would be fighting experienced guys who had been around the block. Ray and I were probably the most unlikely gold medallists there. I was only seventeen and he was a late replacement on the team,' recalls Ward.

However, he wasn't the youngest gold medallist in Ankara. The honour went to light flyweight Salman Alizade from Azerbaijan, who was the youngest since sixteen-year-old Mario Bianchini from Italy won the lightweight title in Budapest in 1930. Still, it was unprecedented for a boxer as young as Ward to win the gold medal in the third-heaviest weight category in the championships.

And for the first time since 1939 Ireland had won two gold medals at the event. Jimmy Ingle was seventeen when he captured the European flyweight title in the National Stadium seventy-two years previously, but Ward became Ireland's youngest ever European champion by a mere three months.

Russia headed the medal table and Ireland was usurped from the runner-up spot it occupied two years previously by the new superpowers in European boxing, Azerbaijan. Ireland finished joint third alongside Wales, who also captured two gold medals.

By the time the Irish squad arrived home their thoughts had already switched to the 2011 World Championships in late September – the first of only two qualifiers for the London Olympics. As is their wont, the IABA became embroiled in an unnecessary tangle with the HPU over team selection. Even before the European Championships, the IABA had scheduled a four-day open unseeded Elite competition in early August 'to assist with their selection process for the Worlds.' However, a week beforehand, the officer board of the IABA's Central Council announced they would be recommending that the winners of the open Elite event make up the team for the Worlds.

This changed the rules of engagement as far as the HPU was concerned, and six of the country's top boxers, Paddy Barnes, John Joe Nevin, Joe Ward, Ray Moylette, Darren O'Neill and Willie McLaughlin, upped the ante by withdrawing from the open tournament, citing injuries. This raised the prospect of Ireland having to send a shadow team to Baku. Not surprisingly the IABA blinked first. As the controversy grew they issued another statement declaring that the Boxing Council (as the officer board of the Central Council is known) would assess 'other relevant performances and factors' as well as the results of the open Elite competition before the squad was selected.

It was a mess, and a seething Billy Walsh opted to bring all the boxers in contention out of the maelstrom to a training camp in Assisi, Italy. There were no surprises at the open competition, although Kenny Egan, who had switched into the heavyweight category, struggled to overcome the challenge of Tommy McCarthy in the semi-final.

'We always do our best work outside Ireland. We brought four extra boxers with us even though I had recommended that other guys be selected instead of them. I sat them down and explained the reasons for my recommendations,' says Walsh.

The squad were in Italy when the Boxing Council formally ratified the team. There were no surprises – all of Walsh's selections were named but it was recommended that Moylette, the newly-crowned European champion, box off with Ross Hickey to decide who would go to Baku. Moylette was furious, but in fairness to the IABA, the Mayo man hadn't won the Elite title and hadn't taken part in the box-off while Hickey had won both competitions. Arguably he deserved a shot at securing a place on the team. In any event, Moylette won the box-off, after a cracking contest, to secure the light welterweight spot.

Walsh revealed later that the boxers knew who had been ratified before he was officially informed of the composition of the team. 'It's a crazy set-up that you cannot select your own team. Even the manager of a junior B GAA team has the authority to pick his own team in consultation with his selectors without having to seek approval from the County Board.' But only a change in the constitution of the IABA would give the HPU full control over team selection. Under the current rules all teams selected for international events must be formally approved by the Central Council of the organisation.

'The whole box-off was a joke even though I took part in it. For me, it was pleasing to fully cement my place on the team for Baku,' suggests Michael Conlan, but for Darren O'Neill the whole episode left a sour taste, not least because it could have cost him his place at the London Olympics.

'Mostly we were protected from the various political fall-outs. But obviously we are aware of issues particularly when they affect us directly. I had damaged cartilage in my hand prior to those box-offs and had a doctor's letter to say that I wasn't fit to box. Yet there was a vote taken on whether I would go to the World championships. I had beaten Jason Quigley twice previously but I only won the vote (against him) 11-9. I thought it was scandalous. I could go on about it all day. I suppose it probably goes on in all organisations,' says O'Neill.

Built on the shores of the Caspian Sea, Baku was used as a location for the 1999 James Bond movie *The World is Not Enough*, starring Irish actor Pierce Brosnan. And in September 2011 ten expectant Irish warriors arrived in the city. Their mission was to qualify for the London Olympics in ten months' time.

CHAPTER 16

BOXING 'BROTHERS'

'I knew that Olympic qualification was at stake and I needed to win that fight. Remember Michael Carruth's jump after he won the gold medal at the Barcelona Olympics. Well, I think I broke his record that day.'

John Joe Nevin

For the three years they boxed together at international level, Darren O'Neill and John Joe Nevin roomed together. So much so that by the time the London Olympics came around Billy Walsh affectionately refereed to them as 'the husband and wife'. 'Well, Darren was definitely the "wife" because he was always whinging about something,' suggests Nevin. Banter aside, a bond developed between the pair which was unique, given their contrasting backgrounds.

At first glance, a friendship between a primary school teacher from Kilkenny and a settled traveller from Mullingar might appear odd but there are few social, economic or racial barriers in boxing. O'Neill and Nevin simply hit it off when they roomed together for the first time in a training camp prior to the 2009 European Union Championships in Odense. Due to underlying tensions between the Nevin and Joyce families in Mullingar, boxers from the two clans rarely spar together in the HPU and don't room together on foreign trips.

'I knew John Joe from around the gym and I volunteered to share with him at a training camp after I won the Elites in 2009 and we just got on like a house on fire. We ended up rooming together on all the trips afterwards. That's the great thing about boxing. Backgrounds go out the window,' says O'Neill.

Nevin was already a fan of the Kilkenny hurling team before he came under O'Neill's influence and they had a common interest in the fortunes of the Kerry football team. Only in their music tastes did they differ radically. In time, though O'Neill became immune to listening to Richie Kavanagh's greatest hits CD first thing in the morning.

'The other boys would come into the room and say "turn off that shite." It was only then I realised I had been listening to it for a couple of hours. We talked about anything and everything. When he lets his guard down he is a one hundred percent different person than the John Joe we see in the media. It's funny, after I was beaten in the 2014 Elite final he roomed with Adam Nolan on trips abroad. So he went from sharing with a teacher to sharing with a guard. He chose well,' suggests O'Neill.

The pair was on a mutual mission of redemption at the World Championships in Baku in 2011, having failed to win a medal at the Europeans in Turkey three months earlier. 'It was the first time we had gone to a championship together and failed to win anything. Qualifying for London was my goal. It was the reason I stuck at boxing after 2008. I had two things on my mind after I won my first Elite title; I wanted to win a major medal and be an Olympian,' says O'Neill.

For Nevin, though, qualifying for another Olympics was never going to satisfy his ambitions. 'I will be very disappointed if I don't win a medal in

London,' he said in advance of the Games, though he did add a rider, 'so long as I give it my best shot I can't be disappointed. I will accept it if I'm beaten by a better man on the day.'

In Grand Prix motor racing there is a saying 'to finish first, first you have to finish.' The same applies in boxing: to medal at the Olympics, first you've got to qualify. This was the harsh lesson that Joe Ward, the then ranked number two light heavyweight in the world with a 10-0 record at the time, discovered to his cost in Baku.

Billy Walsh specifically warned the boxers of the pitfalls. Before a punch was thrown, he lined up Paddy Barnes, Michael Conlan, John Joe Nevin, David Oliver Joyce, Ray Moylette, Roy Sheahan, Darren O'Neill, Joe Ward, Kenny Egan and Con Sheehan and delivered his 'Urbi et Orbi'. 'I said, "Each and every one of you is going to get a chance to qualify. But there will only be one chance and you have to be ready to take it when it comes." Joe [Ward] got his chance in, but he didn't take it.'

Initially, everything ran smoothly – all ten boxers reached the last thirty-two in their respective weight divisions. Even though Ward was the squad's least experienced member, his teammates expected him to reach the last eight, which was the entry requirement for the London Olympics. 'We thought Joe Ward was a dead cert to qualify,' recalls O'Neill. Nonetheless, Billy Walsh made an interesting observation about Ward at the team's final press conference before their departure to Baku. 'He takes a good bit of management,' he suggested.

Outside the ring the teenager's life was changing rapidly. His partner, Julianne, was pregnant; she gave birth to the couple's first child, Joe, two months later. 'This wasn't a distraction. I have a good family,' Ward insists. As the reigning European champion, Ward had a bye into the last thirty-two. He demolished his first opponent, Dilovarshakh Abdurakhmanov from Turkmenistan by 18 points

(22-4) to reach the next round, where he faced an Iranian, Ehsan Rouzbahani, for a place in the last eight and automatic Olympic qualification. Ward had developed a 'modus operandi' which had served him well at underage level but now he needed something different, according to Walsh.

'Joe had so much talent and was so strong for his age that he destroyed fellows at underage level. He had developed the knack of taking it handy early on [during championships] and just doing enough to win fights and then peaking for the final. We must bear in mind that he was still only seventeen. Nowadays, he wouldn't be allowed to fight at the worlds. But once you start boxing at Elite level you need to be more focused. All opponents will be well prepared, particularly at a world championship. The Iranian was a tough bit of stuff, very active, very mobile.

'We thought we had Joe right but this fella was giving it to him. Joe wasn't switched on from the start. So he's four points down going into the last round; then he decided to go for it. Well, he had no choice at that stage. The result went to a countback; he lost it and as it later transpired that was the moment he lost his Olympic place,' says Walsh.

There was no consolation for Ward. He will always remember his first-ever defeat at Elite level. 'I don't remember good things about the fight. I was one win away from qualifying for the Olympics, being beaten on countback made it worse. I never checked what the actual score was. [The AIBA do not release the details of countback scores at the event]. I lacked experience in getting over the finish line as far as the Olympics were concerned and it was all down-hill from there.'

Beijing bronze medallist Paddy Barnes bowed out early as well. His season had been constantly disrupted by injury. He was well below his best going down 20-12 to Mark Barriga from the Philippines. 'The World Champion-ships are my bogey event,' laments Barnes. Barriga lost in the next round to

Barnes's erstwhile rival Olympic champion Zou Shiming, who secured his third world title in Baku.

Unquestionably, the unluckiest Irish boxer in Baku was David Oliver Joyce. The Athy lightweight was literally within seconds of securing his place in London when the cruel hand of fate intervened in the most controversial manner imaginable. Joyce was level 30-30 with India's Jai Bhagwan with four seconds of their quarter-final bout remaining when the referee controversially penalised him for pushing. The Irishman was issued with a public warning and ceded two points. In football terms it was equivalent to conceding a goal from a dubious penalty deep in injury time. He had no time to recover; Bhagwan won 32-30 to claim his spot in London, where he was beaten in the second round.

The decision nearly broke Joyce. 'I was devastated for weeks afterwards. I remember when the result was announced I said, "That's the end, no more. I'm not going through this hard training ever again." I wasn't even thinking about the Olympics. I was ready to pack in boxing.'

Had the fight ended level, Joyce would have comfortably got the verdict on countback. 'This made it all the more disgusting. Actually, I met the referee a few nights later on a night out. He apologized. He didn't know the score when he gave me the warning. He had to do his job, but I felt it was an easy warning to give.

'My opponent came in with his head down a few times during the fight and I just battered down on it. The referee never said anything. Then he gives me a warning at the very end of the fight which cost me two points and the decision. Eventually, Gerry Hussey talked to me and I got my head around it. I went to Turkey for the final qualifier,' recalls Joyce. But like his cousin, Joe Ward, his best chance of making London had slipped by.

'I don't think people realise just how difficult it is for boxers to qualify nowadays for the Olympics. European boxers win seventy percent of the medals at both the Olympic Games and the World Championships, yet European boxers are only allocated thirty percent of the places at the Olympics,' argues Walsh.

Such is the nature of these tournaments that when it comes to the business end of the event there is no time for post mortems. Walsh and Antia had to focus on the boxers still left in the tournament. O'Neill and Nevin were boxing in the same session and travelled together to the stadium. On the bus journey, word filtered through that Ward had suffered a sensational defeat in the last bout of the morning session. 'I didn't believe it; I thought people were messing,' says O'Neill.

However, when the news was confirmed in the dressing room O'Neill felt his confidence seep away. 'We both panicked a bit because we felt he was such a sure thing. It was sort of, "Well if he's beaten how are we expected to win." We pulled ourselves away to one side and had a quick chat. Basically, we said, "To hell with Joe Ward, let's concentrate on ourselves and get our act together."'

O'Neill had beaten his Bulgarian opponent Mladen Manev in the semi-final of the European Championships in Moscow 2010 and expected his opponent to come out with revenge on his mind. Instead, the Bulgarian was apprehensive at the start which allowed O'Neill gain an early lead, and it was plain sailing afterwards as the Kilkenny middleweight cruised to a 19-12 win. 'I remember after the final bell walking back to my corner and asking Billy, "Am I going [to the Olympics]?"'

Just as an ecstatic O'Neill was ushered back to the dressing room, John Joe Nevin was stepping into the ring to face his Mongolian opponent Dorjn-yambuu Otgondalai. 'It was payback time for Beijing,' laughs Nevin, who had lost to a Mongolian opponent three years earlier. It was a remarkable fight as Nevin recalls. 'We were level after round one, though he dropped me. He dropped me again in the second round and I was two points down going into the third round. But I pulled it back to make it 18-18 and got the verdict on a countback. No matter how much you're told that it's just another fight, I knew that Olympic qualification was at stake and I needed to win that fight. Remember Michael Carruth's jump after he won the gold medal at the Barcelona Olympics. Well, I think I broke his record that day,' says Nevin.

Back in the dressing room, O'Neill was oblivious to the dramatic action in the bantamweight contest. 'I was over the moon having qualified and I rang my dad with the news. Then Gerry Hussey walked into the dressing room and announced, "John Joe got dropped." I said, "Ah f….," and he adds, "He got dropped twice." Now I go from being over the moon to being completely gutted. Gerry leaves that last line hanging in the air for thirty seconds and then pipes up, "But he got up and won." Well, I nearly did a somersault. It was unbelievable; we both had qualified within a few minutes of each other.'

On seeing the draw in the flyweight category, Michael Conlan would have been forgiven for feeling a degree of self-pity. First up was Alexander Riscan from Moldova, a bronze medallist at the Europeans three months earlier. Conlan nailed him 25-12 to earn a clash with Olzhas Sattibayev from Kazakhstan. 'I still say to this day that he was the best boxer I ever fought. His footwork and movement were phenomenal; his distance was perfect every time.

'I was three points up after the first round but I panicked a bit because it was so early in the fight. His facial expression didn't change when he came out for the second; he was as cool as he was at the start and he won the round by a point. I was now panicking like mad. The third round was tight; he won it by a point which meant I won the fight 18-17.'

Next up was Nordine Oubaali, five years his senior and a bronze medallist in the light flyweight category at the World Championships four years earlier. More significantly, Oubaali had beaten his older brother Jamie in a bout in Ireland when they were both juniors. 'I couldn't believe it when the draw came out. I always remembered him because my old coach Sean McCaffrey said he was the best boxer he had ever seen.'

One suspects, Conlan was slightly spooked at the prospect of meeting the Frenchman who had beaten Paddy Barnes three times before moving up to flyweight and had only lost on a countback to Olympic champion Zou Shiming at the Beijing Olympics. The nineteen-year-old decided to take drastic action before the fight.

'After the weigh-in I decided I to get completely hydrated and drank loads. I just filled myself up. I didn't care what I weighed after the fight so long as I won it. In the first round I let him bully me by showing him too much respect. Near the end of the round I started to push him back and he didn't like it. But I was two points down at the start of the second and Billy [Walsh] told me I needed to keep pushing him back. It was level at the end of that round [11-11] but I knew I had won the fight before the official result. I was the first [Irish] boxer to qualify [for the London Olympics]. But I felt more relief than anything when the decision was announced. I didn't get too excited.'

Conlan's winning margin was three points (20-17). Perhaps his lack of emotion was a reflection of his immediate predicament: the Olympics were nine months away, his next weigh-in was in ten hours' time. He stepped on the scales when he returned to the dressing room and was horrified to discover he was fifty-six kilograms – four kilograms over the flyweight limit. 'I did a training session for an hour in the stadium and lost two kilos. Then I had an interview with RTÉ and I didn't get back to the hotel until one o'clock in the morning. I had to put my gear back on and train again. I got the weight down to fifty-two and a half kilos and I went to bed.

'When I woke up I weighed myself and I was point one of a kilo over. But when I checked again on one of the scales at the official weigh-in I was point two over. Even when I took off my shorts I was still over. So I had to do another training session. I was nearly crying at this stage; I was skipping for ages but I couldn't get a sweat up.'

Conlan ended up being point two kilo under the limit on the official scales. The other scales he had used in the centre were weighing 'heavy'. 'So I needn't have done that last training session.' There is no accurate way of gauging whether it had any impact on his performance against Welshman Andrew Selby in the quarter-final. 'Funnily enough, it was the one fight at the championship that I thought I had won. It was very tight but I felt I won all three rounds.'

The judges saw it differently, however. It was a carbon copy of Conlan's contest against Olzhas Sattibayev – but in reverse. Selby, who ended up winning the silver medal, did the damage in the opening three minutes, gaining a three-point advantage. Conlan won round two and round three by a point but still fell short by a single point (25-24). 'Even though I lost out on a medal, I wasn't devastated because I felt I put in a great performance and got my qualification for the Olympics.'

In terms of Olympic qualification there was no more joy for the Irish. Super heavyweight Con Sheehan got within one win of securing a spot but proved no match for 2008 Olympic champion and two-time world champion, Italian Roberto Cammarelle. In his first foray into the heavyweight division in an international championship, Egan had the misfortune of drawing Cuban José Larduet Gómez, who had won a bronze medal in the lighter 81 kg class at the World Championships in Milan 2009. The Cuban won within the distance.

It was also a bitterly disappointing championship for European title holder Ray Moylette who was comprehensively beaten in a last sixteen contest by India's Manoj Kumar, who lost in the next round to eventual bronze medallist

Thomas Stalker from England. 'I probably didn't have enough work done. I was after winning a European title and I didn't think I needed to do it. What happened was that I stayed in the same position whereas others who were below me improved and I was left behind,' reflects Moylette.

O'Neill's bid for a medal ended in the quarter-finals when he lost 18-9 to Ryōta Murato – a world-class Japanese middleweight who won the silver medal in Baku and was crowned Olympic champion in London. But the manner of O'Neill's defeat was to have serious implications for his preparations for London.

Meanwhile, Nevin became the first Irish male boxer to win two medals at the World Championships. As in Milan two years earlier, he had to be content with the bronze after losing in the semi-final on a countback to England's Luke Campbell, who was beaten in the final by Cuban Lázaro Álvarez. All three renewed their rivalry at the Olympics less than a year later. 'I beat Campbell by seventeen or eighteen points in our first meeting when I was fourteen. Then in 2009 I beat him 13-2 in Denmark in the semi-final of the EU championships. In Baku it was 12-12 and he got the verdict on a countback,' recalls Nevin.

Attention immediately switched to the only remaining qualifying tournament for the London Olympics, scheduled for the Turkish Black Sea port of Trabzon in April 2012. The choice of venue was ominous. Turkish boxing fans are notoriously vociferous and this has the capacity to influence judges' decision-making. Worse still, not a single Turkish boxer qualified for the Olympics in Baku. But the die was cast; the best the Irish contingent could hope for was to avoid Turkish boxers until they had their qualification secured.

In the meantime, there were issues to be tidied up on the home front. These were addressed at the Elite Championships at the start of the year. Any remote possibility that Kenny Egan would make it to London was dashed when he was decisively beaten 29-10 by Joe Ward for a second successive year. Hampered by hand injuries, European champion Ray Moylette did not even make it to the 64 kg final, suffering a shock 15-11 loss to the unheralded Martin Wall in the quarter-finals. Moylette's Olympic dream was over. By contrast, Wexford Garda Adam Nolan revived his ambitions when he beat Beijing Olympian John Joe Joyce 17-15 in the welterweight final.

The Irish squad wound up their preparations for Trabzon at a training camp in the Ukrainian capital, Kiev. There were different criteria for qualification across the categories. Light flyweight Paddy Barnes and lightweight David Oliver Joyce had the widest window of opportunity – a semi-final place would suffice. But light welter Ross Hickey and heavyweight Tommy McCarthy had absolutely no room for error as they had to win gold; Joe Ward needed to reach the light heavyweight final, though he could also make it as a best loser, while Adam Nolan and super heavyweight Con Sheehan needed to reach their respective finals.

Even before the boxing commenced, Ward's dream began to unravel; the draw meant he would almost certainly have to face a Turkish fighter in the quarter-finals. This was precisely what he wanted to avoid, even if his form was excellent. He had underlined his Olympic credentials at the prestigious Chemistry Cup tournament in Halle the previous month when he won the gold medal in his category with a 20-14 win over Egor Mekhontsev from Russia, who was later crowned Olympic champion in London. Billy Walsh, who was in Ward's corner in Halle, can only lament as he reflects on how the respective careers of Mekhontsev and Ward subsequently diverged.

'Joe Ward put the Russian on his arse in the Chemistry Cup, but when Mekhontsev won the Olympic gold medal Joe was sitting at home in Moate,' recalls Walsh. 'I was aware there could be an issue in Turkey. I just had that instinctive feeling and was kinda hoping that I wouldn't draw a boxer from the home nation because they will always be favoured,' says Ward. The Irish camp believed they knew exactly what to expect from Ward's Turkish opponent Bahram Muzaffer. At the Beijing Olympics, back in 2008, the Turk had earned a late call-up but proved no match for Kenny Egan in the second round.

So the scene was set for the showdown between Ward, the number three rated light heavyweight in the world and his twenty-five-year-old opponent, who was born in Uzbekistan and had lived with his family in Russia and Azerbaijan before settling in Turkey in 1996. The Irishman trailed by a point after round one. Muzaffer maintained his slender advantage in the second, to led 12-11 going into the final stanza. The Irishman did all that could be humanly expected. But, in truth, he probably needed a knock-out to be given the decision. The experienced Turk spent most of the final three minutes spoiling. But with the crowd going wild he was awarded six points while Ward could only manage four. So Muzaffer got the verdict 18-15. Joe Ward's Olympic dream was now definitely over.

'I always believed I could beat him and that's what happened. But I just didn't get the verdict. That's the way life is. I was devastated because I knew my Olympic dream was over. But I couldn't have done anything more in the fight,' says Ward. The Irish camp lodged an appeal but, as is the norm, it was rejected.

'In the last round, I thought Joe did all the cleaner scoring. That's what you're up against. 'There's a partisan crowd. Even if Joe is hitting, sometimes they're pressing the wrong button,' Walsh suggested in an interview with Paul McDermott of the Irish Sports Council immediately after the fight.

Ward learned much from the debacle according to Walsh. 'It was difficult to console him afterwards but he learned a hell of a lot from it. He has come back a different guy; physically he works a lot harder now.' According to the IABA's performance analyst Alan Swanton who reviewed the tape of the fight, Ward ought to have won by at least ten points.

'He got a very bad decision,' insists Walsh. 'But it was typical of what went on at that qualifying tournament. Look at the statistics: Turkey failed to get any boxer qualified for the Olympics at the World Championships; they didn't win a medal in London but they got six boxers through in Trabzon.' Ironically, Turkey is to host the key European qualifying tournament at which three boxers in each of the ten weight divisions will qualify for the 2016 Games.

Ward remembers watching as Swanton analysed the video of the fight afterward in Trabzon. 'It was nice to know how I did, but you couldn't turn the clock back. I just had to accept it and get on with life. I've always believed that things happen for a reason,' says Ward. 'It would have been very easy for me to give up boxing afterwards. But it never crossed my mind because I was only eighteen. I have a good head on my shoulders and I always believed that I could get to the next Olympics. A defeat makes you a smarter boxer; you'll never learn if you are always winning because you never feel you are doing anything wrong. It's only when you start losing that you look back on things. It made me a wiser boxer,' he suggests.

In the wake of the infamous 'Le-Hand-of-God' goal in the Republic of Ireland v France World Cup qualifier there was a forlorn hope that Ireland might get a last minute reprieve. There was a similar misguided view that Joe Ward might still somehow make it to London.

The IABA formally wrote to AIBA president Dr Wu Ching-Kuo requesting assistance. Dr John Lynch (Chairman of the IABA's Board of Directors) pointed out that Ward was the highest ranking boxer at light heavyweight not to qualify. 'We should point out that in our one hundred years' existence we have always accepted the rules as set out by AIBA and will continue to do so. However, we would ask that Mr Ward be considered for inclusion in the Olympics in 2012 under the tripartite selection quota or any other avenue.'

Under a tripartite selection quota process, the AIBA and the IOC nominate a specific number of boxers who haven't qualified through the normal selection process to compete at the Olympics. However, these places are earmarked for countries that have had less than seven individual competitors competing in the previous two Olympic Games. The boxer chosen in Ward's weight category was Boško Drašković from Montenegro who, ironically, had been disqualified in his second fight at the 2011 World Championships for persistently head-butting his Indian opponent.

Following the completion of this process one Olympic slot still remained available. Ward lost out again, however – this time to Zdeněk Chládek, a light welterweight, from the Czech Republic. Controversially the Czech was deemed the then best ranked boxer at the 2011 World Championships who had not qualified for the London Olympics. In a final twist to the saga, the issues surrounding Ward's defeat in Trabzon and the subsequent selection of Drašković and Chládek ended up being adjudged upon by the Court of Arbitration for Sport on the eve of the Olympics.

Back in the ring in Trabzon, Ward wasn't the only Irish boxer to lose to a Turkish fighter. Con Sheehan lost to super heavyweight Muhammet Erkan Aci, while Paddy Barnes was beaten 21-14 in the semi-final of the light flyweight category. In terms of Olympic qualification the defeat was academic. Barnes had already qualified for his second Olympic courtesy of a comfortable 17-9 win over Romanian Stefan Caslarov in the quarter-final. Nonetheless, he remained livid about the penultimate contest. 'It was the biggest disgrace ever, honestly. That bout is still on YouTube so anybody can watch it and make up their minds. But the reality is that if I had met him in the quarter rather than the semi-final I would have missed the Olympics in London.'

Other countries suffered too in their bouts against the home nation. Turkey got twenty of the twenty-two decisions prior to the semi-finals and twenty-nine of the thirty-four decisions for the whole tournament. Yet not a single Turkish boxer won a medal at the London Olympics.

Light welter Ross Hickey who missed out on the World and European Championships did not make a fairytale return, losing 24-11 to a Moldovan opponent Dmitri Galagot. Another Moldovan, Vladimir Cheles ended Tommy McCarthy's Olympic ambitions in the heavyweight semi-final with a three-point win.

There was no joy either for David Oliver Joyce, who was so unlucky not to qualify in Baku. In his key quarter-final bout in Trabzon he met the highly rated lightweight Evaldas Petrauskas from Lithuania and lost 19-10. Such was the reputation of the latter – who went on to win a bronze medal in London – that the two boxers who were due to meet him in the semi-final and final in Trabzon conceded walkovers. Turkey's Fatih Keles and Vazgen Safaryants from Belarus, having already earned their passage to London, decided that discretion was the better part of valour. Ironically, in London Keles was beaten in the second round by Petrauskas.

'Even though I hadn't any luck in Trabzon, it wasn't as disappointing a loss as I had endured in Baku,' says Joyce. His plans to retire were put on hold when subsequently he signed with the World Boxing Series, before moving on to the more lucrative AIBA Pro Boxing (APB) series in 2014.

Under the radar, Garda Adam Nolan emerged as the last Irishman standing in the tournament in Turkey. Like Darren O'Neill, Nolan – a native of Ballagh in County Wexford – is a dual sportsman. His father, John, together with Martin O'Connor ran Ballagh Boxing Club. On his mother's insistence he wasn't allowed to attend the club on school nights. He lived for the Friday-night sessions when he worked pads with his dad. His other sporting passion was hurling and he featured on a successful Oulart-The Ballagh squad which won county titles in every grade from U-12 to U-21 through the noughties.

Nevertheless, he continued to excel in the boxing ring as well; he won an All-Ireland youths' title in 2004, defeating Carl Frampton in the final. By then he was boxing out of the St Ibar's/St Joseph's club in Wexford. Billy Walsh was in his corner when he won his first juvenile All-Ireland title in 1999. He quit boxing after winning the youths' title to concentrate on his Leaving Certificate. The sabbatical lasted four years – much longer than he had anticipated. He joined An Garda Síochána and between his training and his hurling commitments he simply didn't have any time for boxing. Stationed in Bray, he decided one night to ramble down to the local Bray boxing club. 'The fact that Katie Taylor was boxing out of the club was a big attraction. Initially I just wanted to maintain my fitness for hurling,' says Nolan.

Under the watchful eye of club coach and Katie Taylor's father, Pete Taylor, Nolan's love for boxing was re-ignited so much so that he won a gold medal at the World Police and Fire Games in Vancouver in 2009. On his return to Ireland he lined out for the Oulart-The Ballagh intermediate team. Standing on the sideline was the club's newly appointed senior team manager Liam Dunne – a folk hero in his native county and an All-Ireland medal winner in 1996.

Nolan experienced mixed fortunes in the game as he recalls: 'I was so fit at the time that I had a stormer and then with five minutes to go I broke my finger. I remember ringing up Pete [Taylor] to tell him and needless to say he wasn't very happy and he gave me an ultimatum; it was either boxing or hurling. I decided to stick with the boxing despite the fact that Liam [Dunne] subsequently asked me to join the club's senior squad.'

Dunne – who now manages the Wexford senior hurling team – coached Oulart-The Ballagh to a hat-trick of Wexford senior titles. Nolan, meanwhile, won an Irish Elite title in the welterweight category in 2011. Then disaster struck a few weeks before he was due to box at the Europeans in Ankara.

While sparring with Irish team colleague Willie McLaughlin, he damaged his knuckle. Any slim chance of being selected for the World Championships in Baku evaporated when he lost to Roy Sheahan in the infamous box-off prior to the event. So Nolan arrived in Trabzon as an unseeded and unheralded boxer, which ultimately worked in his favour. And from the moment he got a bye in the preliminary round, fate seemed to side with him. Unlike Ward, Sheahan and Barnes, he avoided meeting the Turkish welterweight who was in the other half of the draw. Still, he had to reach the final to secure his place.

A 14-9 win over Poland's Tomasz Kot set up a quarter-final bout against Tamerlan Abdullayev from Azerbaijan, which Nolan won 17-13. He controlled his crucial semi-final clash against Romanian Ionuṭ Gheorghe to win 19-10. And, just for good measure, he secured the gold medal when he won the final against Germany's Patrick Wojcicki – who had beaten the Turk in the other semi-final – on a countback.

So, for the second successive Olympics Ireland qualified five male boxers – two of whom, Paddy Barnes and John Joe Nevin had competed in Beijing. The three rookies were Michael Conlan, Darren O'Neill and Adam Nolan. And none of them hailed from the country's biggest and second biggest centres of population, Dublin and Cork. It was a bitter-sweet moment for Irish coach Billy Walsh. He felt that Ward and Joyce should have made it to London as well. But on a personal level the achievements of O'Neill and Nolan were particularly sweet. 'I had known Adam [Nolan] since he was a baby and had coached him, while I knew Darren [O'Neill] from when he was a kid as his father boxed at the same time as I did.'

Ahead of the London Olympics the Irish public was focused on the prospects of one boxer – Katie Taylor. It took much of the limelight away from the men's squad, which suited them perfectly, not least because their build-up was fraught with difficulties.

CHAPTER 17

LONDON CALLING

'Paddy was trying to talk to me when I came into the gym, but I wouldn't look at him I was so focused. We got into the ring and he battered me. He just wouldn't stop punching me. We have been close mates since.'

Michael Conlan

Less than six months before the opening ceremony of the London Olympics, Ireland's leading male medal contender in boxing John Joe Nevin fractured his jaw. He was boxing for the Paris United franchise in the World Series of Boxing, a semi-professional competition which the AIBA had established after the Beijing Olympics.

Nevin picked up the injury in an accidental clash of heads in the opening thirty seconds of a bout against Serbian native Branimir Stankovic. He went on to win the fight on a split decision. But he knew something was amiss, though the diagnosis wasn't confirmed until he visited a specialist in Dublin on his return from Paris. He didn't seem too perturbed as he explained to IABA public relations officer Bernard O'Neill how the injury would impact on his preparations for the Olympics. 'I'll have to give up sparring and boxing for four or five weeks. I should be fine after that.'

Nonetheless, the injury ebbed away at Nevin's confidence. Worst still, he suffered a devastating personal loss. His cousin, occasional sparring partner and close friend, twenty-five-year-old David Nevin died suddenly from a heart attack in February. David, who won national titles and boxed for Ireland, had planned to travel to see his cousin in action at the London Olympics.

Nevin's colleague and room-mate, Irish captain Darren O'Neill, was also experiencing a dip in confidence. His difficulties originated in his medal fight at the World Championships in Baku the previous November when he lost to Japan's Ryōta Murato. 'He was a bit of a tight-guard specialist. I wanted to be ready for him if we met at the Olympics so I decided I needed to work on my in-close fighting. The plan was to improve my tactics in this area then get back to my old style. As it transpired, I put too much emphasis on the former. For the first time in my career I was struggling with my confidence.'

Understandably, between the World Championships in Baku and the final European Olympic qualifying tournament five months later in Trabzon, the coaching staff in the HPU focused on the boxers who had not yet qualified for London. The result was that O'Neill's difficulties were not addressed. His worst fears were realised at the prestigious Chemistry Cup tournament in Halle in March when he lost 14-9 in the quarter-final to Donabek Suzhanov from Kazakhstan.

Ireland's final competitive event before the London Olympics was a four nations' round-robin tournament involving the hosts, France, Germany and Morocco in Berck, an hour's drive from the port of Calais in early June. The event was an unmitigated disaster for Nevin, who was struggling with his weight and boxed in the 60 kg lightweight division rather than at bantam-weight. He lost two of his three bouts. It was becoming apparent to his team-mates that something was amiss.

Michael Conlan could not understand why Nevin was so lethargic when he sparred him in France. 'I was beating him up. I remember saying to him, "Come on here. What's up?" He just stood there on the ropes and let me hit him. Billy [Walsh] was shouting at him as well, but he just stood there and didn't want to know.'

Darren O'Neill also knew that something was amiss. 'Normally we would bounce things off each other. After his [Nevin's] unusually poor performance in the first fight, I tried to instigate a discussion but he just changed the subject. I don't know, maybe there was tension between Billy, Zaur and himself, but I noticed that between rounds in that fight he was looking up at me in the crowd.' Nevin went on to win his last fight in France, but when the squad reassembled in Dublin for a training camp with the visiting Indian and Tunisian Olympic squads, he requested a meeting with the HPU coaching staff.

Billy Walsh, together with Zaur Antia and team psychologist Gerry Hussey met with Nevin. He poured out his innermost feelings and insecurities. 'Basically he told us he couldn't handle the pressure,' says Walsh. 'His family, friends and everybody he met thought he was going to win a medal. But he didn't want to go to the Olympics. I said, "You must be joking. Half the world would give their right arm to go. But you don't want to go even though you have a ticket." I advised him to calm down, relax, stay for the ten days of the camp and see how he felt.'

Hussey took Nevin on a run along the South Circular Road after the meeting. By the time they returned Nevin had agreed to stay in the camp. 'John Joe is a bit of a freak in the sense that he has the capacity to get fit and sharp very quickly. He had four test bouts at the end of the camp and I predicted he would be flying by then and as it happened he was,' says Walsh.

Darren O'Neill's crisis of confidence also came to a head around this time. 'I was finding training a bit difficult and really, really struggling the week before the Indian Olympic boxing squad was due in Dublin. We were doing this combat stuff, which basically means you have to follow specific rules about what punches you throw in the ring. It's technical stuff. I hate it; it just drives me up the wall. I wanted to get out of the ring one day but Adam Nolan got me to finish the round.

'Billy called me into his office later that morning because he knew something was up. I said, "Look, I'm off form. I'm not boxing well. I'm doing too much of this combat stuff and I need to get back boxing the way I should be boxing."

'Billy just said, "If the combat stuff is not working out, just turn it into a spar. Whatever boxer you are sparring against will hit you back because they won't let you beat them up." So Adam and I beat each other round the ring.'

O'Neill took the next four days off and returned to his home in Paulstown. 'I trained with my dad and went back to basics. When I came back for the camp I felt re-energised. But you cannot turn on performances overnight. I had struggled all year and my performances at the Olympics reflected that. I performed averagely. It was far from my best.'

Billy Walsh fretted about the Games being in London and was adamant that the team's final pre-Olympic camp would take place outside the country. Since the inception of the HPU the squad had done better in faraway locations. The London Games were effectively a 'home' Olympics for Ireland. Would the pressure get to the boxers? The awarding of the Games was outside his control but not the choice of venue for the last camp. So he turned down an opportunity to join the Cuban and Australian teams in Queen's University, Belfast.

'Obviously the Cubans wanted us to go there but I said, "No way." Two of our team were from Belfast and if they were at that camp, they would be mobbed every day. We needed to get out of Ireland. Our best work has always being done outside the country where there are no distractions. So we went to Assisi in Italy.'

It was at this training camp that the Irish squad had their biggest scare of all. Michael Conlan sustained a broken nose. 'It wasn't even a full blow,' he laments. 'I was sparring against the Italian 48 kg guy [Manuel Cappai] and he threw a shot which hit the side of my nose. It wasn't even a hard punch. It was more the way he hit me. The middle of my nose swelled up internally.'

Conlan was diagnosed with a haematoma. 'The doctor wanted to slice it open and drain the blood. Had he done that I would not have been able to box for twenty-eight days and would have missed the Games. I opted instead to try nasal and anti-inflammatory medications. As the swelling subsided, I could feel the blood squirting into my nose. I think it is now a bit flatter. And we kept quiet about the injury during the Games.'

His room-mate Paddy Barnes wasn't impressed because he snored incessantly due to his haematoma. 'I was doing Paddy's head in.' The pair are close mates now, but this wasn't always the case. After Barnes returned from the Beijing Olympics with his bronze medal, Conlan, who had just turned seventeen, put the word around Belfast that he didn't rate him and that he fancied his chances against Barnes in the ring.

The following year Conlan got an opportunity to test his theory when the pair clashed in a spar. 'Paddy was trying to talk to me when I came into the gym, but I wouldn't look at him I was so focused. We got into the ring and he battered me. He just wouldn't stop punching me. We have been close mates since.' Nonetheless, when the latter joined with the HPU three years later he did not room with Barnes. 'I tried to avoid sharing a room with him when we went to training camps because he did my head in asking me what I weighed every morning,' says Barnes.

As the Belfast pair and the rest of the Irish squad settled into the athletes' village in Stratford, Joe Ward made one final desperate and ultimately futile bid to join them. He took a case to the Court of Arbitration for Sport (CAS) in Lausanne. The ad hoc division of the Court, comprising of its president Massimo Coccia and arbitrators Martin Schimke and Maidie Oliveau, heard the case. The respondents were the International Olympic Committee (IOC), International Boxing Association (AIBA) and the Association of National Olympic Committees (ANOC). The Olympic Council of Ireland (OCI), the Montenegrin Olympic Committee and their light heavyweight boxer Boško Drašković were listed as 'interested parties'.

'I knew what was going on in the background,' says Joe Ward. 'I always had a little hope even though I kinda knew it wasn't going to happen. Someone financed the case; I'm not going into too many details. Sometimes when people don't get behind it is very hard to get there.'

Ward declined to elaborate on his latter statement or say if he felt the OCI could have been more supportive of his case. 'I won't get into that conversation. Maybe it happened for a reason. There is no point crying about split milk. I just have to look forward and make sure that I'm number one on the podium the next time.'

On 24 July, three days before the scheduled start of the Games, Ward filed a thirty-eight page application with CAS. He was represented at the hearing in London's Grosvenor House Hotel by solicitor Frank Walsh and barrister David Casserly, who specialises in sports law. Ward's case focused on two issues. Firstly the qualification process was flawed, and secondly his personal rights were violated because the refereeing in the April Olympic qualifying tournament in Turkey was alleged to have been corrupt and, thus, he was unjustly eliminated. An anonymous witness was prepared to give evidence to support the allegation of corruption, while one of the HPU's coaches, Eddie Bolger, would also give evidence. However, the panel, having heard oral submissions at the start of the hearing, ruled that they did not have jurisdiction on the alleged corruption practices at the tournament in Trabzon. Therefore, they would not entertain any submissions or evidence on this issue.

The other element of Ward's case centred on a contention that the Montenegrin Olympic Committee should not have been considered for inclusion under the rules that govern the Tripartite Commission's decision to award 'wild card' places as they had nineteen athletes (six individuals and a Water Polo team) competing at the Beijing Olympics. Accordingly, the place in the 81 kg category should have been reallocated to Ward as he was the next best ranked boxer not yet qualified at the 2011 World Championships. Crucially, however, due to his elimination in the second round at the 2011 World Championships, Ward was ranked sixteenth at that event, even though in the overall AIBA light heavyweight ranking list he was in third place in 2011.

The panel delivered their twelve-thousand-word judgment hours before the opening ceremony. The background to the case was outlined, as was the legal correspondence between Ward's solicitor which began the previous June when the AIBA officially informed the IABA that Ward that had not been given a place in London under the 'wild card selection' process. Ruling against Ward, the panel said they did not have jurisdiction to deal with the case but even if they had, the challenge would have been dismissed. They ruled that the Tripartite Commission was correct to use the ranking list based on results achieved at the 2011 World Championships rather that the AIBA overall ranking list.

Having made this finding, the panel declared that they did not need to address the issue of whether team athletes should be included in the calculation made by the Tripartite Commission. 'The application filed by Mr. Joseph Ward on 24 July 2012 is denied,' concluded the panel. Joe Ward's Olympic dream was finally dead in the water. The 'wild card' Montenegrin Boško Drašković was beaten 16-11 in the preliminary round by Oscar Bravo from Nicaragua at the Olympics, while the two boxers who had beaten Ward in Baku and Trabzon respectively, Ehsan Rouzbahani and Bahram Muzaffer, clashed in the second round in London, with the Iranian winning 18-12.

Ward watched the action from his home in Moate. 'I sat down and watched the Irish guys and I watched the fights in my weight division. I would have liked to have been there but it wasn't to be.'

As is his wont, Paddy Barnes stole the show from an Irish perspective during the opening ceremony. He would have liked to follow in the footsteps of Wayne McCullough in Seoul in 1988 and carry the Irish tricolour into the Olympic stadium. Instead, that honour went to Katie Taylor. Still, it was too good an opportunity to miss for a wind up. The forecast was for scattered showers; the other boxers presented Paddy with an umbrella with a suggestion that he hold it over Katie's head to keep her dry while she carried the tricolour. It didn't rain but Paddy was determined to grab the limelight. So he wrote on a sheet of paper: 'Open for Sponsors @ Paddyb-ireland (twitter)' and held it up for the camera as he paraded around the in-field. It was a bit of light-hearted banter before the action began. As Katie later remarked, Paddy doesn't know the meaning of the word embarrassment.

In contrast to the Beijing Olympics, the IABA's High Performance programme was the second-best funded in 2012 with an allocation of €807,874, though it still lagged behind Athletics Ireland's programme, which received €887, 874. And, overall, the IABA itself still lagged behind in terms of their grant allocation from the ISC. But when it came to the business of winning medals in London, the boxers delivered once again.

CHAPTER 18

ECSTASY AND AGONY
IN THE EXCEL

'Of course, he should have won it, one hundred percent. If he didn't have the potential to beat Campbell, it wouldn't have mattered. Why didn't he win? He didn't focus. You can see it as he's walking to the ring.'

Zaur Antia

The first boxing session at the London Olympics was virtually a sell-out. It was a portent of things to come. 'I've never seen a better atmosphere at an Olympic tournament. The Irish turn up everywhere but I was taken aback by the sheer number of them. It was phenomenal,' recalls Irish coach Billy Walsh.

Bantamweight John Joe Nevin was the first Irish boxer in action and, according to Walsh, he was taken aback by the atmosphere. 'He was looking out at the crowd during the first round. When I got him back into the corner, I told him, "Get your head back into the ring; you can enjoy the crowd after."

'Our psychologist [Gerry Hussey] spotted what had happened and he

Kenny Egan celebrates with Irish coach Billy Walsh after winning his quarter-final bout against Brazil's Washington Silva at the Beijing Olympics in 2008, to guarantee himself a bronze medal. He ended up winning a silver.

Above: The late Darren Sutherland in a reflective pose in the HPU gym, prior to the Irish team's departure to the World Boxing Championships in Chicago in 2007.

Left: A beaming Darren Sutherland celebrates after winning his second professional fight against Siarhei Navarka in Wigan, March 2009.

Above: Ireland's Beijing Olympic medallists, Darren Sutherland, Paddy Barnes and Kenny Egan, show off their haul following their arrival back in Dublin Airport.

Below: Middleweight Darren O'Neill, a silver medallist at the 2010 European Championships in Moscow, taught in Holy Trinity National School in Donaghmede, Dublin, while training for the championships. Pictured here, together with school principal Jerry Grogan (**left**) and Gary Keegan, founder of the HPU and now director of High Performance Management at the Irish Institute of Sport.

Above: Joe Ward celebrates after beating Russia's Nikita Ivanov to win a bronze medal in the light heavyweight category at the World Boxing Championships in Almaty in 2013.

Below: A tearful Michael Conlan is consoled by Irish coaches Billy Walsh (**left**) and Zaur Antia moments after losing his Olympic flyweight semi-final to eventual gold medallist Robeisy Ramírez Carrazana from Cuba.

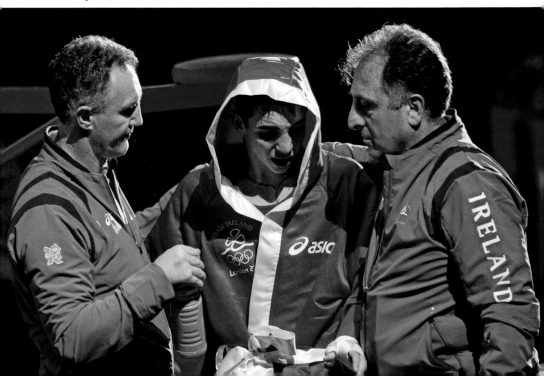

Right: John Joe Nevin celebrates after winning the European bantamweight title in Minsk in 2013, to become the first Irish male boxer to wins medals at the World and European Championships, as well as the Olympic Games.

Left: John Joe Nevin's dream of securing the gold medal in the Olympic bantamweight final ends in bitter disappointment as Luke Campbell's hand is raised in victory in London's ExCel Arena.

Left: Paddy Barnes puts Olympic champion Zou Shiming under pressure in the light flyweight semi-final bout in London, which the Irishman lost narrowly on a countback.

Below: Ireland finished second in the medal table at the European Boxing Championships in Minsk in 2013 headed only by Russia. The medalists (**from left**) were Paddy Barnes (silver, light flyweight), John Joe Nevin (gold, bantamweight), Jason Quigley (gold, middleweight), and Michael Conlan (silver, flyweight).

Above: Paddy Barnes: double Olympic bronze medallist, European gold and silver medalist and two-time Commonwealth Gold medallist; he is also the only Irish boxer to qualify for three Olympic Games.

Right: Mayo's Ciara McGinty, who was named Best AIBA Junior Woman Boxer in 2013.

Above: Katie Taylor (**left**) in action in the lightweight final at the London Olympics against Russia's Sofya Ochigava.

Below: Newly-crowned Olympic champion Katie Taylor at the homecoming celebrations in her native Bray, together with coach Zaur Antia and, in the background, Adam Nolan, who also boxed for Ireland at the London Olympics.

recorded the atmosphere during the fight. He put it on his laptop and later played it back to the other lads. They all uploaded it on to their iPads so they could get accustomed to the noise.'

'But the real thing was 100 percent different,' says flyweight Michael Conlan. 'It's just not the same as closing your eyes, listening to the tape and imaging you're walking out into the arena. I lost myself until the end of the first round in my first fight. I was saying, "What's going on here?" The crowd just sucked me in.'

In a significant change from the Beijing Olympics only the three closest aggregate scores counted; two of the five judges' scores were discounted. In truth it mattered little to the boxers, though it threw up the usual quota of inconsistent decisions. Even if he was slightly distracted, John Joe Nevin was 5-2 ahead after the first round of his bantamweight bout against Dennis Ceylan, the only Danish boxer to qualify for the Olympic Games. One judge, indeed, scored the round 8-2 in favour of the Irishman.

Nevin, who had beaten Ceylan at the 2008 EU Championships, was simply in a different class. Trailing by seven points at the end of the second round, the Dane knew his Olympic dream was over. So much so that Nevin remembers his opponent initiating a conversation when they resumed boxing. 'He said, "You're boxing very well, John Joe," and that kind of gave me a little buzz. I was talking to him as well trying to slow him down," says Nevin who went on to win the contest 21-6. When the result was announced the Irish boxer pointed his right and left index fingers towards the sky and looked upwards in a gesture of thanks to his late cousin David Nevin.

Nevin's male colleagues, middleweight Darren O'Neill, welterweight Adam Nolan, light flyweight Paddy Barnes and Michael Conlan, all breezed through their opening assignments. The Belfast pair, Barnes and Conlan received byes in the first round which meant they were two wins away from securing bronze medals. It also left them with ample time to indulge in harmless mischief around the Olympic village. 'We used to head off to the nearby Westfield Shopping Centre and the casino. Paddy was winning loads, whereas I was losing big money. I often said to Paddy, "You're going to lose your fights because you can't have that much luck."

'Any time I lost money I always won my fights. So I was delighted to be giving money to the casino,' says Conlan. 'We always played cards when we went away, usually a game called Guts. Billy hated it. He always worried in case we lost too much money.'

Darren O'Neill was the first Irish boxer to exit the tournament, losing 19-12 to German middleweight Stefan Härtel in the second round. Even though the Irish captain comfortably beat the rangy Nigerian Muideen Akanji 15-6 in the opening session, he never regained the form he showed at the World Championships the previous year. Looking back, O'Neill admits, 'I wasn't totally surprised at how it turned out in London. I wouldn't say I struggled with my confidence but my form was down. I twice sparred with that German. In the first spar I clearly got the better of him, but my form was off the second time and he gave me a hiding.

'I thought I would be fine against him at the Olympics. I think if I had the chance to box him the year before or the year after it might have been a different story. I came out disappointed that I didn't perform as well as I could. But I gave it all I could on the day and that's all I could do.' Härtel was beaten in the next round by England's Anthony Ogogo who went on to win the silver medal.

Adam Nolan also bowed out, losing 18-9 to the highly rated Russian Andrey Zamkovoy, a silver medallist at the World Championships in Milan in 2009. In London Zamkovoy was surprisingly defeated in the semi-final, so had to be content with a bronze medal. Within a couple of weeks of the closing ceremony Nolan was back on beat duty in Bray. He would treasure his Olympic experience and his 14-8 win over Carlos Sánchez Estachio from Ecuador.

Still, by the time Nevin stepped into the ring to meet 2009 world feather-weight bronze medallist Óscar Rafael Valdez Fierro from Mexico the Irish bandwagon had gathered considerable momentum. Barnes, Conlan and Katie Taylor were all within touching distance of a podium finish. Earlier that day Nevin's favourite GAA football team Kerry had suffered a shock defeat to Donegal in the All-Ireland quarter-finals in Croke Park. But in the ring Nevin was on a roll. He had beaten Kanat Abutalipov from Kazakhstan 15-10 in round two to secure a medal fight against Valdez, who as a seventeen-year-old had boxed at the Beijing Olympics. Having boxed as a featherweight at the 2009 World Championships, Valdez was forced to revert to the lighter ban-tamweight category after the 57 kg weight division was dropped from the Olympic boxing programme.

Like Nevin, he had lost to the eventual gold medallist Enkhbatyn Badar-Uu-gan from Mongolia at the Beijing Olympics. The Irishman and the Mexican were level, 5-5, at the end of the first round. But Nevin's ability to hit cleanly with his right hook when he got within range of his opponent ensured that he won the second round 7-4, to take a three-point lead into the final three min-utes. The Mexican possessed a lethal punch which he finally landed on Nevin's midriff with fifty seconds left in the contest. Nevin was forced to go down on one knee to catch his breath.

Nevin can easily recall what happened next. 'I remember thinking, this is going to be a long minute. It was a brilliant shot and I just had to go down. Either that or get knocked out. He's a very hard hitter. He hit me a few head shots. I knew my tactics. I didn't want to stand there with him trading shots. I wanted to annoy him.' With relative ease, Nevin survived Valdez's increasingly desperate attempts to land a knock-out blow in the closing seconds. The Irish boxer won 19-13 to guarantee himself an Olympic bronze medal.

It was Ireland's twenty-fourth medal in Olympic history, thirteen of which had been won by boxers. As he had done throughout the tournament, Nevin blessed himself and pointed to the sky when the verdict was announced. His late cousin David was never far from his thoughts, and Nevin believes it was David who 'told me I'd go all the way. It was him that inspired me.'

In terms of the preparation for the fight, Nevin knows it was coaches Billy Walsh and Zaur Antia who provided the blueprint for the win: 'They're phenomenal coaches. I think the best in the world. They do the tactics and tell you how best to fight a lad. I just go along with them because they're not going to tell you the wrong thing. I might have been thinking different things myself, but I just went with the boys' strategy and it worked.'

Michael Conlan was apprehensive about his flyweight quarter-final medal clash against Frenchman Nordine Oubaali, even though he had beaten him in a tournament in Berck seven weeks earlier as well as at the World Championships in Baku in 2011. 'It is just so hard to beat anybody three times in a row. I knew it was going to be a nail-biter. I had to dig deep, but I wanted it more and I broke him in the end to win 22-18.'

There was more than just an Olympic bronze medal at stake when Paddy Barnes climbed into the ring in his 48 kg quarter-final against Indian Devendro Singh Laishram, who he had sparred in Dublin during a training camp prior to the Olympics.

Barnes has vivid memories of the pressure he was under. 'I was fighting for my life. I was after buying a house in Belfast and needed to win a bronze medal to secure my funding from the Sports Council. Otherwise I wouldn't have been able to pay the mortgage. Had I lost I would have had to go down to Tesco looking for a job. The biggest problem with the High Performance programme is that while the funding provides you with enough money to live on there is no job security.' In a tight contest Barnes prevailed 23-18 to become the first Irish boxer to win two Olympic medals.

So, for the second successive Olympics three Irish male boxers were through to the Olympic semi-final – an achievement only surpassed in 1956 when four Irish boxers made it to the penultimate stage of the Melbourne Games.

Twenty-four hours after Katie Taylor's historic gold medal triumph at the ExCel centre, it was the turn of Barnes, Conlan and Nevin to grab the limelight. Outside of the team expectations were muted. There are no soft touches at this level in the Olympics and, despite their heroics up until then, few expected the trio to advance past their Chinese and Cuban opponents. The team management knew exactly what their charges were facing. After nine years in existence they had accumulated a database on every rated amateur boxer in the world. Once the draws were made, the HPU performance analyst Alan Swanton switched on his laptop and searched for contests involving boxers the Irish team were due to face. As a result, when they entered the ring they knew what to expect.

For Barnes it was a case of déjà vu. For the second successive Olympics and the third time in all, he faced his Chinese nemesis Zou Shiming who had beaten him at the 2007 World Championships and in the semi-final in Beijing. This time around the Irishman felt his time had come: 'When I saw the draw at the start of the tournament I said, "That's perfect because I am going to beat him in the semi-final." I just felt it was my time.'

Much to Barnes' chagrin, the judges in Beijing failed to award him a single point. It was a different story in the ExCel. Shiming however, is difficult to pin down in the ring. Apart from being two centimetres taller than Barnes, his bone structure belies the fact that his boxing weight is 49 kg. He had the edge over Barnes in the first round which was reflected on the judges' scorecards – a three-point lead for the defending Olympic champion. The second round was cagier and tighter which the judges marked 3-3. Barnes knew he had to step up his challenge in the final three minutes and he responded magnificently. Such was the frenetic nature of the exchanges that at times it was difficult to ascertain who was landing the scoring punches.

The two boxers raised their gloved hand to signify they felt they had won when the final bell sounded. It is a meaningless gesture really. Barnes actually felt he had lost when the contest ended. There was a two-minute delay before the official result was announced during which he watched some of the highlights of the final round on the big screen in the arena, and says, 'Having looked at it I thought I had thrown more punches.'

An expectant hush fell over the arena when the announcer began, 'Ladies and gentlemen, the judges have scored the contest 15-15. The winner on countback in the red corner ...' Shiming had maintained his one hundred percent record over his Irish rival. But the victory was literally by the slimmest of margins – a single point (45-44). In the countback all five judges' scores are taken into account. Barnes had won the last round by three points (7-4), but it wasn't enough.

Before the tournament had begun, Walsh had stressed to the team the significance of winning the first round. Analysis done within the HPU had revealed that eighty-five percent of boxers who are ahead after three minutes go on to win the fight. His words of wisdom came back to haunt Barnes. But it was despairingly close. Had Barnes been credited with two more scoring punches, he would have been in an Olympic final.

In 2008 he had suggested that bronze medals were for losers. He was more philosophical about his near-miss in London. Nevertheless, having watched the fight again a couple of days later, he definitely felt he should have got the decision: 'I was so close. I didn't feel cheated because it was so close and he was the defending champion. Still, I think I would have done well in the final as

Kaeo Pongprayoon was smaller than me and would have suited me more than Shiming.' Shiming successfully defended his Olympic title against Pongprayoon, an army officer from Thailand. The latter was inconsolable afterwards and he had the crowd's sympathy. When the verdict was announced it was loudly booed.

Even though they fought three times, Barnes and Shiming never spoke. Barnes says that Shiming 'speaks no English whatsoever but he used to smile at me when we met and he obviously knows who I am.' The Irish boxer's dream is to challenge the Chinese fighter, who has now turned professional under famous American trainer Freddie Roche, in a $1 million purse fight for a title.

There was no joy either for Michael Conlan in the semi-final. He was outclassed 20-10 by Cuban Robeisy Ramírez Carrazana who won the gold medal twenty-four hours later. Despite his tender years and relative lack of experience at this level, Conlan was devastated: 'I really thought it was my Olympic Games. I know not too many people get a medal [at the Olympics] but I was heartbroken. It took me two days to get over it. Once I took part in the medal presentation ceremony I was okay. I was jealous of the winner but I enjoyed it and it was great that my parents were in the arena to witness it.'

Regardless of what John Joe Nevin achieves during his professional boxing career, in terms of performance it is difficult to imagine it surpassing his nine minutes of magnificence against Cuban world champion Lázaro Álvarez Estrada.

It was a fight redolent of Michael Carruth's gold medal contest against another Cuban, Juan Hernández Sierra at the Barcelona Olympics twenty years earlier. 'It's the outstanding memory from my career so far,' says Nevin. 'Everything I tried that day worked. It seemed as if all I had to do was put out my hand and it connected.'

In truth, Nevin undersells his performance. Muhammad Ali was talking about himself when he proclaimed, 'Float like a butterfly, sting like a bee.' But the greatest athlete of the twentieth century would surely have acknowledged that Nevin gave a near-perfect exhibition of the philosophy on that famous Friday afternoon. Thin Lizzy's 'The Boys are Back in Town' blared through the sound system as Nevin made his way to the ring. Within half a minute of the opening bell, he had laid out his stall, catching Álvarez with a textbook right. He didn't relent for the rest of the round and should have been more than 5-3 at the end of it.

The reaction in the Cuban corner betrayed their emotions. The coach slapped the side of Álvarez's headgear as if to remind him that this was an Olympic semi-final and Cuba were struggling to fill their usual quota of places in the finals. But Álvarez didn't want to know. After shipping two more rights and then a short left, the Cuban southpaw was down on one knee early in the second round. He finally responded with a barrage of punches, but Nevin landed more scoring shots in the final thirty seconds and won the round 7-6. Nevin now led by three points. It was not an unassailable advantage but the Cavan Boxing Club boxer had built his career on avoiding punches. Essentially the Cuban needed to knock out him out if he was to advance.

By now, though, Nevin was operating in a different stratosphere. Any trace of fear had drained from his body. His adrenalin-pump was in overdrive. From somewhere deep in the recesses of his muscle memory he remembered his first-ever fight as an eight-year-old and his attempt to recreate the shuffle which his boyhood boxing hero Prince Naseem had patented. In the most important fight of his career Nevin did the shuffle again. 'Sure, we'll call it the Mullingar Shuffle,' suggested Walsh afterwards.

As it had done fifteen years earlier, the 'Mullingar Shuffle' provoked a reaction from the Cuban, who charged forward and caught Nevin on the ropes and landed a couple of punches. But Nevin slipped away and caught Álvarez again before the final bell.

There was no doubt about the result: a 19-14 win for Nevin, who became the sixth Irish boxer to qualify for an Olympic final and the third bantamweight, following in the footsteps of John McNally and Wayne McCullough. The word in the ExCel Centre afterwards was that the Irishman was a contender for the vaunted Val Barker Trophy, awarded to the best boxer at the Games. The problem was that the final was less than thirty hours away.

Marathon Olympic silver medallist John Treacy understood the dilemma Nevin faced. 'His semi-final performance was phenomenal. I believe if he had one more day to rest he would have secured the gold. But he was after eliminating the number one bantamweight in the world and it was very difficult to bounce back from that.'

Nevin's opponent was England's Luke Campbell, who had a comfortable 20-11 win over Japan's Satoshi Shimizu in the other semi-final. The host nation had three boxers: welterweight Fred Evans – who was actually from Wales – and super heavyweight Anthony Joshua together with Campbell in the finals. So for the first time during the tournament the Irish fans wouldn't be the loudest in the arena and UK supporters obviously wouldn't be rooting for Nevin. Nonetheless, he held most of the other aces and was the bookies' favourite.

Darren O'Neill knew exactly what his room-mate needed to do in final. 'I've often said it to John Joe. "When you hit form there is nobody in the world who can beat you." He proved that against the Cuban. When he hits form, he is gifted. I kept telling him before the final, "Don't rush this lad. Wait for him, wait for him." I felt the whole fight would hinge on who kept their nerve the longest. I told him, "Campbell is fighting in front of his home crowd, he will crack first". But John Joe went in and attacked him. I could have cried,' says O'Neill. Katie Taylor revealed in her autobiography that O'Neill did cry when the verdict was announced.

'There was no way I could see him being beaten,' says Walsh, though he was concerned about the short time lag between the two contests. 'Boxers can go four or five days without a fight at the Olympics and then their most crucial bouts are straight after one another.'

Zaur Antia becomes particularly animated when he reflects on Nevin's defeat. 'It was obvious that he had a very special talent from his early days with us. John Joe could have been the Olympic champion. He broke my heart forever in the final. Of course, he should have won it, one hundred percent. If he didn't have the potential to beat Campbell, it wouldn't have mattered. Why didn't he win? He didn't focus. You can see it as he's walking to the ring.'

In footage of Nevin walking to the ring, the boxer is smiling and looking up at the crowd. Alongside him, Antia has a pronounced scowl on his face and he's clearly barking instructions at his boxer. 'I was telling him to focus, focus, focus. Look how Katie Taylor or the other boxers focus before a fight,' declares Antia who demonstrates by walking across the room with his head resting on his chest.

'But with John Joe he is smiling and looking around. The boxer should never do that before a fight; it should happen after the competition. As you can see in the clip, I'm not happy. Three times I said, "Listen, John Joe, stop smiling now. Sit down and think about what you are going to do." But he's not listening. I am talking to him but he is not there. I am thinking, "We are fucked." I was not happy.'

Darren O'Neill questions Antia's theory. 'John Joe was like that before every fight. Look, if he had fought Campbell an hour later or the day after he probably would have won.'

The Irish coaches reviewed the two previous fights at senior level between Nevin and Campbell. The former won the first 13-2 at the EU Championships in Denmark, while the Hull southpaw, who won a European title in Liverpool in 2008, beat the Irishman on a countback in the World Champion-ships semi-final in Baku in 2011. They had no doubt about how Nevin should approach the fight, as Antia explained. 'In the first fight it was seventy percent counter-attack and thirty percent attack. At the World Championships it was fifty/fifty. Billy and I thought it was still the wrong verdict. John Joe sat down and watched the video. We tell him sixty percent counter-attack; and forty percent attack will make you champion.'

In reality, it wasn't going to be quite so simple. Walsh and Antia knew that the English coaching team would have done their research as well. 'They would be thinking the same way as we were thinking. So the fight would not be so much physical as emotional. So we said to John Joe, "You must be focused. No attacking no matter what happens, keep feigning, keep edging." But then once the fight started he seemed to forget. It was so difficult," sighs Antia.

Walsh is slightly more sympathetic in his assessment. 'We knew that Camp-bell was going to wait. He knew that if he came forward he was going to be hammered. So it was about John Joe feinting and hitting him with body shots in the meantime. I think John Joe got a bit excited with the crowd and once he went behind he felt he had to go chasing.'

Campbell's grandparents are Irish. Indeed, during a period when he was unsettled in the British Podium Squad due to personality clashes and a dip in form, he explored the possibility of declaring for Ireland. The arrival of Rob McCracken as Performance Director for the British team in November 2009 persuaded him to stay and give it another go. Ironically, had Campbell declared for Ireland, the odds are that he would have ended up fighting Nevin not for an Olympic gold medal but for a place in the qualifiers.

Minutes before the bantamweight final, British runner Mo Farah had won the 5000-metre final, five miles away in Olympic Park, to become the first athlete since Lasse Virén in 1976 to complete what is regarded as the near mythical 5000 metres/10,000 metres double gold at the Olympic Games. So, the thousands of British fans in the ExCel were feeling positively heady when the boxers walked in. Two years older than his Irish rival, Campbell was unfazed, despite the rising decibel levels.

In truth, the contest was decided in the final two and a half minutes of the first round. Nevin started out following his corner's instructions. Indeed, neither boxer threw a punch of note in the opening thirty seconds. Then Nevin went over on his ankle and this clearly fazed him. Campbell started to score with his long right counter-punches. The favourite finally hit his target in the latter stages of the round. It was Campbell who had succeeded in impressing the judges, and he led 5-3 at the end of the three minutes. Psychologically, Campbell now held the aces. As a southpaw he was more comfortable counter-attacking and he had a ten centimetre longer reach than his opponent. Nevin had no option but to go on the offensive. Against the odds, the Irish boxer won the round 5-4, which left Campbell with a precarious one-point advantage going into the final stanza. For a brief moment, it seemed the pre-fight favourite might mine the gold after all.

The final turning point came midway through the last round. As Nevin stepped forward to throw a shot, his opponent slipped the punch and countered with a left hook to the temple. Nevin wobbled, having turned on his ankle in the earlier round, and went to the canvas. He was on his feet within seconds but referee Jonas Kennedy gave him a standing count. Campbell only earned a point for the punch, but it changed the momentum of the contest. His confidence grew and he kept out of harm's way for the remainder of the round, which he won 5-2 for an overall 14-11 success.

Immediately after the fight and, indeed, in the intervening years Nevin has never made any excuses for his loss. 'I feel like a failure' was his first comment to the media afterwards. 'I would have taken bronze coming here but after I got so far I wanted to go the whole way. I feel like a failure because I beat him well before. I'm heartbroken. I wanted to go home and join the club with Katie Taylor and Michael Carruth. But if it's not meant to be, it's not meant to be.'

The boxer demonstrated his humility by remembering the four victims of a horrific car accident in Tullamore the previous day. Brothers Darren, David and Ryan Doyle and their friend Lee Bryan had reportedly watched Nevin's semi-final win before the accident 'I'd just like to say I'm very sorry for the families of the four chaps that died in that crash. My heart goes out to them. I'm here standing with a silver medal and those poor families are arranging funerals.'

Months passed before Nevin gave a more reflective view on what was arguably the biggest disappointment of his career. 'Fair play to Campbell, the better man won. Maybe people don't understand on the day before the final I had beaten the world champion. It was hard to come down after that fight. I was trying to get myself nervous for the final but I couldn't. Campbell told me after the fight that he was worried because Álvarez had easily beaten him before. In the first minute I went over on my ankle. When you're boxing the pain goes away. At the medal presentation Billy Walsh and one of the other lads had to lift me on to the podium.'

Nowadays he is at pains to stress that he has no explanation to offer for what happened. 'I have no excuses. I have never used one excuse. I tried my best, but my best wasn't good enough on the night. Maybe on another day my best might have been different.'

The next forty-eight hours were a whirlwind of homecoming celebrations for the Irish team. Compared to 2008, the squad and their families were better informed as to what would happen. A month before the start of the London Games, the HPU organised a family day for the boxers' parents, partners and coaches. 'Basically we outlined what was going to happen at the Games; how it was going to happen; how we were going to communicate with them during the Games and how they could get tickets,' recalls Walsh. Beijing silver medallist Kenny Egan and his mother Maura addressed the gathering. 'My mam just explained to the parents what happens,' says Egan.

Two days after the squad returned from London they attended a debriefing. A week later, the HPU brought the families together again. 'We told them the emotions they would experience coming down after an Olympic experience. We used the analogy of what happens climbers on Mount Everest. Eighty percent of the fatalities on the mountain happen on the way down,' says Walsh. Within a month of the closing ceremony the boxers were back in full-time training. 'Their routine was established again.'

Nevertheless, the celebrations were still memorable and in the case of Nevin, poignant. One Direction's Niall Horan was on the stage in Cusack Park in Mullingar for Nevin's official homecoming. Later the boxer went to Ballyglass Cemetery in Mullingar to pay his respects at the grave of his grandparents John Joe and Mary and his cousin David. 'No matter where I go, I will always come back to my grandparents' grave. I believe they look down on me and help me along the way. It's very sad to have lost them and I just like to be out here and bring the medal to them. It means a lot to me to have such people in my life,' he told the *Irish Independent*.

Meanwhile, it was party time for Paddy Barnes and Michael Conlan, who spun a yarn that they were planning to holiday in Bundoran; they actually went to Ibiza. 'My life was changed, it went upside down for a while,' recalls Conlan. 'We came back on Monday and got our Olympic tattoos on Tuesday. Skinworks in Belfast did it for free; Paddy had one already from Beijing. He got another and I got the Olympic rings tattooed on to my left pectoral.

'I never actually stayed at home that week; I was out every night, only returning home to change my clothes. The holiday was brilliant. It was crazy how much we were recognised in Ibiza, but I suppose the tattoos kinda gave us away. We had been told beforehand that all this would happen so that was definitely a help. I had never been off the rails before. But I could never become an alcoholic because I don't like alcohol. I can't drink beer; the only thing I can drink is vodka. I couldn't drink loads of it because I would be tossed.'

Conlan was back boxing in early September; he headed off to the US on a tour with Paddy Barnes' Holy Family Club. Barnes opted to stay at home to watch his close friend Carl Frampton win the Commonwealth and IBF Inter-Continental super bantamweight title at the Odyssey Arena in Belfast.

The London Olympics was an unqualified story success for the HPU. The odds are that Katie Taylor would have won gold regardless of their existence. She is a one-off; a remarkable athlete whose talent has been nurtured and honed for more than a decade by a voracious work ethic. For the second successive Olympics the Irish male boxers brought home three medals – one silver and two bronze – a feat only bettered by the one silver and three bronze garnered by the boxers in Melbourne in 1956. Nevin, Conlan, Barnes and Taylor received bonus payments of €10,000 each from the ISC for their exploits in London which meant that their total income under the carding scheme in 2012 was €50,000 each. O'Neill received €40,000 and Nolan €20,000.

In international terms these payments are a pittance. According to a survey in AIPS magazine at the most recent Olympics, the Winter Games in Sochi in 2014, Russia – who headed the medal table with thirty-three, including thirteen gold – paid out five million euro in bonus payments. Obviously all the countries were not quite as extravagant. Still, Belarus paid their gold medal-winning freestyle skiers, Anton Kushnir and Alla Tsuper $150,000 (€128,000) each in bonus payments, while at the other end of the scale, Armin Zöggeler from Italy, who won a bronze in the luge, earned a bonus payment of $68,000 (€58,510).

Ireland was only one of twenty countries to win boxing medals in London. For the first time ever the USA failed to win a medal in the men's boxing. France, Germany, Turkey and Hungary also returned home empty-handed. Great Britain made the most of the traditional 'host country bounce' in boxing by topping the ranking list with five, including three gold. Ireland's tally of four medals elevated them to an all-time high fifth place alongside Kazakhstan. Apart from Great Britain, the other countries placed higher were Ukraine, Cuba and Russia. Yet Irish coach Billy Walsh couldn't quite shake off that gnawing feeling that London could have been better. His dream of securing that elusive Olympic gold medal had passed him by again.

Like John McNally, Fred Tiedt and Kenny Egan, John Joe Nevin ought to have won an Olympic title but fell short. So Michael Carruth remains the only Irish male boxer to have garnered that famous piece of metal manufactured of copper with a diameter of sixty millimetres, a thickness of three millimetres and covered with six grams of pure gold: an Olympic gold medal.

Twenty months after the London Games Nevin had to endure a far more traumatic life event than the loss of an Olympic final. His right shin bone was broken in two places, and his left fibula was fractured in a fracas near his home at Ardleigh in Mullingar.

For weeks his boxing career hung by a thread. He had to have a steel rod inserted between the knee and the ankle of his right leg. 'Of course I feared for my future when I was in Tullamore hospital. It was a natural feeling with top doctors telling me that I might never box again. I'm still young and I had my whole life in front of me. Boxing was the only thing I ever wanted to do and the only thing I knew how to do. It was like killing me off there and then.'

Three weeks after the incident Nevin discarded his wheelchair; seven weeks later he was off the crutches. Badgered by his coach Brian McKeown, he resumed running. 'I was cursing him the next day because my ankle had all swelled up.' Following consultations with his surgeons, they removed screws which had been inserted during the initial surgery. 'Ever since then the leg has been perfect. Fretting over the wins and losses seems irrelevant, even petty-minded now. I'm just going to cherish what's left of my boxing career,' says Nevin.

While he made a successful comeback in the ring in November 2014, chalking up his third win in the professional ranks with a first round TKO (Technical Knock Out) win over Jack Heath in Dublin's 3 Arena, his life outside the ring continues to be problematic. In February 2015 he appeared at Mullingar District Court on a criminal damage charge, while in April he was barred from every pub in County Westmeath, pending a court case, following a brawl outside a bar in the town on Easter Monday night. On 21 May he appeared before Judge Seamus Hughes in relation to a different incident outside a pub in Mullingar just after Christmas 2014. Nevin admitted a public order offence arising from his involvement in what was described as a 'general melée' which spilled out of a pub in the town.

Nevin told the court that he was now off drink and training for his next professional fight. Addressing the boxer, Judge Hughes said, 'I want you to do your fighting inside the ring and not outside it.' He told Nevin he was a national and international figure and that people looked up to him, but he was blighting his reputation by occasional instances of bad behaviour. 'For your sake, stop the messing you're doing,' the judge said. He ordered Nevin to pay €500 to the court poor box.

CHAPTER 19

LIFE AFTER LONDON

'Look, I don't want to be anywhere else, though there are nice places which have a better climate where we could go. But we don't need to be anywhere else because we have the talent here; we have built a nice system around which we are continuously trying to improve.'

Billy Walsh

The euphoric mood among Irish fans at the London Olympics was deflated on the eve of John Joe Nevin's gold medal fight when they read in the *Irish Independent* that coaches Billy Walsh and Zaur Antia were being tempted with lucrative offers from other boxing federations. Clearly the success of the boxers – the team had effectively rescued the Games from an Irish perspective – put Walsh and Antia into an enviable bargaining position. On an emotional level, neither wanted to leave Ireland, and Walsh stressed that he didn't want to be portrayed as 'moaning and whingeing'.

Nonetheless, he didn't mince his words in an interview with sports journalist Vincent Hogan when he compared their plight to the then Irish soccer boss Giovanni Trapattoni and his rugby counterpart Declan Kidney. 'When you consider Mr Trapattoni is on a million euro just to qualify [for the European finals]. Declan Kidney is on a fantastic contract. Now, I've the utmost respect for those men. I'm happy for them, but we're not valued for what we do. We're making history, bringing more medals into this country than any other sport. I know for a fact that I'm the lowest paid High Performance manager, or whatever you want to call it, of all sports.

'I don't mind about titles. Everybody knows I lead a good team, but we need to be rewarded for that going forward. When you consider that before the World Cup, Declan Kidney got a massive contract. Before the Euros, Trapattoni the same. Nobody tried to secure us. That says it all, doesn't it?'

Nicolás Cruz once told Walsh, 'What you didn't have around your neck as a boxer, you will have in your hand as a coach.' By the time the London Games ended, the HPU had delivered seven Olympic medals. Cruz's remark had proved prophetic. But Walsh and Antia felt that their pay cheques did not reflect boxing's dominant position on the Irish sporting landscape. In the end, though, Walsh and Antia signed up for another four-year cycle. 'The offers at the time were realistic and they are still there if we need to go. But we're Irishmen; Zaur classes himself as being Irish at this stage,' says Walsh.

'Look, I don't want to anywhere else, though there are nice places which have a better climate where we could go. But we don't need to be anywhere else because we have the talent here; we have built a nice system around which we are continuously trying to improve.' In the four-year Olympic cycle leading up to the London Games the government through the ISC invested €6,441,331 in boxing; this figure includes the annual grant to the IABA, the funding of the HP programme and the individual grants paid to boxers through the carding system.

So, in crude mathematical terms, the four Olympic medals at the London Games cost the taxpayer €1.2 million each. Of course, in real terms the figure was much less. Not all of the €6.4 million was spent on the elite boxers; the grants covered all aspects of the sport. Even if the figure was €1.2 million per medal, judged by international standards it represents extraordinary good value. In the aftermath of the London Games, UK Sports published details of their spending on each Olympic sport in Great Britain since the 2008 Games.

The largest amounts were spent on rowing €36.16 million (£27 million), cycling €34.82 million (£26 million) and athletics and swimming €33.48 million (£25 million each). They invested €12,792,291 (£9,551,400) in boxing, which proved the most cost effective. British boxers won five medals putting the average cost of a boxing medal at €2.54 million (£1.9 million); still more than double the comparable figure in Ireland.

Furthermore, compared to the return from other sports in Ireland, the investment in boxing performed better than a hot share tip from Warren Buffet. Between the Beijing and London Games, the ISC invested €8,987,393 in athletics, €5,784,061 in equestrian; €5,566, 245 in swimming and €4,281,832 in sailing. This total investment of €24,619,531 yielded one Olympic medal – a bronze for Cian O'Connor in show jumping.

Six months after their exploits in London the squad were brought back to earth at the 2013 Elite Championships, though, as usual, nobody was willing to take on gold medallist Katie Taylor. In an exhibition she beat Poland's Karolina Gracyk 28-8. However, there is never a shortage of able challengers for her male colleagues, as Olympian and four-time Irish middleweight title holder Darren O'Neill discovered in the quarter-finals.

He suffered a shock defeat to twenty-one-year old Jason Quigley. In a cracking contest, the pair tied 13-13 after O'Neill made up a two-point deficit in the last round. But the Donegal pugilist got the verdict 49-38 on a countback. The win represented a significant breakthrough in Quigley's career. Although he had underlined his potential by winning the European Youth title in 2009 and the European U-23 crown three years later, O'Neill repeatedly thwarted him at senior level, defeating him in the 2010 and 2011 Elite finals. In a desperate effort to make the breakthrough, Quigley shed more than six kilos to qualify as a welterweight for the 2012 Elite Championships. But the experiment backfired when he was beaten by a seasoned international Willie McLaughlin, who coincidentally also hails from county Donegal.

The defeat marked a watershed in Quigley's career. Remarkably, he won his next thirty-two fights on the spin before losing his last bout as an amateur – a historic World Championship decider.

Quigley first laced up a pair of gloves in the kitchen of the family home in the Donegal village of Laghey. The table was pushed to one side to enable the youngster to skip, shadow box and do some work on the pads with his father Conor. A former Irish national champion, Conor had a profound influence on his eldest son's career.

Conor and his partner Muriel were teenagers when Jason was born. His mother went back to school to complete her Leaving Certificate while his dad worked as a plasterer. Life began in a one-bedroom flat over a pub in Donegal town and Jason initially joined St John Bosco Club. The family also lived in Laghey before moving to Stranorlar when Conor founded the Finn Valley Boxing Club, based in neighbouring Ballybofey. Quigley made his competitive debut at a show in Jackson's Hotel in the town. He was ten years old. His opponent, Noel McBride, was from Annagry, and they have stayed in touch ever since. 'I won it. It was an unbelievable feeling,' Quigley recalls. He won his first national title a year later and by the age of twelve had earned his first international vest. A year later, he lost his first national final and these defeats continued for another two years.

When it came to sport Quigley was an all-rounder in his early teens. But boxing had the strongest hold on him and he opted to concentrate on it. His gold medal win at the European Youth Championships in 2009 vindicated this decision, but his transition into the senior ranks was problematic.

The losses Quigley endured against Darren O'Neill cut deeply into his psyche as he revealed in an interview with *The Sunday Times*. 'I kept everything deep down inside me. I knew this was what I was put on the planet to do – to box. I just got my head right and used all that hurt and disappointment to my advantage.' Having failed to secure an Elite title in three championships on the spin, Conor Quigley reckoned they needed to do something different. So the father and son headed to Bargoed, a small town in the Rhymney Valley in south Wales for a training camp.

They got a chance to spar against Nathan Cleverly, the then WBO professional light heavyweight champion who, coincidentally, was also trained by his father, Vince. Once Quigley survived Cleverly's initial onslaught he looked comfortable. When he returned to Bargoed a few months later, he won nine of the ten rounds of their spar. 'I was learning. I was improving. My confidence just rose to a different level.' says Quigley. Winning the Irish Elite title secured Quigley a place on the Irish team for the European Championships in Minsk the following June. This would be his first foray into an international championship event at senior level.

Meanwhile, Olympic bronze medallist Michael Conlan fine-tuned his preparations for the Irish Elite Championships with a clash against the Welshman Andrew Selby, who had surprisingly failed to medal at the London Games. The latter, together with John Joe Nevin and Joe Ward, was boxing for the British Lionheart franchise in the semi-professional World Series of Boxing. Conlan was signed by the USA Knockout team based in Rio, Nevada and moved up to the bantamweight category.

The boxers wore no headgear or vests and the contests were over five rounds. Conlan dropped a unanimous points decision against Selby when they clashed in Bethnal Green in London. Nevin and Ward won their contests the same night. 'I had only two fights in the series because I couldn't make the weight,' recalls Conlan. 'It was a great experience. I was making great money even though I wasn't fighting. The food in Rio was amazing and, guess what, when I came back I had put on weight.'

Conlan did make the 52 kg limit for the Elite Championships in February, though he knew his days as Ireland's top flyweight were numbered. 'I barely made the weight. Somebody remarked that I looked like death warmed up at the weigh-in and I was probably lucky to pass the medical.' In any event he comfortably retained his title – defeating Chris Phelan 20-9 in the final.

After his Olympic disappointment, Joe Ward bounced back to inflict a third successive defeat in the lightweight final on Kenny Egan, who announced his retirement in the ring afterwards. It was Egan's thirteenth consecutive appearance in an Elite decider, but his dream of winning a record-breaking eleventh Elite crown remained unfulfilled. Ward seemed hell bent on stopping him.

'He was throwing out big bombs,' acknowledges Egan, who stayed the distance – though the twenty-point defeat he endured was the biggest margin in any of the men's finals. Although Ward won the glory, it was Egan took all the honour as the crowd rose to give him a standing ovation afterwards.

By the time the fortieth European Championships rolled around in June, five of Ireland's men's squad were ranked in the top-ten in the world. Olympic medallists Nevin, Conlan and Barnes together with defending European title holders, Joe Ward and Ray Moylette (both of whom had missed the London Games), were the ranked boxers. The squad completed their preparations at the training camp in Kiev.

The computer scoring system had been replaced which left the boxers with a sense of trepidation. The new system was similar to that used in professional boxing where a boxer who wins a round is awarded ten points. Depending on how his opponent performs, he is awarded nine or less points. As the scorecards of only three of the five judges counted, it meant that majority decision would feature again for the first time since the Seoul Olympics in 1988.

Minsk, the capital of Belarus, was the venue for another memorable performance from the boxers. The championships began on the worst possible note. Ward was cruising to a routine last sixteen win over Mateusz Tryc from Poland when twenty seconds from the end there was an accidental clash of knees in the ring. The luckless Ward buckled over and had to be helped back to his corner having dislocated his left knee cap. His dream of becoming the first Irish boxer to retain a European title was over. 'The chief doctor at the venue immediately put the knee cap back in its place. I didn't feel a lot of pain because the adrenalin was flowing. I did a lot of ligament damage, though, and it took me about three months to recover,' he recalls.

Ireland's other defending title holder, Ray Moylette, also had a forgettable experience, exiting on a unanimous points decision to Turkish light welterweight Huseyin Karslioglu. All three scoring judges voted the contest 29-28. Nonetheless, Ireland ended up with five boxers in the quarter-finals. Heavyweight Tommy McCarthy was the luckless one. He dropped a unanimous points decision to the eventual silver medallist Teymur Mammadov from Azerbaijan in his medal fight. The other four, Barnes, Conlan, Nevin and Quigley, all guaranteed themselves bronze medals – the latter beating Germany's Stefan Härtel who had ended Darren O'Neill's medal ambitions at the London Olympics.

The quartet then defied the odds as they all won their respective semi-finals. For the first time in the 102 year history of the IABA, four Irish senior boxers reached the finals of a major championship. Unfortunately for Barnes his luck ran out at that point. He had to withdraw with a badly broken nose. He had been fortunate to survive until the semi-final.

'To be honest it was broken before I went to Belarus but I didn't tell anybody. It was just a hairline crack. It didn't bleed in my first fight. But in the quarter- and semi-finals it just bled and bled. Jesus Christ, I remember my nose was so unstable it was shaking. I knew then I wouldn't make the final. I could have done serious damage,' says Barnes. So he had to be content with a silver medal. In typical forthright fashion he declared that the medal meant nothing. 'It's just a piece of metal.' Nonetheless, it brought his championship medal tally to four – two Olympic bronze and two Europeans (a gold and a silver).

Weight was not an issue for Michael Conlan in Minsk. He comfortably made the 52 kg limit. 'I took the weight down gradually and kept it down. I fought well in the competition, stopping a Bulgarian in my medal fight and then beating a Russian in the semi-final.'

He faced his nemesis Andrew Selby in the final. It was a desperately close contest but for the third time in a row the Welshman got the nod, albeit on a majority 2-1 decision. One judge gave the Belfast pugilist all three rounds, but his two colleagues favoured the Welshman who was crowned European champion on a 30-27, 29-28, 28-29 scorecard. 'It's always war when we meet,' says Conlan. 'He just has my "number". We know each other well outside the ring as well and he keeps saying, "I don't want to meet you again," and I hope he doesn't.'

The vagaries of boxing were underlined later when Jason Quigley was on the right side of a split decision in the middleweight decider against the number two seed Romanian Bodgan Juratoni, a bronze medallist at the 2011 World Championships in Baku. Quigley – sporting two black eyes in the final – had announced his arrival on the world stage in the semi-final when he fashioned a unanimous 3-0 points win over the 2011 world champion and number one seed Evhen Khytrov from the Ukraine.

Buoyed up by this performance, Quigley began the final in confident fashion and all three judges gave him the first round. However, Juratoni upped his performance in the second and two of the judges gave him the round. Quigley looked to be visibly tiring and shouts of 'wake-up' rang in his ears as he left the corner. He responded magnificently and won the round on two of the judges' cards to give him the title on a split decision (30-27, 29-28, 28-29).

Unlike the Olympic Games nine months earlier, Irish coaches Billy Walsh and Zaur Antia did not fret for one second during John Joe Nevin's final against Ukranian Mykola Butsenko. Twenty-four hours previously, on his twenty-fourth birthday, the Olympic silver medallist had comfortably seen off the challenge of Russian Vladimir Nikitin. He gave an equally impervious performance in the final. His nimble footwork and ability to box off the back foot had the Ukranian in trouble from the start. Nevin won the first two rounds on all three judges' cards, which effectively left him in an unassailable position. His intensity levels dropped in the third, and two of the judges gave the round to his opponent. It mattered little as Nevin cruised to a unanimous win (30-27, 29-28, 29-28).

Nevin had toyed with the idea of turning professional in the immediate aftermath of the London Olympics. Indeed, in a television interview he indicated that he planned to link up with Amir Khan, the former two-time world champion who had won a silver medal at the Athens Olympics in 2004. However, Nevin felt there was unfinished business to be dealt with in his amateur career. No Irish male boxer had ever won championship medals at European, world and Olympic level. In Minsk, Nevin squared that circle. His gold medal meant that Ireland pipped Ukraine to finish second behind Russia in the medal table. Not surprisingly the Irish squad were never invited back to a training camp in Ukraine, though the current unrest in the country rules it out of bounds in any case.

There was another bonus for Nevin. His win elevated him to number one spot in the bantamweight division in the AIBA World rankings – the first Irish male boxer to achieve that accolade and he also won Boxer of the Tournament at the championships. 'I finally got one up on Paddy Barnes,' he recalls. 'I can rub that in his face. I was the only Irish amateur boxer to be ranked at number one. So I have something over him.'

Nevin never fought for Ireland again. Not surprisingly, he finally turned professional in October 2013 when he signed a management deal with Philadelphia-based Green Blood Boxing and Berkley Sports and Media from London. 'This is the next step up for me. I've done everything I wanted to do in the amateur business. If I could change the colour of the Olympic medal I would, but that's not possible. Now it's time to move on and hopefully bring a world professional title to Ireland,' he says.

Meanwhile, halfway across the globe in Almaty, the former capital of Kazakhstan, the five Irish boxers who had qualified for the quarter-finals at the World Amateur Championships were preparing for battle. The absence of Nevin from the Irish squad proved a blessing in disguise for Conlan, who switched from the flyweight to the heavier bantamweight category at the championships. The decision to switch weights was made at the squad's final training camp in Almaty.

Conlan remembers the impact of the weight change. 'It was so hard for me at that camp. I would do okay for thirty seconds in a spar, but then I was getting battered by boxers that I'd normally take care of. I ended up crying because I couldn't do it.'

The weight issue is also a perennial one for Barnes, though the only time he didn't make the 49 kg limit was in Almaty and he has since switched back to light fly. 'Weight and eating wise I was trying to do everything on my own at the time.' His eating regime has remained virtually the same since he joined the HPU in late 2007. When training, he rolls out of bed and on to the weighing scales. The result dictates his mood and food for the rest of the day. Breakfast consists of porridge, poached eggs or beans. He eats fish and rice for lunch and chicken, sweet potato or salad for dinner. 'Actually the only way to make the weight is to eat properly. I hate those heavyweights,' he says with a smile.

The lateness of Conlan's and Barnes's decisions to switch weights probably cost Hughie Myers, the then reigning Elite light flyweight champion, an opportunity to compete in the championships. Meanwhile, Barnes's foray into the flyweight category failed to end his World Championship jinx. As far as he was concerned, the fault lay with the AIBA. In another controversial rule change they decreed that male boxers would no longer be permitted to wear protective headgear. Self-evidently the decision greatly increased the chances of boxers being injured in a clash of heads which had been virtually eliminated with the use of headgear. Fifteen seconds before the end of the first round of his quarter-final, Barnes's legs and those of his opponent Jasurbek Latipov from Uzbekistan became tangled and they both fell to the canvas. Latipov drove his knee into Barnes's forehead after the Irishman went to ground, momentarily knocking him unconscious.

'I remember thinking, "What the hell happened there?"' recalls Barnes. 'I got up, but my head was in agony and my legs were like jelly. My vision was blurred for the rest of the fight.' Unsurprisingly, Barnes dropped a unanimous 3-0 decision (29-28, 30-27, 29-28) to Latipov. He went on to beat the 2011 world silver medallist Andrew Selby in the semi-final but lost to the Russian defending title holder Misha Aloyan in the final.

Barnes believes the AIBA must address fundamental safety issues in the wake of their controversial decision to ban headgear. 'The headgear needs to be retained unless the format for tournaments is changed. They cannot expect amateur boxers to fight day in, day out. Professional fights may last twelve rounds but the boxers then have two months off. Amateurs box every week and the pace and intensity of their fights is often greater than the professional bouts. It takes two weeks at least to recover from a fight. I've often lost one kilo during a fight.'

Russian Vladimir Nikitin probably came to Almaty expecting to face European title holder John Joe Nevin once more. Instead, it was Michael Conlan who stood between the Russian and a place on the podium. Conlan obsessed about winning a medal at the championships. 'It was the one I wanted because it would have meant I had won medals at all three championships which would have equalled John Joe's [Nevin] achievement. But I would have done it in a shorter time frame.

'The Russian won it on a unanimous 3-0 decision which left me disgusted and sickened. I couldn't contain myself. I thought I had killed him in the first round. I couldn't believe the decision.'

Heavyweight Tommy McCarthy was out of luck as well. As in the European Championships, he fell agonizingly short of winning a medal and was beaten in the last eight on a split 2:1 decision by an Argentinian fighter, Yamil Peralta, who bowed out in the semi-final.

But it wasn't all a tale of woe for the Irish on quarter-finals' day. European champion Jason Quigley underlined his growing reputation with his thirty-first win on the spin – a unanimous 3-0 points decision over Hungarian Zoltán Harcsa. Just ten months after securing his first Irish Elite senior title, Quigley became the seventh Irish boxer to medal at the World Championships.

Less than forty-five minutes later Joe Ward became the eighth to do so. His victory also marked another milestone in the history of the HPU; for the first time ever Ireland had won two medals at the same World Championship event.

Ward dismantled the defences of reigning Russian European champion

Nikita Ivanov, whom he had beaten in the European final two years earlier when he was only seventeen. In Almaty the Russian sustained a cut over his left eye and was retired less than two and half minutes into the first round. Under the rules, if a fight is stopped because of injury the boxer that is ahead on points – Ward was 10-9 up on all three cards – wins the bout. But Ward couldn't repeat that performance in the semi-final, where he bowed out on a unanimous 3-0 decision to the defending title holder Julio César de la Cruz. The classy Cuban captured the gold medal twenty-four hours later.

'It's unbelievable, a European gold and a world bronze at nineteen years of age. I'm enjoying every moment of it,' Ward told journalists after the fight.

Reflecting on it now, he suggests he could have turned the bronze into gold. 'After dislocating my knee cap at the European Championships I wasn't sure whether I would be fit to box at the Worlds. But I made the final training camp in France where I won two fights. It was my world championship debut at senior level. I got the bronze but it easily could have been gold.'

Joe Ward had become the first Irish boxer to medal in three different weights and age classes at world championship events. The father of two has had countless offers to turn professional but has one ambition remaining before doing so – he wants to box at the Rio Olympics next year.

'After that my dream is to turn professional. I'll only be twenty-three. I'm doing this in the best interests of my family. I want to get as much as possible out of boxing so I can give them as good a life as possible,' says Ward, whose second son Gerry was born in April 2014.

Quigley's epiphany performance as an amateur boxer came in the semi-final against Russian Artem Chebotarev. Three years older than the Irish boxer, the Russian had won the European title in Moscow in 2010. But he was outsmarted in the World Championships by Quigley, who achieved a 3-0 win, thus becoming the first Irish boxer to qualify for a World Championship final.

Interviewed after the fight, Quigley outlined his game plan. 'We went through our tactics last night and we pulled them off to a T today. I picked him off as he came at me. I knew I had the speed and the skill to beat him.'

The unanimous verdict, however, disguised the fact that it was a gruelling contest. Quigley got the first round on two of the judges' cards. There was a brief moment of panic in the second when he was given a standing count after a stumble when the boxers' legs tangled. However, all three judges still gave him the round. He dominated the final stanza, even though the referee twice called for a time-out to allow the ringside doctor check on Chebotarev's bloodied nose.

Unluckily for Quigley, twenty-year-old local favourite Zhanibek Alimkhanuly received a walkover in the other semi-final when England's Anthony Fowler had to withdraw due to a wrist injury. This swayed the pendulum in Alimkhanuly's favour. Quigley had twenty-four hours and ten minutes between his semi-final and final, while Alimkhanuly had exactly twice that.

So there was no gold medal coronation for Quigley on finals' day, when the host nation Kazakhstan announced itself as the new superpower in world boxing. The former central-Asian Soviet state had boxers in six of the ten finals. They won four gold, two silver and two bronze medals, to top the ranking list for the first time ever at the World Championships.

Alimkhanuly fashioned a superb performance against Quigley. Despite being a southpaw, he didn't rely on counter-punching to chalk up points against the Irishman. He came forward and scored regularly. The Finn Valley boxer was literally on the back foot from midway through the first round when he got caught off balance by a big left. He spiralled on the canvas and took a standing count. All three judges gave the round 10-9 to Alimkhanuly, which left Quigley facing an uphill battle. Though Quigley lacked nothing in effort, his opponent also won the second round on all three judges' cards. So to win the fight, Quigley needed to knock out Alimkhanuly in the final three minutes. One judge gave him the final stanza, but Alimkhanuly deserved his 30-27, 30-27, 29-28 win.

'It's just a shame that I couldn't go that step further,' said an emotional Quigley when he spoke to journalists afterwards. 'It was a dream of mine to win from day one; not only mine but also my family who are over here and have put everything into boxing. I would have loved to bring home the gold.'

Walsh put Quigley's achievement into context when he spoke to journalists in Almaty. 'He had five really tough contests in the championships and his semi-final was a real grueller. And to have to go back in twenty-four hours later, while his opponent had a walkover, that was telling. I could see the fatigue in him; he wasn't as sharp as usual. But, by God, did he leave everything in there. He went to the soles of his boots. Hats off to him.'

The Irish coach had predicted that, even without John Joe Nevin, Ireland would win two medals: he was vindicated again. Ireland finished in a record joint-sixth place in the medal table at the championships behind Kazakhstan, Cuba, Azerbaijan, Russia and Italy, who between them have a population of two hundred and forty million. Within months, however, the HPU had suffered a significant setback when Jason Quigley turned his back on the amateur game and signing a professional contract with the high profile Los Angeles-based Golden Boy Promotions. The company is overseen by Olympic gold medallist and former professional world champion Oscar de la Hoya.

Later that year, the Louis Fitzgerald Hotel at Newland's Cross, in Clondalkin, hosted the IABA's annual awards dinner. For all its perceived failings, no other national sporting organisation in Ireland came close to boasting the range of international successes which Irish boxers achieved in 2013. In the six-month period between June and December 2013 they won forty medals in eight World and European men's and women's Elite, Youth, Junior and school tournaments. In five of the eight tournaments Ireland claimed the Best Boxer Awards, courtesy of John Joe Nevin, Katie Taylor – who won her fifth successive EU title in Hungary that summer – Jordan Myers, Gary Cully and Ciara McGinty. The latter also won the Best AIBA Junior Woman Boxer of the Year award. Joe Ward became the first – and youngest – boxer to win a hat trick of AIBA medals in three different age classes. And, just for good measure, Athy lightweight Eric Donovan was a member of the Astana Arlans Kazakhstan squad which won the 2012–13 World Series of Boxing. In this worldwide series, boxers are recruited by franchises based in different cities in Europe, Asia and the US. Up until 2014 it was a team competition, though it is now a designated qualifying event for the Rio Olympics.

A decade after the foundation of the HPU, Irish boxing had come of age. Billy Walsh was there from its inception and sums it all up: 'These guys have not let us down over a ten-year period. I have watched them deliver. Sometimes I'm sitting at ringside and saying, "Wow where did that come from? They love winning medals. They have the drive and ambition to be the best in the world. We were ranked fifth after the London Olympics; we want to be number one in Rio. This is our strategy. We want to be the best nation in the world and the whole team has that ambition.'

The clocking is ticking. Twenty-four hours after the opening ceremony of the Games of the XXXI Olympiad in Rio de Janeiro on 5 August 2016, the boxing begins.

CHAPTER 20

THE KATIE TAYLOR SHOW

'I had no fear at all. I just wanted to get in against the best, and I know that young girls coming on to the scene now have the same attitude towards me.'

Katie Taylor

Most of the business conducted at the 1997 Annual Convention of the Irish Amateur Boxing Association was routine. Acting president Breandán Ó Conaire was returned unopposed. But the delegates who gathered in the National Stadium did make one momentous decision – they unanimously supported the introduction of women's boxing in Ireland. Four weeks earlier, Katie Taylor had celebrated her eleventh birthday. A self-confessed 'tomboy', she was the busiest eleven-year-old living in Oldcourt, a housing estate in Bray. She played soccer with St Fergal's Football Club, Gaelic football for Bray Emmets, camogie for Fergal Óg, ran with Bray Runners and boxed with Bray Boxing Club.

Were it not for the fact that her father, Pete ran the boxing club, it is doubtful whether Taylor would ever have laced on a pair of boxing gloves. Women's boxing, not just in Ireland but worldwide, was frowned upon for most of the twentieth century. It did appear in the Olympic Games in St Louis, USA, as a demonstration sport in 1904, but was banned in most countries. It was revived by the Swedish Amateur Boxing Association in 1988. The pioneer of women's boxing in Ireland Deirdre Gogarty had to move to the United States from Drogheda, county Louth, and turn professional in order to fulfil her sporting ambitions.

In 1996 Gogarty caught the attention of the world's boxing media in Las Vegas. Boxing on the undercard of a world heavyweight title fight between Mike Tyson and Frank Bruno, she fashioned a heroic performance when losing to the then superstar of women's pro boxing, Christy Martin. This contest, which was the first-ever female pay-per-view fight, is generally regarded as the one that 'made' women's professional boxing in the US. A year later, the Drogheda woman won the world professional featherweight title in New Orleans. One of the congratulatory letters she received afterwards was from Katie Taylor, who expressed the hope that one day women would be allowed to box in the Olympics.

Taylor recalls meeting Deirdre Gogarty a few times in the St Saviours Olympic Boxing Academy in Dublin's inner city, where Pete Taylor used to bring his daughter for sparring sessions. 'She [Gogarty] was an incredible boxer but didn't get the recognition she deserved. Women's professional boxing was flourishing at the time and I followed her career.'

Born in Leeds, Pete Taylor came to Ireland in 1975 when he was sixteen to work in an amusement arcade in Bray. While his parents returned to the UK, within a year Pete had decided to put down his roots in Ireland, though he returned home briefly to complete his education. The reason he stayed in Ireland was straightforward. He had met and fallen in love with his future wife, Bridget, who later became Ireland's first female boxing judge.

Pete had done some boxing as a teenager in England and took up the sport again once he settled in Ireland. His own career climaxed in 1986 when he won an Irish intermediate title. Taylor's first memories of boxing are of watching her father train in the kitchen of their Bray home.

On Tuesday nights he would drop Taylor off to athletics on his way to train in Enniskerry Boxing Club, where he was a member at the time. The weather was so bad one night that the athletics training was cancelled and Taylor went to the boxing instead.

'Thank God for the Irish weather,' laughs Taylor. 'That's how it all started. Before then, I had just been kinda messing around and doing a bit of boxing with my brothers at home.'

'I remember the night well,' recalls Pete. 'It was my last year boxing and I was getting ready for the All-Irelands. I looked around at one stage and Katie was inside the ring sparring with one of the lads. She had no gum shield or anything but she loved it straight away.'

Having reached the mandatory retirement age of thirty-five, Pete had to hang up his boxing gloves. He decided to set up a new boxing club, St Fergal's, based in Bray. The first three members were his children – Peter, Lee and Katie. At the time, there was still no official IABA-sanctioned competitions for women boxers.

From the time she joined, Taylor always sparred with male opponents. And she took them on in underage tournaments. Her father tucked her hair under her headgear before they left the dressing room and she would simply be listed as 'K Taylor' on the programme. But that ruse had a limited time span. 'By the time she was twelve, she was sparring all the time with boys and I remember she beat the U-15 All-Ireland boys' champion,' recalls Pete.

Despite voting to allow women's boxing in 1997, it wasn't until 31 October

2001 that the first-ever sanctioned contest took place at the National Stadium. Pete had begged, cajoled and ultimately persuaded the IABA to implement their decision. 'They were sick of me ringing the office. It the meantime, I was putting Katie up against boys [in club tournaments] which wasn't going down too well either.'

Another key figure in the campaign to persuade the IABA to implement their 1997 decision was Mercedes Taaffe, a native of Coolaney, County Sligo. She came from a martial arts background and won a European title in kick-boxing in 1994. 'I always found that I was better at the hand element compared to the kick element of it, and my interest in boxing developed from there.'

But with women banned from competing, Taaffe decided to train as a boxing coach. There were still obstacles to be overcome when she applied to attend her first coaching course in 1990. 'I was told by one official that I couldn't do the course. But I'll give him his due, he stood up in a ring a few years later and said he was wrong, and I also received fantastic support from Joe Hennigan who is still involved. [Now Vice President of the IABA, Hennigan will manage the Irish boxing team at the 2016 Olympics.]

Within a decade of securing her coaching badges, Taaffe was recognised as one of the leading boxing coaches in the country. She guided Sligo brothers Stephen and Alan Reynolds to win Elite titles and represent Ireland at international level; they both boxed at the World Championships in Belfast in 2001.

Taaffe's ambition to compete herself never waned, however, and when she discovered that the first-ever women's World Boxing Championships had been scheduled for Scranton, Pennsylvania, in November 2001, her interest was rekindled. There was one technical problem, though. She was too old. 'I turned thirty-five in 2001, and the age limit was thirty-four,' she recalls. 'I actually thought about altering my passport, but given that the championships were in the US, I thought better of it.'

Together with Joe Hennigan's daughter Fiona and Sadie Duffy – both qualified referees and judges – Taaffe worked with the IABA to recruit female boxers for the historic show on Halloween night 2001.

She persuaded Dundalk-native Sallie McArdle, a ten-time world and European kick-boxing champion, to switch codes and together with Debbie Rogers from the Westside Boxing Club in Tallaght they prepared for their respective bouts against English boxers, Julia Fields from Surrey and Leeds-born Nicola Adams, who like their Irish counterparts were boxing in their first international contest.

'We fought and fought until they agreed to hold the first women's international fight in the National Stadium. It wasn't a monster event, but its significance was huge, and I doubt if any of the women fighting today even realise what went down to make it happen,' remembers McArdle. She was blown away when she saw Katie Taylor in action for the first time. 'A short time before the show in the stadium I was down training in the National Stadium with Nicolás Cruz and this little fifteen-year-old was doing the session.

'She blew my mind. Mercedes told me who she was and how hard she trained and we agreed instantly that this incredible little machine had to be on the bill. She was going to be magic and without doubt the future of the sport.'

Taaffe was well aware of Taylor's prowess, as she explains, 'A few years earlier I had brought one of my boxers to Bray, to spar with Katie's father, Pete. I remember watching Katie beat up some young fella in the ring, and I felt sorry for him.'

On the 2001 Halloween-night show Taylor beat Alanna Audley [now Audley-Murphy] from Belfast 23-12 over three ninety-second rounds. Her reputation had preceded her, as Jimmy Magee, who was ringside that night, recalls. 'Everyone was talking about her beforehand.' The President of the IABA Dominic O'Rourke called the event 'a momentous day for Irish boxing'.

Taylor's abiding memory of the contest is being disappointed with her performance. Her father recalls how she had just returned three days earlier from Switzerland, having played soccer for Ireland at underage level. 'She had no boxing training done and she was underweight on the night and Alanna was much heavier but she still beat her.'

Future Olympic gold medallist Nicola Adams beat Debbie Rogers, but McArdle trounced her opponent. 'I'm pretty sure I was expected to lose as well so a few people could say they were right about women boxers not being ready.'

Having taken leave of absence from her work in TV to prepare for her international debut, McArdle now stepped up her preparation ahead of the World Championships. She headed to Limerick to link up with Taaffe, who was studying for a degree in sports science in Limerick University. McArdle assumed the IABA would rubber-stamp her selection.

The decision of GB Boxing not to enter a team for the world event until women's boxing became more firmly established probably didn't help her cause. Nevertheless, the *Irish Independent* reported that the IABA's National Coaching Committee, having reviewed the entry list for the championships, were looking favourably at the idea of sending her. All the Elite male boxers and their coaches were supportive of the idea as well.

Then, days before she was due to depart, came the dreaded phone call. 'The words still ring in my ears,' says McArdle. '"We have decided to hold off on anyone travelling to the worlds as we have a duty of care, and we don't know what the standard is like."There was no standard; it was the first world championships. As for "duty of care", I swear if I ever hear that phrase again in my life, it will be too soon.'

'Those excuses are a load of bollix,' suggests Taaffe. 'They just didn't want to spend the money. The (IABA) wouldn't exactly be renowned for being leaders; they're more followers.'

Coincidentally, both women now live on the opposite side of the world. Taaffe moved to Australia in 2006, where she is still involved in boxing as a coach and competitor; she competed in the World Masters Boxing Championships in New York in 2015. McArdle, who is now living in New Zealand where she runs a specialist food business, never boxed again. 'I felt I couldn't respect a group of people who would do that to any athlete. I knew that the ball was in motion and they couldn't stop it.'

There was a poignant finale to her career in martial arts. Two years after settling in New Zealand, her husband, Carl, passed away in June 2011 when their son, Cian, was four months old. 'My husband made me promise to win one more world title so I returned to the ring in 2013 to do it.'

McArdle won a seniors world title at the World Association of Kickboxing Organisations (WAKO) championships in Antalya, Turkey, in December 2013, more than a decade after missing out on the inaugural women's World Amateur Boxing Championships in 2001. Indeed, it wasn't until the third women's World Championships in 2005 that Ireland finally sent a team consisting of Alanna Murphy and Katie Taylor.

For most of her teenage years, Taylor was arguably better known as a soccer player. When she was thirteen, she played in the prestigious Kennedy Cup tournament, which featured most of the country's male soccer prodigies. Shortly afterwards, she was called into the Irish U-17 women's soccer squad and later captained the team. By the time she was sixteen she was featuring on the Irish women's soccer squad.

On reflection, Pete Taylor believes that her involvement in so many sports – she was also a decent 1500-metre runner and an even better sprinter – ultimately benefitted her boxing career because it involved so much cross-training.

'I believe it made her the boxer she is today.'

As a boxer, Taylor came of age just before her eighteenth birthday in 2004. Even though she had won her first international tournament the previous January in Norway, she was still a rookie when she headed to Italy for the prestigious Torneo Italia Women's Tournament in Cascia. She could hardly contain her excitement when she noticed that Jennifer Ogg, the reigning world champion in Taylor's lightweight category, had entered the tournament. 'She was the girl I wanted to box,' remembers Taylor. 'It was such an exciting opportunity to test myself against the best in the world.'

Her father was less enthusiastic, and his reservations deepened as the tournament progressed. 'Katie was only a child and had only fought five times at international level; Ogg was a thirty-two-year-old experienced international and a southpaw. She had stopped the two girls she fought in the tournament, whereas Katie had been given a count in the first round by an Italian girl Emanuela Pantani [who later won world professional titles in two different weights], though she recovered to comfortably win the fight. Apart from the fact that she was my daughter, as a coach I had a duty to protect my boxer.'

Pete Taylor hardly slept a wink on the eve of the final. He sought counsel from Gary Keegan back in Dublin. Deep down, he knew his daughter could beat Ogg, who was a policewoman back in her native Canada. After all, Taylor had proved more than a match for the best males she had sparred against in training, and he knew how much she wanted the fight. 'I had no fear at all,' says Taylor. 'I just wanted to get in against the best and I know that young girls coming on to the scene now have the same attitude towards me.' Taylor went on to comfortably outpoint Ogg 41-30.

Ultimately though, it proved impossible to combine her boxing and soccer careers. The issue came to a head prior to her first appearance at the Women's European Amateur Boxing Championships in October 2004 in Riccione, Italy.

Her preparations were curtailed as she had to play four soccer games in the space of ten days – three for the U-19 Republic of Ireland team which was bidding to qualify for the European Championship finals and a cup final with her club.

Fatigue caught up with her at the boxing tournament in Riccione. She tasted defeat for the first time in her career, losing 27-12 in the first round to eventual bronze medallist Yuliya Nemtsova from Russia. 'All my losses have impacted on me but I've always learned from them,' confesses Taylor. 'Going into that championship I had this fear of losing. But once that went away it freed me up.' Taylor continued, however, to play soccer for Ireland until 2009, winning a total of nineteen caps, although from 2004 onwards boxing took priority.

In May 2005 she captured her first European title. She defeated her then nemesis, defending title holder Gülsüm Tatar in the semi-final. It was desperately close: they were tied 12-12 at the end of the scheduled four rounds, but Taylor – who had lost to the Turk a month earlier – prevailed 29-28 in the countback. It was also close in the final against the 2004 European silver medallist Eva Wahlström. Taylor was 19-17 ahead when the referee stopped the contest after the Finnish boxer suffered an eye injury. Six weeks shy of her nineteenth birthday, Katie Taylor became only the sixth Irish boxer and first female from these shores to capture a European crown.

At that time, though, she was a mere mortal in the ring as evidenced by the fact that five months later at the Women's World Championships in Podolsk, Russia, she lost 28-13 to a North Korean opponent, Kang Kum-hui, in the quarter-final. The latter was beaten in the next round by the eventual gold medallist Tatyana Chalaya from Russia. Taylor then lost for a second time to Gülsüm Tatar – the eventual gold medallist – in the quarter-finals of the 60 kg class at the European Union Championships in Porto Torres, Sardinia, in June 2006.

Significantly, it was the last time she fought abroad without her father. In the wake of her defeat at the 2004 Euros, the HPU had experimented with the idea of sending other coaches with Taylor to a couple of international tournaments. 'They decided to change things around,' says Pete Taylor, 'and they didn't want me to go away with her. After she got beaten in Sardinia, they sent another coach with her to a tournament in Italy. But I went over anyway and did her corner and she got Best Boxer. The next tournament was in Norway; somebody else was due to go, but they pulled out, and I ended up going and she won again.'

Ever since then Taylor's father has been in her corner and the results speak for themselves: sixteen championship titles, consisting of one Olympic, five world, five European and five European Union crowns, with just three defeats – all of which were controversial.

In May 2007 Taylor lost for a third time to Gülsüm Tatar (16-13) in the final of the Ahmet Cömert tournament in Istanbul. She then embarked on a remarkable forty-two bout unbeaten sequence over a two-and-half-year period. It ended when she lost to her future arch-rival, Russian Sofya Ochigava (8-1) in the semi-final of a multi-nation tournament in the Czech Republic in March 2010. It was suggested afterwards that two of the judges were Russian and possibly biased.

Forty-eight hours later, Taylor was due to join President Barack Obama for the St Patrick's Day celebrations in the White House. She was so distraught at her defeat that she contemplated not going. In the end she relented and used her free time during the trip for reflection and scripture reading. Looking back on that controversial decision, Taylor says, 'It's heart-breaking when you know you've won a fight but the judges don't give you the decision. I did a lot of reflection after that loss.'

Possessing a deep Christian faith, Taylor listens to worship songs on her iPod and reads a passage from the bible before every fight. She recalled in her autobiography, *Katie Taylor, My Olympic Dream*, how she returned from Washington with a deep conviction that God had a great plan for her. It proved a prophetic statement. Other than a bizarre 5-1 loss to Denitsa Eliseeva from the host country Bulgaria in the final of a multi-nation tournament in February 2011, she remains unbeaten since 2010. The respected boxing trade paper *Boxing News* described the decision to award the fight to Eliseeva as 'the worst decision they had ever seen'.

Aside from boxing aficionados, the Irish public were largely indifferent to Katie Taylor's remarkable achievements throughout this period. 'It took a while to get any recognition. She had been world champion a couple of times before the interest started. We never craved it, to tell you the truth,' says Pete Taylor. 'We just would have liked for RTÉ to show her European and world title fights.'

In truth the situation is similar in men's boxing. The Irish public only become truly engaged in the fortunes of Irish boxers when they compete in the Olympic Games. Still, the notion that one day the Irish nation would holds its breath as Taylor bid for gold at an Olympic Games seemed so far-fetched that it wasn't worth dreaming about.

In 2005, the International Olympic Committee (IOC) turned down a request from boxing's world-governing body, the AIBA to include women's boxing on the Olympic programme. Nonetheless, the Taylor family decided to give it their best shot regardless. Pete Taylor sold his electrical business in order to concentrate full time on Taylor's career, while she dropped out of UCD. An old boat shed near Bray harbour, which Pete acquired, became the epicentre of the project. It's a picturesque setting, but facilities in the newly-named Bray Boxing Club were basic. It wasn't until Taylor won her fourth world title in 2012 that a toilet was installed. Up until then everybody had to run down the road to use the bathroom facilities in the Harbour Bar.

Taylor, though, was ready for the Olympics. The key issue was whether the IOC was ready for her. A defining moment came during the 2007 world men's championships in Chicago. The President of the AIBA, Dr Wu Ching-kuo, invited her and five other women boxers to take part in three demonstration bouts. Members of the IOC, including the then president Jacques Rogge, were present. Taylor couldn't disguise her competitive instincts, even though she was boxing in the unfamiliar light welterweight category. She stopped her opponent Canadian Katie Dunn, a three-time Pan-American champion, in the first round. She believed there was now a chance of women's boxing being included in the Beijing Olympics. Realistically, London was always a more likely option.

Dr Wu cleverly played the gender card, pointing out, 'Of all the Olympics sports, we were the only ones without women.' The last thing the IOC needed was a law suit claiming they were biased against women boxers. On 14 August 2009, the fifteen-member IOC executive board announced, after a meeting in Berlin, that it had approved the inclusion of women's boxing in the schedule of events in London. The decision did not require approval from a full session of the IOC as the sport was already on the Olympic programme.

Ireland's Pat Hickey was not a member of the executive at the time but played a key behind-the-scenes role in ensuring the proposal received the green light. Hickey and Dr Wu are personal friends, having begun their respective administrative careers in the IOC at the same time. Hickey's skills as a lobbyist are renowned and he put his full weight behind Dr Wu's campaign. Long before the crunch meeting in Berlin, Hickey knew what the outcome would be. 'Everybody was well disposed towards putting women's boxing on the Olympic programme, including the President Jacques Rogge who wanted gender equality in the Games.'

'Dr Wu is Katie Taylor's greatest fan,' says Hickey. 'He never stops talking about what she has done for women's boxing.'

There were just three weight categories for women – fly, light and middle. The featherweight category was dropped from the men's programme and the total number of boxers allowed to compete in London remained unchanged at 286. The notion that the golden girl in women's international amateur boxing might not qualify for the London Games was simply never entertained by the Irish public. Inside the Taylor camp, nothing was taken for granted however. There was a quota system at the Olympic pre-qualifying tournament which doubled as the 2012 World Championships. It was staged in the Chinese city of Qinhuangdao. And for the first time in Katie Taylor's career, RTÉ sent a crew to report on her performance.

The qualification process was complicated, owing to the decision of the IOC to introduce the quota system to ensure that women boxers from around the world qualified for London. In Taylor's lightweight category, ten of the boxers who reached the last sixteen in Qinhuangdao were European and six of them qualified for the quarter-finals. It looked like the Bray boxer might have to reach the final to secure her place in London.

In the event, her qualification was almost an anti-climax. Injury forced her quarter-final opponent, Mihaela Lacatus from Romania, to concede a walk-over. Then, when Mavzuna Chorieva from Tajikistan – the eventual bronze medallist in London – beat France's Estelle Mossely, it secured Ireland's boxer her place in London. Taylor had been too nervous to watch that fight go down. Appropriately, it was her father who rushed into the dressing room to give her the good news. 'That moment was one of the best of my career,' she recalls.

But as far as she was concerned, the job wasn't finished yet; she wanted to go to the Olympics as the reigning world champion. She achieved her ambition by beating Chorieva in the semi-final and then, in what was a dress rehearsal for the Olympic final, she edged out the Russian southpaw Sofya Ochigava (11-7) to secure her fourth world title on the spin. Ireland now had a gilt-edged gold medal prospect ahead of the London Olympics. Up until then Katie Taylor was one of the most talked-about women in sport but the least seen in action. All that was about to change. Irish sporting fans were determined not to miss the opportunity to witness her mine Olympic gold. The date of the Olympic lightweight women's final, 9 August 2012, had entered the collective Irish consciousness long before the Irish boxer had even qualified.

However, expectations brought pressure. An injury, a slight dip in form or a skewed judgment decision could all derail the Taylor express. At the Atlanta Games in 1996, Ireland's best-ever female athlete Sonia O'Sullivan ran below expectations in the 5000 metres and 1500 metres, having expected to medal in both races. Four years later, in Sydney, Cathy Freeman delivered for Australia but the look of fear in her eyes before the 400-metre final was as haunting as it was revealing.

The Taylor camp could not control the country's clamour for gold, but Taylor herself stayed out of the limelight. Apart from accepting an invitation to carry the tricolour during the opening ceremony, she avoided all other public engagements prior to the Games.

There was just a six-week gap between the World Championships and the Olympic Games which left no room for mistakes in the build-up. Former European bronze medallist Eric Donovan, together with Dean Walsh, nephew of Billy Walsh, and current Irish Elite light welterweight champion, travelled to Assisi for the final training camp. The pair were specifically chosen as sparring partners for Taylor. Donovan was a southpaw specialist like the Russian Olympic hopeful Sofya Ochigava, while Walsh's height and technique replicated those of China's Dong Cheng. The chances were that Taylor would have to beat both Ochigava and Cheng in London if she was to capture the gold medal.

In mid-July Assisi is like an open-air sauna. There was no air conditioning in the gym, with the boxers regularly shedding three kilos during a session. There was a regimental routine: Taylor weighed herself every morning at seven-thirty. She would spar at ten o'clock – often doing ten two-and-a-half minute rounds. Nobody batted an eyelid at the sight of her exchanging blows with the males in the ring.

One of the most celebrated Irish YouTube boxing clips features a sparring session between Taylor and light flyweight Paddy Barnes. Taylor would be just over ten kilos heavier than Barnes. Understandably, he was initially reluctant to hit her when they first sparred. 'I was saying, "Jesus, I can't hit her. She's a girl." Then she started belting me,' Barnes recalls. 'We did nine rounds toe to toe. We were killing each other. Anyone who wins an Olympic gold medal and five world titles has to be admired.'

After her sparring sessions, Taylor would work on pads and other drills before taking a break for lunch at eleven-thirty. The afternoon programme was more demanding – at least mentally. Her father marked out a 600 metres long course on a nearby football field. Her challenge was to complete a series of runs over the distance in less than two minutes. She has acknowledged that these interval sessions took her to the edge both mentally and physically. She readily says, 'I hate running. For me the worst part of training are the running sessions. But from a physiological and mental viewpoint, it is important to do the things you hate.

This extraordinary work ethic is complemented by a Spartan-like lifestyle. A teetotaller, Taylor's only vice is an occasional raid on a box of chocolates. 'It's her lifestyle that sets her apart,' says Billy Walsh. 'If I could get the lads to even adopt a quarter of her lifestyle, we would have won a lot of gold medals over the years. Naturally we use her as a role model. She likes the craic and the banter and is very witty and funny herself. She loves a good laugh and the boys treat her as another teammate.'

Her Twitter fans got an insight into her sense of humour after she won the world title in 2014. Tongue–in–cheek Barnes tweeted: 'Ya may have five world titles but have ya 2 Commonwealths?'Taylor's reply was sharp and fast: 'Haha, the Commonwealths?! Sure my Ma would win a gold medal in that!!'

Being number one seed in London gave Taylor a bye into the quarter-final. So, on her Olympic debut the pressure was full on; she would be fighting straight off for a medal. It was the scenario the Taylor camp had hoped to avoid.

Pete Taylor says, 'The last thing I wanted was for Katie to be facing a boxer from the home nation especially if they had a fight under their belt. Katie felt the pressure but I felt it more. But I did my best to take some it off her by saying that she wouldn't be defined as a person regardless of whether she won the gold medal or not.'

Taylor's quarter-final opponent, Liverpudlian Natasha Jones, received the perfect boost ahead of the showdown with a spectacular 21-13 win over American Queen Underwood. The latter had come within seconds of securing a sensational victory over Taylor – who was ill at the time – in the semi-finals at the World Championships in Barbados in 2010.

On 6 August, Katie Taylor made her long-awaited Olympic debut. From the moment she appeared in the auditorium, until the result was announced the atmosphere was extraordinary. The decibel level hit 113.7 – the highest recorded at any venue during the Games.

The contest was a resounding endorsement for those who advocated the inclusion of women's boxing in the Olympics. Taylor led 5-2 after two minutes. Jones, however, dominated the early stages of the second round. Then the Irish favourite pressed her turbo drive after hearing her father scream, 'You have got to be the first against her!' It was 10-7 after round two. Jones was forced to take two standing counts in the final two rounds as Taylor cruised to a 26-15 win which guaranteed her a bronze medal. Jones was magnanimous in defeat. 'I could have thrown the kitchen sink at her or driven a bus over her and it wouldn't have worked today.'

As part of Taylor's overall development as an international boxer, Pete Taylor had accepted an invitation from promoter Brian Peters for Taylor to fight on the undercard of Bernard Dunne's 2009 world title fight at the 02 Arena. It had given the Bray boxer an invaluable insight into what it was like to box in front of a boisterous and expectant audience. So, unlike her male counterparts, Taylor wasn't fazed by the atmosphere in the ExCel centre during the Olympic showdown.

'Being honest,' recalls Pete. 'I wasn't thinking of the Olympic Games at the time. Brian Peters is a good friend of ours and I knew it would be a great opportunity to showcase her talent. There was opposition to the idea and we had another battle to get the go-ahead. Experience-wise, it worked unbelievably well and she knew what to expect when it came to the reaction of the crowd at the Olympics.'

An Olympic boxing semi-final can never be described as routine. Still, the truth is that nobody inside the ExCel Centre was expecting anything other than a comfortable win for Taylor who had beaten Mavzuna Chorieva at the World Championships six weeks earlier. Their Olympic clash was a tactical affair, with Chorieva content to sit back and allow Taylor to attack. Chorieva's approach never changed even though she trailed throughout the eight minutes. The one-sided nature of the contest was reflected on the scorecard – an emphatic 17-9 success. Taylor was now guaranteed a silver medal.

However, all her Irish fans were not going to be satisfied with the silver. Their sights were firmly set on Olympic gold. Expectations were through the roof, and there was a tangible, heightened level of tension inside the ExCel Arena for the final.

By this stage in their careers, Taylor and Sofya Ochigava knew each other well, having boxed on the same circuit during the preceding seven years. The Russian, who is thirteen months younger than Taylor, originally made her name in lighter weight divisions. A two-time world champion, she won gold at flyweight in 2005 and at bantamweight in 2006. She also won a bronze medal at featherweight at the world championships in 2008. At European level she was a three-time champion, with wins in the flyweight (2005), bantamweight (2007) and featherweight (2009) divisions.

She moved up to the lightweight category in 2010 and marked her arrival by fashioning that controversial 8-1 success over Taylor in the multi-nation tournament in Ústí nad Labem in the Czech Republic. Taylor avenged that defeat in the final of the European Championships in Rotterdam in October 2011 and then beat the Russian in the World Championship final in China. Unusually for a Russian boxer, Ochigava is comfortable speaking English and she did a lot of trash-talking in the run-up to the final – a first in women's boxing and, indeed, in Olympic boxing at any level.

'When you go in to box against her [Taylor], you begin with minus ten points,' Ochigava declared. 'It's difficult. You're boxing with all the judges around the table, and it's difficult, boxing against all the system. AIBA's goal is to give her gold. They want to make her a superstar.' In an unverified comment on Twitter, translated by Russian journalist Slava Malamud, the Russian boxer is also alleged to have declared: 'Ireland is in a financial crisis because they've spent all their money on Taylor's referees.'

The Taylor camp simply ignored the Russian's taunts and concentrated on perfecting their tactics. They knew there was no possibility that the final would be a repeat of the high-scoring slug-fest between Taylor and Jones. Instead, it would be a tactical low-scoring affair.

Up to the final, Pete Taylor had called every fight in the 60 kg category correctly – even down to the scoring. 'I said Queen Underwood would lose to Natasha Jones by eight points, and while everybody thought that China's Dong Cheng would beat Mavzuna Chorieva in the quarter-final because she is more than six inches taller than her, I tipped the Tajikistani boxer to win by two or three points. She won 13-8.'

Taylor convinced his daughter that even if she fell behind she was capable of capturing the gold medal. 'I knew the Russian girl would try and get ahead so there was a possibility that Katie would go behind. Everybody thought that whoever went ahead would go on and win the fight. That kinda annoyed me a bit because I knew Katie could change up a fight. I knew that if the Russian went ahead she would relax a little bit. It's a tactical game. Technically, at this level, all the boxers are good, so it's tactics that win.'

Final day began with an 8am weigh-in. Then Taylor breakfasted alone in her room in the Olympic village. Later, she went for a walk around Olympic Park with her father. At two o'clock her mother arrived to plait her hair and they prayed together. Then, together with her father and coaches Billy Walsh and Zaur Antia, they took a thirty-minute coach ride to the ExCel Centre.

As always during her warm-up, Taylor wore a red-coloured t-shirt with the words 'It is God who arms me with strength' printed on the front, and on the back, 'He trains my hands for battle.'

As she walked to the ring wearing her trademark red-coloured robe with the words 'The Lord is my Strength and my Shield' embroidered on the back, the boxer repeated to herself Psalm 37 – which contains the lines 'Delight yourself in The Lord and he will give you the desires of your heart' – to challenge any negative thoughts. For the first thirty seconds Taylor remembers feeling lethargic. 'I think it was nerves. Maybe it was something more but I was very tense.' Then suddenly the cloud lifted and the Bray boxer was back in her rhythm.

The same couldn't be said for the crowd. When the 2-2 score flashed up on the electronic scoreboard at the end of the round the 'Mardi Gras' atmosphere was punctured. The mood became even more sombre at the halfway point. Ochigava was 4-3 ahead. It was as if Pete Taylor's prophecy had come to pass. 'I was probably the calmest person in the stadium at that moment,' recalls Pete Taylor. 'Once she was in front, the Russian assumed that Katie was going to chase her and her tactics were based on that assumption. But I told Katie to simply keep on doing what she had done in the first two rounds but just get in very close before she attacked.'

For Taylor, being down one point was nothing more than what she described as the 'ebb and flow' of the contest. She remained composed. Her confidence, allied to her father's tactical nous, was justified. At the end of the third round she was 7-5 ahead. It was the pivotal round and one in which she showed her class by winning 4-1. The initiative now rested with the 'lady in red'. At face value, a two-point lead was precarious. Still, it would be difficult to pull it back in the 120 seconds remaining. And it was against Ochigava's natural instincts to come forward and attack. Essentially, Taylor just needed to stay off range and the gold was hers. She performed this task very efficiently. Nevertheless, it was incredibly tense. When the final bell sounded, an expectant hush descended. Taylor looked to her corner and mouthed, 'Is it me?'

The tension was palpable across Ireland and particularly on the seafront and main street in Bray, where thousands had gathered to watch the fight on giant screens. There were concerns that the decision would go to a countback which could turn the result into a lottery. In the end, Taylor didn't hear the official announcement as it was drowned out by the roar from the crowd. When the referee raised her arm, Taylor fell to her knees, closed her eyes and expressed thanks to God. The dream had become a reality.

The President of the OCI, Pat Hickey, presented the Bray boxer with her gold medal and Amhrán na bhFiann was given a particularly lusty rendition by the now delirious crowd. Ironically, another Irishman nearly usurped Hickey that day. All IOC members have the right to prioritise what Olympic events to attend to present medals.

Hickey was dismayed when his attempts to put the women's lightweight boxing final top of his list was blocked by the computer system. 'When I got to London, I went to the girl who was in charge of the list and discovered that the medal ceremony after Katie's fight had already been allocated to Pat McQuaid. [the then president of the International Cycling Union, who was also a member of the IOC]. I went ballistic. I wrote to Jacques Rogge, who has the final say, pointing out that I was President of the OCI and the senior member of the IOC from Ireland and I had to be allocated Katie's fight. I spoke to him as well and he roared laughing at the thought that somebody had tried to pull one over me. Presenting the gold medal was one of the proudest moments of my life,' says Hickey.

The hours after the medal ceremony were hectic for Taylor. Following the obligatory doping test, there was a formal press conference at which she declared, 'I'm no good at these interviews.' Later, though, she gave a hint of her deadpan sense of humour. When asked where she would keep her Olympic medal she replied, 'We might get a safe.'

Among those who sat alongside her at the top table was Ireland's Olympic silver medallist Sonia O'Sullivan, who was Ireland's chef de mission in London. She was one of Taylor's role models. Such was Taylor's own athletic prowess in her early school days that one of her teachers had even suggested that she could become the next Sonia O'Sullivan.

Afterwards, the gold medallist was whisked off to Central London for a link-up with the Six One news on RTÉ. She then attended an OCI celebration at the Irish House near King's Cross. Finally, the hunger pangs set in.

Together with her parents and sister, she made it to McDonald's restaurant near Trafalgar Square and ordered a chicken nugget meal just before closing time at 2am. The four of them took seats at the window and ate their meal. The gold medal was safely tucked away in the pocket of Pete's tracksuit bottoms. 'It was the best way to celebrate; just spending time with my family,' recalls Taylor. 'It was great,' remembers Pete. 'Nobody recognised us.'

Even though her father stated that he would have liked to see her hang up her gloves afterwards, Taylor – who had also won the best Female Boxer award at the London Games – had other plans. She remains on target to equal the feat of hammer thrower Pat O'Callaghan, the only Irish athlete to successfully defend an Olympic title.

In the aftermath of her gold-medal triumph there was grandiose talk that Ireland would host the 2013 European Women's Amateur Boxing Championships. In the end, the event was postponed. While the decision was outside the control of the IABA, it became controversial after it emerged that the association had neglected to tell Pete Taylor that the championships had been postponed ahead of him answering questions about the possibility of Ireland hosting the event at an IABA press conference. The decision to postpone the event had been taken by the European Boxing Federation twenty-four hours earlier. But relations between the association and Pete Taylor have sometimes been strained as evidenced by the fact that he is employed by the ISC rather than the IABA.

Taylor eventually returned to the ring in the spring of 2013 and took part in two sell-out exhibition shows in the Bord Gáis Energy Theatre in Dublin. Later on, she collected her fifth European Union title in Keszthely, Hungary. She maintained her winning form in 2014. Firstly she retained her European title in Bucharest in June. She beat Bulgarian Denitsa Eliseeva – the last boxer to officially beat her – in the semi-final and Estelle Mossely in the final. The latter had earlier inflicted a shock defeat on Sofya Ochigava.

The Korean island of Jeju was the venue for the eighth Women's World Amateur Boxing Championships in November 2014. Surprisingly, there was no seeding, and Taylor was due to meet her erstwhile rival Ochigava in the quarter-final. But the latter did not turn up for the weigh-in, having apparently picked up an injury in her fight the previous day. Taylor stopped Chinese opponent Yin Junhua in the semi-final; the Chinese boxer's corner threw in the towel at the start of the last round.

The final was a tactical, tight affair against southpaw Yana Alekseevna, who was representing Azerbaijan, though she is a native of Ukraine. Taylor won on a unanimous 3-0 verdict. She was the only boxer to retain her title. More significantly, her fifth consecutive world title equalled the achievement of India's Mary Kom, a pioneering and revered figure in women's amateur boxing.

Taylor and Alekseevna clashed again in the semi-final of the inaugural European Games in Baku in June 2015. Younger and taller than the Olympic champion, and fighting in her adopted country, the omens favoured the underdog.

The outcome couldn't have been tighter. Three judges from Poland, Finland and China all scored the contest 38-38. The Polish and Finnish judges gave rounds two and four to Taylor, while the Chinese judge awarded her rounds one and three.

It was reminiscent of the scoring in Fred Tiedt's Olympic final in Melbourne. But unlike Tiedt, Taylor got the rub of the green with the Polish and Finnish judges giving her the nod for a majority 2-1 win. Twenty-four hours later, Katie comfortably outpointed France's Estelle Mossely to secure her eighteenth championship gold medal.

On New Year's Day 2016 Taylor will have been the world's number one ranked female lightweight boxer for a decade. No boxer, male or female, has achieved that. Truly, we will never see the likes of her again.

EPILOGUE

'I had no idea of the other result but as I stepped out of the ring Paddy [Barnes] came running at me and jumped on me, like a leprechaun, shouting, "You're going to the Olympics too." All I could say was, "You'd better not be joking."'
Michael Conlan

On a sweltering night in the Venezuelan port city of Maiquetía, in April 2015, Michael Conlan stepped into the ring of the 2500-seater José María Vargas sports centre for what he believed would be his final fight as an amateur boxer.

In the three years previously he had secured an Olympic bronze medal, a European silver and a Commonwealth gold. His philosophy in life is summed up in his frequent comment: 'If it's meant to be; it's meant to be.'

But as the bell sounded to signal the start of his fight in Maiquetía, the Belfast bantamweight was convinced that he wasn't meant to box at the Rio Olympics in 2016. Instead, the time was ripe for him to join his older brother Jamie in the pro ranks.

In the preceding thirteen weeks both Conlan and his fellow Olympian Paddy Barnes had each racked up more than thirty thousand air miles as they criss-crossed the world in pursuit of a spot at the Rio Games.

The Olympic qualifying process in boxing has changed significantly since the London Games in 2012. In a groundbreaking decision in 2013, the AIBA, the world governing body of amateur boxing, announced that professional boxers who had fought fewer than fifteen times in the pro ranks would be eligible to compete in the Olympics.

As a result, the Olympic qualifying system was radically overhauled with the creation of a fully professional AIBA Pro Boxing series (APB) through which boxers could secure Olympic qualification. In another innovation, Olympic places were also reserved for boxers who topped the ranking lists in the semi-professional World Series of Boxing (WSB), where the participants are recruited by professional franchises based in cities in Europe, Asia and the Americas.

Cousins Joe Ward and David Oliver Joyce were the only Irish boxers recruited for the groundbreaking APB series. Ward's fights in the light heavyweight division took place in the Bulgarian capital Sofia while Joyce's light weight division was based in Almaty, the largest city in Kazakhstan. The boxers wore no headgear or vest in the contests, which were decided over six three-minute rounds.

Ward lost his first fight, which effectively ended his hopes of winning the overall title, but then won three on the spin. Joyce was beaten in two of his four contests. They both made the semi-finals, leaving them two wins away from qualifying for the Rio Olympics.

However, neither made it past the penultimate phase. Joyce was beaten on a unanimous, though controversial, 77-75 verdict by Hurshid Tojabaev in Tashkent, the capital city of the victor's native country Uzbekistan. Even though Tojabaev was on the back-foot for almost the entire eight rounds he still did enough in the judges' eyes to get the verdict.

There was no doubt about the outcome of Ward's light heavyweight contest against French professional boxer Mathieu Bauderlique, who was unbeaten after nine fights in the pro ranks before opting to join the APB series. The referee stopped the fight in the fourth round as Bauderlique overwhelmed Ward. It was the first time the Moate pugilist had suffered a TKO (technical knock-out) in his career.

Meanwhile, welterweight rivals Steven Donnelly and Adam Nolan, Gary Sweeney (heavyweight), and Dean Gardiner (super-heavyweight) together with Barnes and Conlan joined the World Series of Boxing, which heretofore was primarily viewed by the boxers as a way of earning a few bob away from the pressure of championship events. Now, with Olympic places at stake, the High Performance Unit decided to dispatch coaches with the boxers when they travelled abroad to WSB events.

Barnes and Conlan were drafted by the Milan-based Italia Thunder team; neither were interested in the money, nor in Barnes's case the air travel – he hates flying. He becomes so uptight while in the air that he can't sleep, read or watch movies. In fact, while travelling to the series he couldn't even sip water, never mind have a beer, in case he failed to make the 49 kg weight limit. All they were interested in was Olympic qualification.

The odds were stacked against them. In Barnes's case only one Olympic place was reserved for light flyweight boxers. 'I don't know why this was the case. I think it's discrimination,' he suggests. There were two spots up for grabs in Conlan's bantamweight division. But at the tail end of 2014 Conlan suffered a big setback when he broke his thumb while sparring.

There were seven contests in each weight division. Crucially, Barnes and Conlan forfeited their appearance fees and win bonuses – believed to be in the region of €5,000 per fight – to ensure they were selected by Italia Thunder for all seven.

While their Irish colleagues were battling for Elite titles in the National Stadium in January of 2015, Barnes and Conlan and his father, John – who is on the coaching staff of the HPU – were in the city of Guba in north eastern Azerbaijan to face the local Azerbaijan Baku Fires franchise in the first round of the 2015 WSB. The visitors experienced a torrid evening, going down 4-1. Barnes was the only winner, securing a unanimous 3-0 win over

Magomed Ibiyev. Conlan, whose preparations were badly hampered by his broken thumb, lost 3-0 to Magomed Gurbanov.

For the next three months there was no respite for the Irish duo. The sixteen franchises in the WSB are divided into two divisions of eight, which meant the boxers had to keep a watchful eye on how their main rivals were faring in the other division. Ultimately, they had no control over these boxers' fates as they wouldn't meet in the ring during the series.

After winning his second Commonwealth gold medal in Glasgow in 2014, Barnes was awarded an MBE in Queen Elizabeth's 2015 New Year Honours list. Despite being the country's highest-profile boxer his luggage was mislaid on the way to Palermo in Sicily for round two of the WSB series at the end of January.

Even though he was forced to wear a pair of boxing boots two sizes too big for him, Barnes recorded another unanimous win to earn five ranking points. Conlan bounced back after his setback in Baku. The referee halted his scheduled five-round bout against Anthony Chacon Rivera from Puerto Rico after fifty-four seconds of the third round.

By the end of March the Irish pair had been to Konin in Poland, Almaty in Kazakhstan, as well as two Italian cities, Pescara and Milan, as Group B of the WSB reached a climax. By then, Barnes was on the cusp of making history by becoming the first Irish boxer to qualify for three Olympics. He had breezed through the series; he stopped one opponent and recorded unanimous wins in his other five contests. Being a history-maker didn't interest him however. 'I'm not interested anymore in just qualifying for major championships. I want to win medals at them. Just going to another Olympics means nothing,' he insists.

Facing the long journey to Venezuela, Barnes had thirty ranking points – the maximum number. He had been the beneficiary of an unexpected slice of good fortune on the journey. His chief rival for the single Olympic spot available was Hasanboy Dusmatov, a light flyweight from Uzbekistan who was boxing for the Ukraine Otamans franchise in Group A. Like Barnes, he was unbeaten.

In week nine of the series the Ukraine squad were in London to face the British Lionhearts in York Hall. Dusmatov's opponent Ashley Williams, who had won a bronze medal at the 2014 Commonwealth Games for Wales, conceded a walkover. As a result, Dusmatov only received three ranking points, which gave Barnes a crucial two-point advantage going into the final round. Essentially, a majority win, which would earn him four points, would suffice for Barnes, regardless of how his rival fared in his last fight.

By contrast, Conlan's chances were hanging by a thread. In Almaty, Conlan suffered a controversial 2-1 defeat to local favourite Kairat Yeraliyev, even though one of the judges had awarded the Irishman all five rounds. As a result, his two principal rivals, Vladimir Nikitin from Russia – who had beaten him at the World Championships in Almaty in 2013 – and Magomed Gurbanov from Azerbaijan were in pole position to secure the two available spots.

Effectively, Conlan needed to win his fight in Maiquetía by a unanimous decision and hope that either Nikitin or Gurbanov slipped up. On the night before Conlan's bout, Nikitin was in action in Kiev and secured a comfortable 3-0 win to nail down his Olympic spot.

'I was distraught when the results came through,' says Conlan. 'I thought my Olympic chance was gone. There was no way I felt the Azerbaijan boxer would lose as I had fought him myself in the first round. I didn't see the point in getting into the ring.'

It took all the persuasive powers of his father, John, HPU head coach Billy Walsh – both of whom travelled to Venezuela – together with Conlan's mother, brother and his partner, Shauna Olali – who had given birth to the couple's first child, Luisne, the previous month – to convince him not to concede a walkover.

First though, it was the turn of Barnes to step into the ring. Dusmatov's unanimous 3-0 win the previous night in Kiev in his final bout meant that he actually led the ranking list on thirty-three points – three ahead of the Irishman. So Barnes needed to maintain his one hundred percent winning record to secure his Olympic place.

Inside the stadium the heat was oppressive and the atmosphere hostile as the locals roared on eighteen-year-old Yoel Segundo Finol Rivas, who had lost just one of his previous five bouts in the WSB series. Barnes momentarily silenced the crowd when he put the teenager on the canvas in the first round, and he went on to dictate the contest, despite a spirited effort by Rivas, particularly in the fifth round.

Barnes knew he was Rio-bound as soon as the final bell sounded. Nothing though can ever be taken for granted in amateur boxing. The British judge Raymond Morley inexplicably gave the verdict to Rivas on a 48-47 score. But the other two officials voted decisively 49-45 for Barnes, which secured him the victory and the four ranking points he needed to overtake Dusmatov at the top of the 49 kg ranking list and formally qualify for the 2016 Olympics.

Forty minutes later, the bell rang to signal the start of Conlan's fight against José Vicente Diaz Azocar. Though it was entirely unplanned, the Irishman's fate was effectively decided 880 km away in the Puerto Rican capital of San Juan at exactly the same time. The unbeaten Magomed Gurbanov from Azerbaijan looked set for a routine win over an unheralded Puerto Rican who had only fought once previously in the series. Gary Mackay, a journeyman professional soccer player from Edinburgh, embedded himself in the consciousness of the Irish nation when his late winning goal for Scotland against Bulgaria secured the Republic of Ireland a place in the 1988 European soccer championships. Among the Irish boxing fraternity, Mackay now has a rival as the country's most beloved non-Irish sporting hero: step forward Puerto Rican bantamweight, Hector Luis Garcia Mora. All three judges gave the Puerto Rican the decision over Gurbanov by a three-point margin.

Inside the ring in Maiquetía, Conlan was unaware of the dramatic turn of events in San Juan. He lost his third round on all three judges' cards but won the other four on his way to a unanimous 3-0 win. It felt like a pyrrhic victory. 'I had no idea of the other result, but as I stepped out of the ring Paddy [Barnes] came running at me and jumped on me, like a leprechaun, shouting, "You're going to the Olympics too!" All I could say was, "You'd better not be joking."

'I just couldn't believe it. Even the next morning as soon as I got up I checked the results again to make sure there was no mistake. Quite honestly I had never heard of the Puerto Rican boxer before,' says Conlan.

Conlan pipped Gurbanov by a single point (26-25) to secure the second qualifying spot. The single point he secured from his controversial split-decision loss in Almaty gave him the edge, though he would still have qualified had the pair finished level as he had boxed in all seven rounds, whereas Gurbanov had missed one.

And in another stroke of good fortune, the Olympic gold medallist Robeisy Ramírez Carrazana who beat Conlan in the semi-final in London, only boxed twice in the series. Fears that the twenty-one-year-old – regarded as one of the hottest properties in Cuban boxing – might defect and turn professional are believed to have prompted the Cuban authorities to withdraw him. Ironically, his replacement Andy Cruz Gomez won his five fights, to finish in joint third spot along with Gurbanov.

The magnitude of what Barnes and Conlan achieved cannot be underestimated. In a thirteen-week period Barnes boxed thirty-four rounds and Conlan thirty-three – almost the equivalent of three full-length World professional title fights.

By way of comparison, Ireland's IBF world super bantamweight champion

Carl Frampton fought seventeen rounds between September 2014 and February 2015, a period of twenty-five weeks, while WBO world middleweight champion Andy Lee fought eighteen rounds between December 2014 and April 2015, a time span of seventeen weeks. So regardless of how Barnes and Conlan fare, if they are fit to box in Rio, nobody can deny that the pair of London bronze medallists earned their blazers.

Maybe Paddy Barnes will fulfil another lifelong ambition and carry the tricolour at the head of the Irish delegation in the famous Maracanã Stadium, Rio de Janeiro, on 5 August 2016, at the opening ceremony of the XXXI Olympiad. Nobody deserves the honour more.

Meanwhile, at the inaugural European Games in Baku, in June 2015, the seven-strong men's team collected three medals. Together with Katie Taylor's gold, it elevated Ireland to third place in the medal table behind Azerbaijan and Russia respectively.

Michael O'Reilly from Portlaoise was the hero, winning the middleweight title. His potential was never in doubt. In 2011 he was very unlucky to lose 16-15 to a Russian in the final of the European Youth Championships in Dublin. In Baku O'Reilly defied the odds when he fashioned a unanimous 3-0 win in the decider against local favourite Xaybula Musalov.

Nineteen-year-old Belfast teenager Brendan Irvine battled his way through to the light flyweight final, beating Azeri and Ukrainian opponents in his medal contests before succumbing to Russia's Bator Sagaluev on a split decision. In the lightweight category another Belfast boxer, Sean McComb, picked up a bronze medal before bowing out in the semi-final to Albert Selimov from Azerbaijan who went on to win the gold medal.

Based on these performances, the HPU's 'Medal Factory' looks set to continue to mint medals for a long time to come.

ACRONYMS

AA – Alcoholics Anonymous

AIBA – International Boxing Association*

AIPS – Association Internationale De La Presse Sportive

ANOC – Association of National Olympic Committees

APB – AIBA Pro Boxing

BBBC – British Boxing Board of Control

CAS – Court of Arbitration for Sport

EABA – European Amateur Boxing Association

EUBC – European Boxing Confederation

EU – European Union

FIFA – Fédération Internationale de Football Association

GAA – Gaelic Athletic Association

IABA – Irish Amateur Boxing Association

IBF – International Boxing Federation

INSEP – National Institute of Sport and Physical Education

IOC – International Olympic Committee

ISC – Irish Sports Council

HPU –High Performance Unit

NCTC – National Coaching and Training Centre

OCI – Olympic Council of Ireland

TKO – Technical knockout

USSR – Union of Soviet Socialist Republics

WAKO – World Association of Kickboxing Organisations

WBA – World Boxing Association

WSB – World Series of Boxing

* formerly known as the Association Internationale de Boxe Amateur

BIBLIOGRAPHY

BOOKS

Carruth, Michael (with Peter Byrne), *Ring of Gold*. Dublin: Blackwater Press, 1992.

Dunne, Bernard, *My Story*. Dublin: Penguin, 2010.

Egan, Kenny (with Ewan McKenna), *Kenny Egan: My Story*. Dublin: Paper Weight Publications, 2011.

Flynn, Barry, *Legends of Irish Boxing: Stories Seldom Told*. Belfast: Appletree Press, 2007.

Flynn, Barry, *Best of Enemies: John Caldwell vs. Freddie Gilroy*. Dublin: Liberties Press, 2014.

McGuigan, Barry, Cyclone: *My Story*. London: Virgin Books, 2011.

Jennings, Andrew, *The New Lord of the Rings: Olympic Corruption and How to Buy Gold Medals*. London: Simon & Schuster, 1996.

Naughton, Lindie & Watterson, Johnny, *Irish Olympians*. Dublin: Blackwater Press, 1992.

Taylor, Katie (with Johnny Watterson), *My Olympic Dream*. London: Simon & Schuster, 2012.

Wallechinsky, David, *The Complete Book of the Summer Olympics*, 1996 Edition. Toronto: Little, Brown & Company, 1996.

MAGAZINES

Beltran, Maria Pia and Nikcevic, Sonja, *Breaking the Bank*. AIPS Magazine, January, 2015.

TV DOCUMENTARIES

Gallimore, Andrew, *Tales from a Neutral Corner*. Dublin: Midas Productions, 2011.

WEBSITES

www.iaba.ie

www. amateur-boxing.strefa.pl

www.aiba.ie

www. worldseriesboxing.com

www.aibaproboxing.com

www.eubcboxing.org

www.thesweetscience.com/article-archive/2008/6448-tss-prospect-
watch-darren-sutherland

www. irishsportscouncil.ie

www.olympic.org

JOURNALS

Ó Conaire, Breandán. 'Punching above our weight? Irish boxing and the Olympic Games' in *History Ireland*, 20th-century/Contemporary History, Features, Issue 4 (July/August), Vol 20. Dublin: 2012.

NEWSPAPER AND MAGAZINE ARCHIVES

Boxing News
Irish Examiner
Irish Independent
Irish News
Irish Star
Sunday Independent
Sunday World
The Irish Press
The Irish Times
The Sunday Times

ACKNOWLEDGEMENTS

I had an inauspicious start to my career as a boxing reporter. My first-ever foreign assignment with the *Irish Press* was the 1989 European Boxing Championships in Athens. The five-member Irish team, including future Olympic gold medallist Michael Carruth, were all beaten within twenty-four hours of my arrival in the Greek capital.

How times have changed. On my last overseas trip to report on the Irish boxers they won four medals at the London Olympics in 2012. The story behind the revival of Irish amateur boxing over the last decade and a half provided the genesis for this book.

Of course, it would not have been possible to tell the story were it not for the co-operation, generosity and frankness of those who tasted action inside the ring. Boxers are natural story-tellers; they're utterly dedicated to their craft but there is also an inherent honesty and openness about them. Firstly, I want to thank all the boxers, past and present, who told their stories, and the coaches and officials from the boxing community who were just as forthcoming and frank.

Thanks also to my journalistic colleagues, in particular the doyen of Irish boxing writers Gerry Callan, for his practical help; to Jimmy Magee, whose infectious enthusiasm for boxing rubbed off on me and to Barry Flynn, a pioneering figure in terms of chronicling the exploits of Irish boxers in his three excellent books.

I also wish to thank Colm MacGinity, Editor of the *Sunday World* and Eamon Gibson, sports editor, for encouraging me to write about boxing and sending me to the Sydney, Beijing and London Olympic Games. Thanks also to my friend and colleague Ray McManus of Sportsfile for allowing me to delve into his wonderful archive of boxing pictures, and to Conor McCaughley, my guide when I visit Belfast.

This book would probably have remained an idea in my head were it not for the fact that Helen Carr, a fellow member of Raheny Shamrock Athletic Club, introduced me to Michael O'Brien, the founder of O'Brien Press. Thanks to Michael for taking a punt on this project.

A particular word of thanks to the book's editor, Susan Houlden, and to Emma Byrne for her evocative cover design.

A special word of thanks to my sons, Paul and Colm, for their encouragement. Finally, I thank my wife, Mary, for her fortitude, patience and practical support. She had the unenviable task of reading the first draft of the book and her judicious use of a red felt pen proved an invaluable aid in moulding the final draft.

INDEX

Roche, Michael, 115, 124-26, 128
Rodgers, John, 37-38, 39
Rogers, Debbie, 318, 319
Rouzbahani, Ehsan, 258, 279
Russell, Hugh, 41, 44-47
Ryan, Jim, 185, 198-99

Sagaluev, Bator, 344
Saitov, Oleg, 104
Sarsania, Zurab, 121, 122-23
Sattibayev, Olzhas, 261
Selby, Andrew, 263, 302-3, 305, 308
Sharkey, Pat, 22, 23
Sheahan, Roy, 165, 166, 168, 171, 211-12, 271
Sheehan, Con, 184, 209, 214, 241, 250, 263, 268
Sheehan, Tommy, 180
Shiming, Zou, 173, 201-2, 285-87
Shynaliyev, Yerkebulan, 204, 209
Sierra, Juan Hernández, 95, 97-98, 100
Silva, Washington, 201
Sinclair, Neil, 118
Smart, Kelvin, 46
Smyth, Martin, 22-23
Song Kyung-sup, 55, 70, 71
Stalker, Tom, 251, 264
Stankovic, Branimir, 272
St Brigid's Boxing Club, 114, 226, 229
Stepanov, Boris, 23
Steward, Emanuel, 163
Stewart, Don, 108
St John Bosco Boxing Club, 22, 245, 301
St Joseph's Boxing Club, 112, 115
St Michael's Boxing Club, 166, 167, 211
Storey, Gerry, 41, 44, 52, 169
St Saviours Olympic Boxing Academy, 229, 315
Sutcliffe, Philip (father), 40-41, 43
Sutcliffe, Philip (son), 214, 248
Sutherland, Darren, 165, 166-67, 171-72, 178, 180-81, 183-84, 187, 193-94, 201-3, 207, 210, 213-14, 224-39
Swanton, Alan, 146, 285
Sweeney, John, 168, 171, 172

Taaffe, Mercedes, 317-18, 319-20
Tatar, Gülsüm, 322, 323
Taylor, Katie, 207, 241, 279, 295, 314-36
Taylor Pete, 270, 315-16, 323, 335
Tibua, Zurab 'Rob', 134, 135, 136
Tiedt, Fred, 22, 25-27, 29-30
Thompson, Shay, 114
Thompson, Tommy, 114
Todorov, Serafim, 89, 94
Tojabaev, Hurshid, 338
Tracey, Edward 'Eddie', 35
Transport Boxing Club, 111
Traynor, Eugene, 52
Traynor, Frank, 12-13
Treacy, John, 44, 107
Tuifao, Maselino, 92, 93

Underwood, Queen, 329, 332

Valdez Fierro, Óscar Rafael, 283-84
Valentino, Domenico, 167, 172, 246

Wahlström, Eva, 322
Walasek, Tadeusz, 25, 27
Walker, Keith, 55, 71
Walsh, Billy, 57-58, 64-65, 66, 68-69, 71-72, 75-82, 111-13, 120, 131-33, 138-39, 142-43, 192-93, 214, 216-17, 222, 253-54, 298-99
Walsh, Dean, 327
Ward, Joe, 241-44, 250, 251-52, 253, 257-58, 265-68, 277-79, 302-3, 304, 309-10, 338
Ward, Steven, 241
Winters, Mark, 89, 91, 118
Womens' European Amateur Boxing Championships 2004, Riccione, 321-22
Women's World Boxing Championships 2001, Scranton, United States, 317-18
2005, Podolsk, Russia, 322
2012, Qinhuangdao, China, 326, 330
2014, Jeju, South Korea, 336
World Boxing Championships 1974, Havana, Cuba, 39
1986, Reno, United States, 66-67

1989, Moscow, Soviet Union, 74, 93
1991, Sydney, Australia, 77-78, 93
1993, Tampere, Finland, 101
1997, Budapest, Hungary, 104, 119, 123
1999, Houston, United States, 151
2001, Belfast, Northern Ireland, 62, 103, 128-29, 148, 170, 173
2003, Bangkok, Thailand, 149-50, 153
2005, Mianyang, China, 156, 164
2007, Chicago, United States, 166, 167-68, 171-75, 188, 201, 204, 213, 325
2009, Milan, Italy, 214-16, 246
2011, Baku, Azerbaijan, 256, 257- 64, 268, 273, 278, 284, 291, 305
2013, Almaty, Kazakhstan, 307-10
WSB (World Series of Boxing), 338, 339-40
Wu Ching-kuo, 60-61, 188, 267, 325-26

Yeraliyev, Kairat, 341
Yin Junhua, 336

Zamkovoy, Andrey, 282
Zhang Xiaoping, 192, 204, 205-6, 232-33